# Disability Theory

# CORPOREALITIES: Discourses of Disability

David T. Mitchell and Sharon L. Snyder, editors

Books available in the series:

# Disability Theory

*Tobin Siebers*

The University of Michigan Press

*Ann Arbor*

Copyright © by the University of Michigan 2008
All rights reserved
Published in the United States of America by
The University of Michigan Press
Manufactured in the United States of America
⊛ Printed on acid-free paper

2011   2010   2009   2008      4   3   2   1

*A CIP catalog record for this book is available from the British Library.*

Library of Congress Cataloging-in-Publication Data

Siebers, Tobin.
     Disability theory / Tobin Siebers.
         p.     cm. — (Corporealities)
     Includes bibliographical references and index.
     ISBN-13: 978-0-472-07039-8 (cloth : alk. paper)
     ISBN-10: 0-472-07039-8 (cloth : alk. paper)
     ISBN-13: 978-0-472-05039-0 (pbk. : alk. paper)
     ISBN-10: 0-472-05039-7 (pbk. : alk. paper)
     1. Disability studies.   2. Sociology of disability.   3. People
with disabilities—Social conditions.   I. Title.
     HV1568.2.S54     2008
     305.9'08—dc22                              2007052247

# Contents

# Chapter One
# Introduction

*Disability Theory* pursues three interlocking agendas. First, it makes an intervention from the perspective of disability studies in some of the major debates of the last thirty years in critical and cultural theory. My objective here is to address the two audiences at this convergence point: on the one hand, to demonstrate for critical and cultural theorists how disability studies transforms their basic assumptions about identity, ideology, politics, meaning, social injustice, and the body; on the other hand, to theorize the emerging field of disability studies by putting its core issues into contact with signal thinkers in the adjacent fields of cultural studies, literary theory, queer theory, gender studies, and critical race studies. Some of these debates include the possibility of ideology critique in the wake of increasingly powerful claims for the relation between ideology and unconscious thought; the authority of psychoanalysis in critical and cultural theory; the battle over the usefulness of identity politics; the impact of social construction theories in matters of gender, sexuality, and race; the assumptions underlying body theory as a field of study; the future of minority studies and whether one should be able to study what one is; the value of personal experience for theorizing social justice; the epistemology of passing in queer theory; the future alignment of the sex/gender system; and the ongoing struggle to theorize a viable model of human rights for the global world. The chapters to follow depend on the content specific to these great arguments and on the theorists who have best addressed them, but the goal remains in each case to use disability as a lever to elevate debate, not only by asking how the theories of our most influential critical and cultural thinkers advance disability studies but also by asking how disability theory might require these same thinkers to revise their own claims.

Second, I offer an extended discussion of the broad means by which disability relates to representation itself. This second agenda may also be thought of as an intervention in the field of theory, although at the most general level, because the status of representation has been one of the most significant issues in critical and cultural theory since the emergence of structuralism in the 1960s. The structuralists and their heirs embrace language as the dominant model for theorizing representation, interpreting nearly all symbolic behavior in strictly linguistic terms. Two consequences of this so-called linguistic turn concern disability studies. First, because linguistic structuralism tends to view language as the agent and never the object of representation, the body, whether able or disabled, figures as a language effect rather than as a causal agent, excluding embodiment from the representational process almost entirely. As Jean-Luc Nancy puts it, in emblematic fashion, there is "no such thing as *the* body. There is no body" (207). *Disability Theory* echoes recent calls by Linda Martín Alcoff (2006), Donna Haraway, and N. Katherine Hayles to take the mimetic powers of embodiment seriously. Disabled bodies provide a particularly strong example of embodiment as mimesis because they resist standard ideas about the body and push back when confronted by language that would try to misrepresent their realism. Second, theorists influenced by the linguistic turn infrequently extend the theory of representation from mimesis properly speaking to political representation. This lack of flexibility has made it difficult to critique ideology within mimetic theory, to push discourse theory in the direction of a broader consideration of the real as a domain in which words and things exist in relations of verifiable reciprocity, and to account for social and political representation beyond narrow ideas of social constructionism. A focus on the disabled body encourages a more generous theory of representation that reaches from gestures and emotions to language and political representation. It also opens the possibility of classifying identity as an embodied representational category, thereby inserting the body into debates about identity politics.

Third, this book theorizes disability as a minority identity, one whose particular characteristics contribute to the advancement of minority studies in general. While seen historically as a matter for medical intervention, disability has been described more recently in disability studies as a minority identity that must be addressed not as personal misfortune or individual defect but as the product of a disabling social and built environment. Tired of discrimination and claiming disability as a positive identity, people with disabilities insist on the pertinence of disability to the human condition, on the value of disability as a form of diversity, and on the power of disability as a critical concept for thinking about human identity in general. How does disability resemble or differ from race, gender, sexuality, and class as a marker of identity? Which issues ally disability studies to other minority studies? How does the inclusion of disability change the theory of minority identity? Feminism, critical race studies, and queer theory have transformed critical and cultural theory by requiring us to account for the experiences of different identities. I believe that increased literacy about disability identity and its defining experiences will transform critical and cultural theory yet again.

## Disability Identity

Disability has been a medical matter for as long as human beings have sought to escape the stigma of death, disease, and injury. The medical model defines disability as an individual defect lodged in the person, a defect that must be cured or eliminated if the person is to achieve full capacity as a human being. The study of disability as a symbolic network is of more recent date. Unlike the medical approach, the emerging field of disability studies defines disability not as an individual defect but as the product of social injustice, one that requires not the cure or elimination of the defective person but significant changes in the social and built environment. Disability studies does not treat disease or disability, hoping to cure or avoid them; it studies the social meanings, symbols, and stigmas attached to disability identity and asks how they relate to enforced systems of exclusion and oppression, attacking the widespread belief that having an able body and mind determines whether one is a quality human being. More specifically, disability studies names the states of social oppression unique to people with disabilities, while asserting at the same time the positive values that they may contribute to society. One of the basic claims of disability studies is that the presence of disabled people in any discussion changes not only the culture of the discussion but also the nature of the arguments used in the discussion. For example, disability studies frames the most contested arguments of our day, such as debates about abortion, assisted suicide, and genetic research, in entirely new and unfamiliar terms.

Disability is not a physical or mental defect but a cultural and minority identity. To call disability an identity is to recognize that it is not a biological or natural property but an elastic social category both subject to social control and capable of effecting social change. Nevertheless, as a marker of social identity, disability sometimes works in contradictory ways, and it is necessary to remark on these contradictions before moving forward, since they pervade many discussions in the field of disability studies. To put it simply, disability has both negative and positive usages in disability studies, and unless one remains vigilant about usage, a great deal of confusion will result. Undoubtedly, the central purpose of disability studies is to reverse the negative connotations of disability, but this pursuit tends to involve disability as an identity formation rather than as a physical or mental characteristic. Many disability theorists—and I count myself among them—would argue that disability as an identity is never negative. The use of disability to disparage a person has no place in progressive, democratic society, although it happens at present all the time. As a condition of bodies and minds, however, disability has both positive and negative valences. For example, many disabled people do not consider their disability a flaw or personal defect—and with good reason. They are comfortable with who they are, and they do not wish to be fixed or cured. But these same people may be ambivalent about acquiring other or additional disabilities. A woman proud of her deafness will not automatically court the idea of catching cancer. Nor will a man with post-polio syndrome look forward necessarily to the day when he turns in his crutches for a power chair—although he may. These ambivalent attitudes spring not only from the preference for able-bodiedness, which appears as a conceptual horizon beyond which it is difficult to think, but also from the intimate and beneficial connections between human identity and embodiment. It is a good thing to feel comfortable in one's skin, and when one does, it is not easy to imagine being different. For better or worse, disability often comes to stand for the precariousness of the human condition, for the fact that individual human beings are susceptible to change, decline over time, and die.

As a discipline, disability studies contains these contradictory usages and attitudes about disability, developing its own understanding of disability as a positive contribution to society and both critiquing and comprehending society's largely harmful views about disability. On one level, it is easy to believe that disability is only negative if one has insufficient schooling in disability studies, whereas on another level from a disability perspective, it is difficult to see disability as anything but positive. Increasingly, theorists of disability are arguing, as I will here, more nuanced and complicated positions. Susan Wendell, for example, makes the case that changes in the built environment will not improve the situation of some people with painful disabilities. The reality of certain bodies is a fact, while harsh, that must be recognized (45). If the field is to advance, disability studies needs to account for both the negative and positive valences of disability, to resist the negative by advocating the positive and to resist the positive by acknowledging the negative—while never forgetting that its reason for being is to speak about, for, and with disabled people.

The presence of disability creates a different picture of identity—one less stable than identities associated with gender, race, sexuality, nation, and class—and therefore presenting the opportunity to rethink how human identity works. I know as a white man that I will not wake up in the morning as a black woman, but I could wake up a quadriplegic, as Mark O'Brien did when he was six years old (O'Brien and Kendall 2003). Able-bodiedness is a temporary identity at best, while being human guarantees that all other identities will eventually come into contact with some form of disability identity. In fact, a number of disability theorists have made the crucial observation that disability frequently anchors the status of other identities, especially minority identities. David Mitchell and Sharon Snyder argue that "stigmatized social positions founded upon gender, class, nationality, and race have often relied upon disability to visually underscore the devaluation of marginal communities" (1997, 21). Douglas Baynton reveals that discrimination in the United States against people of color, women, and immigrants has been justified historically by representing them as disabled. These oppressed groups have gained some ground against prejudice, but when their identities are tied to disability, discrimination against them is justified anew. Disability marks the last frontier of unquestioned inferiority because the preference for able-bodiedness makes it extremely difficult to embrace disabled people and to recognize their unnecessary and violent exclusion from society.

The more we learn about disability, the more it will become apparent that it functions at this historical moment according to a symbolic mode different from other representations of minority difference. It is as if disability operates symbolically as an othering other. It represents a diacritical marker of difference that secures inferior, marginal, or minority status, while not having its presence as a marker acknowledged in the process. Rather, the minority identities that disability accents are thought pathological in their essence. Or one might say that the symbolic association with disability disables these identities, fixing firmly their negative and inferior status. What work is disability doing, without being remarked as such, in matters of sex, gender, class, nationality, and race? Why does the presence of disability make it easier to discriminate against other minority identities? In which other ways does disability inflect minority identity and vice versa? If disability serves as an unacknowledged symbol of otherness rather than as a feature of everyday life, how might an insistence on its presence and reality change our theories about identity?

My practice of reading here strives to reverse the influence of this strange symbolism by purposefully interpreting disability as itself, while attending to its value for intersecting identities. When minority identities are pathologized by association with disability, the effect is never, I claim, merely metaphorical—a simple twisting of meaning a degree or two toward pathology. The pathologization of other identities by disability is referential: it summons the historical and representational structures by which disability, sickness, and injury come to signify inferior human status. The appearance of pathology, then, requires that we focus rigorous attention not only on symbolic association with disability but on disability as a reality of the human condition.

## The Ideology of Ability

We seem caught as persons living finite lives between two sets of contradictory ideas about our status as human beings. The first contradiction targets our understanding of the body itself. On the one hand, bodies do not seem to matter to who we are. They contain or dress up the spirit, the soul, the mind, the self. I am, as Descartes explained, the thinking part. At best, the body is a vehicle, the means by which we convey who we are from place to place. At worst, the body is a fashion accessory. We are all playing at Dorian Gray, so confident that the self can be freed from the dead weight of the body, but we have forgotten somehow to read to the end of the novel. On the other hand, modern culture feels the urgent need to perfect the body. Whether medical scientists are working on a cure for the common cold or the elimination of all disease, a cure for cancer or the banishment of death, a cure for HIV/AIDS or control of the genetic code, their preposterous and yet rarely questioned goal is to give everyone a perfect body. We hardly ever consider how incongruous is this understanding of the body—that the body seems both inconsequential and perfectible.

A second but related contradiction targets the understanding of the human being in time. The briefest look at history reveals that human beings are fragile. Human life confronts the overwhelming reality of sickness, injury, disfigurement, enfeeblement, old age, and death. Natural disasters, accidents, warfare and violence, starvation, disease, and pollution of the natural environment attack human life on all fronts, and there are no survivors. This is not to say that life on this earth is wretched and happiness nonexistent. The point is simply that history reveals one unavoidable truth about human beings—whatever our destiny as a species, we are as individuals feeble and finite. And yet the vision of the future to which we often hold promises an existence that bears little or no resemblance to our history. The future obeys an entirely different imperative, one that commands our triumph over death and contradicts everything that history tells us about our lot in life. Many religions instruct that human beings will someday win eternal life. Science fiction fantasizes about aliens who have left behind their mortal sheath; they are superior to us, but we are evolving in their direction. Cybernetics treats human intelligence as software that can be moved from machine to machine. It promises a future where human beings might be downloaded into new hardware whenever their old hardware wears out. The reason given for exploring human cloning is to defeat disease and aging. Apparently, in some future epoch, a quick trip to the spare-parts depot will cure what ails us; people will look better, feel healthier, and live three times longer. Finally, the human genome project, like eugenics before it, places its faith in a future understanding of human genetics that will perfect human characteristics and extend human life indefinitely.

However stark these contradictions, however false in their extremes, they seem credible in relation to each other. We are capable of believing at once that the body does not matter and that it should be perfected. We believe at once that history charts the radical finitude of human life but that the future promises radical infinitude. That we embrace these contradictions without interrogating them reveals that our thinking is steeped in ideology. Ideology does not permit the thought of contradiction necessary to question it; it sutures together opposites, turning them into apparent complements of each other, smoothing over contradictions, and making almost unrecognizable any perspective that would offer a critique of it. In fact, some cultural theorists claim to believe that ideology is as impenetrable as the Freudian unconscious—that there is no outside to ideology, that it can contain any negative, and that it sprouts contradictions without suffering them (see Goodheart; Siebers 1999). I argue another position: ideology creates, by virtue of its exclusionary nature, social locations outside of itself and therefore capable of making epistemological claims about it. The arguments that follow here are based on the contention that oppressed social locations create identities and perspectives, embodiments and feelings, histories and experiences that stand outside of and offer valuable knowledge about the powerful ideologies that seem to enclose us.

This book pursues a critique of one of these powerful ideologies—one I call the ideology of ability. The ideology of ability is at its simplest the preference for able-bodiedness. At its most radical, it defines the baseline by which humanness is determined, setting the measure of body and mind that gives or denies human status to individual persons. It affects nearly all of our judgments, definitions, and values about human beings, but because it is discriminatory and exclusionary, it creates social locations outside of and critical of its purview, most notably in this case, the perspective of disability. Disability defines the invisible center around which our contradictory ideology about human ability revolves. For the ideology of ability makes us fear disability, requiring that we imagine our bodies are of no consequence while dreaming at the same time that we might perfect them. It describes disability as what we flee in the past and hope to defeat in the future. Disability identity stands in uneasy relationship to the ideology of ability, presenting a critical framework that disturbs and critiques it.

One project of this book is to define the ideology of ability and to make its workings legible and familiar, despite how imbricated it may be in our thinking and practices, and despite how little we notice its patterns, authority, contradictions, and influence as a result. A second and more important project is to bring disability out of the shadow of the ideology of ability, to increase awareness about disability, and to illuminate its kinds, values, and realities. Disability creates theories of embodiment more complex than the ideology of ability allows, and these many embodiments are each crucial to the understanding of humanity and its variations, whether physical, mental, social, or historical. These two projects unfold slowly over the course of my argument for the simple reason that both involve dramatic changes in thinking. The level of literacy about disability is so low as to be nonexistent, and the ideology of ability is so much a part of every action, thought, judgment, and intention that its hold on us is difficult to root out. The sharp difference between disability and ability may be grasped superficially in the idea that disability is essentially a "medical matter," while ability concerns natural gifts, talents, intelligence, creativity, physical prowess, imagination, dedication, the eagerness to strive, including the capacity and desire to strive—in brief, the essence of the human spirit. It is easy to write a short list about disability, but the list concerning ability goes on and on, almost without end, revealing the fact that we are always dreaming about it but rarely thinking critically about why and how we are dreaming.

I resort at the outset to the modern convention of the bullet point to introduce the ideology of ability as simply as possible. The bullet points follow without the thought of being exhaustive or avoiding contradiction and without the full commentary that they deserve. Some of the bullets are intended to look like definitions; others describe ability or disability as operators; others still gather stereotypes and prejudices. The point is to begin the accumulation of ideas, narratives, myths, and stereotypes about disability whose theory this book seeks to advance, to provide a few small descriptions on which to build further discussion of ability as an ideology, and to start readers questioning their own feelings about ability and disability:

- Ability is the ideological baseline by which humanness is determined. The lesser the ability, the lesser the human being.
- The ideology of ability simultaneously banishes disability and turns it into a principle of exclusion.
- Ability is the supreme indicator of value when judging human actions, conditions, thoughts, goals, intentions, and desires.
- If one is able-bodied, one is not really aware of the body. One feels the body only when something goes wrong with it.
- The able body has a great capacity for self-transformation. It can be trained to do almost anything; it adjusts to new situations. The disabled body is limited in what it can do and what it can be trained to do. It experiences new situations as obstacles.
- Disability is always individual, a property of one body, not a feature common to all human beings, while ability defines a feature essential to the human species.
- Disability can be overcome through will power or acts of the imagination. It is not real but imaginary.
- "Disability's no big deal," as Mark O'Brien writes in his poem, "Walkers" (1997, 36).
- It is better to be dead than disabled.
- Nondisabled people have the right to choose when to be able-bodied. Disabled people must try to be as able-bodied as possible all the time.
- Overcoming a disability is an event to be celebrated. It is an ability in itself to be able to overcome disability.
- The value of a human life arises as a question only when a person is disabled. Disabled people are worth less than nondisabled people, and the difference is counted in dollars and cents.
- Disabilities are the gateway to special abilities. Turn disability to an advantage.
- Loss of ability translates into loss of sociability. People with disabilities are bitter, angry, self-pitying, or selfish. Because they cannot see beyond their own pain, they lose the ability to consider the feelings of other people. Disability makes narcissists of us all.

- People who wish to identify as disabled are psychologically damaged. If they could think of themselves as able-bodied, they would be healthier and happier.

To reverse the negative connotations of disability apparent in this list, it will be necessary to claim the value and variety of disability in ways that may seem strange to readers who have little experience with disability studies. But it is vital to show to what extent the ideology of ability collapses once we "claim disability" as a positive identity (Linton). It is equally vital to understand that claiming disability, while a significant political act, is not only political but also a practice that improves quality of life for disabled people. As documented in the case of other minority identities, individuals who identify positively rather than negatively with their disability status lead more productive and happier lives. Feminism, the black and red power movements, as well as gay and disability pride—to name only a few positive identity formations—win tangible benefits for their members, freeing them not only from the violence, hatred, and prejudice directed toward them but also providing them with both shared experiences to guide life choices and a community in which to prosper.

Some readers with a heightened sense of paradox may object that claiming disability as a positive identity merely turns disability into ability and so remains within its ideological horizon. But disability identity does not flounder on this paradox. Rather, the paradox demonstrates how difficult it is to think beyond the ideological horizon of ability and how crucial it is to make the attempt. For thinking of disability as ability, we will see, changes the meaning and usage of ability.

## Minority Identity as Theory

Identity is out of fashion as a category in critical and cultural theory. While it has been associated by the Right and Left with self-victimization, group think, and political correctness, these associations are not the real reason for its fall from grace. The real reason is that identity is seen as a crutch for the person who needs extra help, who is in pain, who cannot think independently. I use the word "crutch" on purpose because the attack on identity is best understood in the context of disability.

According to Linda Martín Alcoff's extensive and persuasive analysis in *Visible Identities*, the current rejection of identity has a particular philosophical lineage, one driven, I believe, by the ideology of ability (2006, 47–83). The line of descent begins with the Enlightenment theory of rational autonomy, which represents the inability to reason as the sign of inbuilt inferiority. Usually, the defense of reason attacked non-Europeans as intellectually defective, but because these racist theories relied on the idea of biological inferiority, they necessarily based themselves from the start on the exclusion of disability. "The norm of rational maturity," Alcoff makes clear, "required a core self stripped of its identity. Groups too immature to practice this kind of abstract thought or to transcend their ascribed cultural identities were deemed incapable of full autonomy, and their lack of maturity was often 'explained' via racist theories of the innate inferiority of non-European peoples" (2006, 22). The Enlightenment view then descends to two modern theories, each of which sees dependence on others as a form of weakness that leads to oppressive rather than cooperative behavior. The first theory belongs to Freud, for whom strong identity attachments relate to pathological psychology and figure as symptoms of ego dysfunction. In psychoanalysis, in effect, a lack lies at the heart of identity (2006, 74), and those unable to overcome this lack fall into patterns of dependence and aggression. Second, in Sartre's existential ontology, identity is alienated from the real self. Identity represents for Sartre a social role, linked to bad faith and motivated by moral failing and intellectual weakness, that tempts the self with inauthentic existence, that is, an existence insufficiently free from the influence of others (2006, 68).

---

Dossier No. 1
*The Nation*
November 6, 2006

Show Him the Money
By Katha Pollitt

I wanted to admire *The Trouble with Diversity*, Walter Benn Michaels's much-discussed polemic against identity politics and economic inequality. Like him, I'm bothered by the extent to which

> symbolic politics has replaced class grievances on campus, and off it
> too: the obsessive cultivation of one's roots, the fetishizing of differ-
> ence, the nitpicky moral one-upmanship over language. Call an ar-
> gument "lame" on one academic-feminist list I'm on and you'll
> get—still!—an electronic earful about your insensitivity to the dis-
> abled....

These two strains of thinking, despite their differences, support the contemporary distrust of identity. Thus, for Michel Foucault and Judith Butler—to name two of the most influential theorists on the scene today—
identity represents a "social necessity that is also a social pathology"
(Alcoff 2006, 66); there supposedly exists no form of identity not linked
ultimately to subjugation by others. In short, contemporary theorists ban-
ish identity when they associate it with lack, pathology, dependence, and
intellectual weakness. Identity in their eyes is not merely a liability but a
disability.

Notice, however, that identity is thought defective only in the case of
minorities, whereas it plays no role in the critique of majority
identifications, even among theorists who assail them. For example, no
one attacks Americanness specifically because it is an identity. It may be
criticized as an example of nationalism, but identity receives little or no
mention in the critique. Identity is attacked most frequently in the analysis of minority identity—only people of color, Jews, Muslims, gay, lesbian,
bisexual, and transgendered people, women, and people with disabilities
seem to possess unhealthy identities. It is as if identity itself occupied a
minority position in present critical and cultural theory—for those who
reject identity appear to do so only because of its minority status, a status
linked again and again to disability.

Moreover, the rejection of minority identity repeats in nearly every
case the same psychological scenario. The minority identity, a product of
damage inflicted systematically on a people by a dominant culture, is
rearticulated by the suffering group as self-affirming, but because the
identity was born of suffering, it is supposedly unable to shed its pain, and
this pain soon comes to justify feelings of selfishness, resentment, bitter-
ness, and self-pity—all of which combine to justify the oppression of
other people. Thus, J. C. Lester complains that "the disabled are in danger
of being changed," because of disability studies, "from the proper object of

decent voluntary help, where there is genuine need, into a privileged and growing interest group of oppressors of more ordinary people." Nancy Fraser also points out that identity politics "encourages the reification of group identities" and promotes "conformism, intolerance, and patriarchalism" (113, 112). Even if this tired scenario were credible—and it is not because it derives from false ideas about disability—it is amazing that so-called politically minded people are worried that a few minority groups might somehow, some day, gain the power to retaliate for injustice, when the wealthy, powerful, and wicked are actively plundering the globe in every conceivable manner: the decimation of nonindustrial countries by the industrial nations, arms-trafficking, enforcement of poverty to maintain the circuit between cheap labor and robust consumerism, global warming, sexual trafficking of women, industrial pollution by the chemical and oil companies, inflation of costs for drugs necessary to fight epidemics, and the cynical failure by the wealthiest nations to feed their own poor, not to mention starving people outside their borders.

My argument here takes issue with those who believe that identity politics either springs from disability or disables people for viable political action. I offer a defense of identity politics and a counterargument to the idea, embraced by the Right and Left, that identity politics cannot be justified because it is linked to pain and suffering. The idea that suffering produces weak identities both enforces the ideology of ability and demonstrates a profound misunderstanding of disability: disability is not a pathological condition, only analyzable via individual psychology, but a social location complexly embodied. Identities, narratives, and experiences based on disability have the status of theory because they represent locations and forms of embodiment from which the dominant ideologies of society become visible and open to criticism. One of my specific tactics throughout this book is to tap this theoretical power by juxtaposing my argument with dossier entries detailing disability identities, narratives, images, and experiences. The dossier is compiled for the most part from news stories of the kind that appear in major newspapers across the country every day, although I have avoided the feel-good human-interest stories dominating the news that recount how their disabled protagonists overcome their disabilities to lead "normal" lives. Rather, the dossier tends to contain testimony about the oppression of disabled people, sometimes framed in their own language, sometimes framed in the language of their oppressors. At first, the dossier entries may have no particular meaning to those untutored in disability studies, but my hope is that they will grow stranger and stranger as the reader progresses, until they begin to invoke feelings of horror and disgust at the blatant and persistent prejudices directed against disabled people. The dossier represents a deliberate act of identity politics, and I offer no apology for it because identity politics remains in my view the most practical course of action by which to address social injustices against minority peoples and to apply the new ideas, narratives, and experiences discovered by them to the future of progressive, democratic society.

Identity is neither a liability nor a disability. Nor is it an ontological property or a state of being. Identity is, properly defined, an epistemological construction that contains a broad array of theories about navigating social environments. Manuel Castells calls identity a collective meaning, necessarily internalized by individuals for the purpose of social action (7), while Charles Taylor argues, "My identity is defined by the commitments and identifications which provide the frame or horizon within which I can try to determine from case to case what is good, or valuable, or what ought to be done, or what I endorse or oppose" (27). Alcoff explains that "identity is not merely that which is given to an individual or group, but is also a way of inhabiting, interpreting, and working through, both collectively and individually, an objective social location and group history" (2006, 42). We do well to follow these writers and to consider identity a theory-laden construction, rather than a mere social construction, in which knowledge for social living adheres—though not always and necessarily the best knowledge. Thus, identity is not the structure that creates a person's pristine individuality or inner essence but the structure by which that person identifies and becomes identified with a set of social narratives, ideas, myths, values, and types of knowledge of varying reliability, usefulness, and verifiability. It represents the means by which the person, qua individual, comes to join a particular social body. It also represents the capacity to belong to a collective on the basis not merely of biological tendencies but symbolic ones—the very capacity that distinguishes human beings from other animals.

While all identities contain social knowledge, mainstream identities are less critical, though not less effective for being so, because they are normative. Minority identities acquire the ability to make epistemological claims about the society in which they hold liminal positions, owing precisely to their liminality. The early work of Abdul JanMohamed and David Lloyd, for example, privileges the power of the minor as critique: "The study—and production—of minority discourse requires, as an inevitable consequence of its mode of existence, the transgression of the very disciplinary boundaries by which culture appears as a sublimated form with universal validity. This makes it virtually *the* privileged domain of cultural critique" (1987b, 9). The critique offered by minority identity is necessarily historical because it relies on the temporal contingency of its marginal position. Different groups occupy minority positions at different times, but this does not mean that their social location is any less objective relative to their times. Nor does it suggest that structures of oppression differ in the case of every minority identity. If history has taught us anything, it is that those in power have the ability to manipulate the same oppressive structures, dependent upon the same prejudicial representations, for the exclusion of different groups. The experiences of contemporary minority people, once brought to light, resound backward in history, like a reverse echo effect, to comment on the experiences of past minority peoples, while at the same time these past experiences contribute, one hopes, to an accumulation of knowledge about how oppression works.

Minority identity discovers its theoretical force by representing the experiences of oppression and struggle lived by minority peoples separately but also precisely as minorities, for attention to the similarities between different minority identities exposes their relation to oppression as well as increases the chance of political solidarity. According to the definition of Gary and Rosalind Dworkin, minority identity has recognizable features that repeat across the spectrum of oppressed people. "We propose," Dworkin and Dworkin write, "that a minority group is a group characterized by four qualities: identifiability, differential power, differential and pejorative treatment, and group awareness" (17). These four features form the basis of my argument about minority identity as well, with one notable addition—that minority status also meet an ethical test judged both relative to society and universally. These features require, each one in turn, a brief discussion to grasp their collective simplicity and power and to arrive at a precise and universal definition of minority identity on which to base the elaboration of disability identity, to describe its relation to minority identity in general, and to defend identity politics as crucial to the future of minority peoples and their quest for social justice and inclusion.

1. Identifiability as a quality exists at the heart of identity itself because we must be able to distinguish a group before we can begin to imagine an identity. Often we conceive of identifiability as involving visible differences connected to the body, such as skin color, gender traits, gestures, affect, voice, and body shapes. These physical traits, however, are not universal with respect to different cultures, and there may be actions or cultural differences that also figure as the basis of identifiability. Note as well that identifiability exists in time, and time shifts its meaning. As a group is identified, it acquires certain representations, and the growth of representations connected to the group may then change how identifiability works. For example, the existence of a group called disabled people produces a general idea of the people in the group—although the existence of the group does not depend on every disabled person fitting into it—and it then becomes easier, first, to identify people with it and, second, to shift the meaning of the group definition. Fat people are not generally considered disabled at this moment, but there are signs that they may be in the not too distant future (Kirkland). Deaf and intersex people have resisted being described as disabled; their future relation to the identity of disabled people is not clear.

Two other obvious characteristics of identifiability need to be stressed. First, identifiability is tied powerfully to the representation of difference. In cases where an existing minority group is not easily identified and those in power want to isolate the group, techniques will be used to produce identifiability. For example, the Nazis required that Jews wear yellow armbands because they were not, despite Nazi racist mythology, identifiably different from Germans. Second, identity is social, and so is the quality of identifiability. There are many physical differences among human beings that simply do not count for identifiability. It is not the fact of physical difference that matters, then, but the representation attached to difference—what makes the difference identifiable. Representation is the difference that makes a difference. We might contend that there is no such thing as private identity in the same way that Wittgenstein claimed that private language does not exist. Identity must be representable and communicable to qualify as identifiable. Identity serves social purposes, and a form of identity not representable in society would be incomprehensible and ineffective for these purposes.

Of course, people may identify themselves. Especially in societies where groups are identified for differential and pejorative treatment, individuals belonging to these groups may internalize prejudices against themselves and do on their own the work of making themselves identifiable. Jim Crow laws in the American South counted on people policing themselves—not drinking at a white water fountain if they were black, for example. But the way in which individuals claim identifiability also changes as the history of the group changes. A group may be singled out for persecution, but as it grows more rebellious, it may work to preserve its identity, while transforming simultaneously the political values attached to it. The American military's policy, "Don't ask, don't tell" in the case of gay soldiers, tries to stymie the tendency of individuals to claim a positive minority identity for political reasons.

2. Differential power is a strong indicator of the difference between majority and minority identity; in fact, it may be the most important indicator because minority status relies on differential power rather than on numbers. The numerical majority is not necessarily the most powerful group. There are more women than men, and men hold more political power and have higher salaries for the same jobs. Numerical advantage is significant, but a better indicator is the presence of social power in one group over another. Dworkin and Dworkin mention the American South in the 1950s and South Africa under apartheid as good examples of differential power located in a nonnumerical majority (12). Minorities hold less power than majority groups.

3. A central question is whether the existence of differential treatment already implies pejorative treatment. Allowing that differential treatment may exist for legitimate reasons—and it is not at all certain that we should make this allowance—the addition of pejorative treatment as a quality of minority identity stresses the defining connection between oppression and minority status. Differential and pejorative treatment is what minority group members experience as a consequence of their minority position. It affects their economic standing, cultural prestige, educational opportunities, and civil rights, among other things. Discrimination as pejorative treatment often becomes the focus of identity politics, those

concerted attempts by minorities to protest their inferior and unjust status by forming political action groups.

The emergence of identity politics, then, relies on a new epistemological claim. While it is not necessarily the case that a group will protest against discrimination, since there is a history of groups that accept inferior status and even fight to maintain it, the shift to a protest stance must involve claims different from those supporting the discriminatory behavior. A sense of inequity comes to pervade the consciousness of the minority identity, and individuals can find no reasonable justification for their differential treatment. Individuals in protest against unjust treatment begin to develop theories that oppose majority opinion not only about themselves but about the nature of the society that supports the pejorative behavior. They develop ways to represent the actions used to perpetuate the injustice against them, attacking stereotypes, use of violence and physical attack, and discrimination. Individuals begin to constitute themselves as a minority identity, moving from the form of consciousness called internal colonization to one characterized by a new group awareness.

4. Group awareness does not refer to group identifiability but to the perception of common goals pursued through cooperation, to the realization that differential and pejorative treatment is not justified by actual qualities of the minority group, and to the conviction that majority society is a disabling environment that must be transformed by recourse to social justice. In other words, awareness is not merely self-consciousness but an epistemology that adheres in group identity status. It is the identity that brings down injustice initially on the individual's head. This identity is constructed in such a way that it can be supported only by certain false claims and stereotypes. Resistance to these false claims is pursued and shared by members of the minority identity through counterarguments about, and criticism of, the existing state of knowledge. Thus, minority identity linked to group awareness achieves the status of a theoretical claim in itself, one in conflict with the mainstream and a valuable source of meaningful diversity. Opponents of identity politics often argue that identity politics preserves the identities created by oppression: these identities are born of suffering, and embracing them supposedly represents a form of self-victimization. This argument does not understand that new epistemological claims are central to identity politics. For example, societies that oppress women often assert that they are irrational, morally de-

praved, and physically weak. The minority identity "woman," embraced by feminist identity politics, disputes these assertions and presents alternative, positive theories about women. Identity politics do not preserve the persecuted identities created by oppressors because the knowledge claims adhering in the new identities are completely different from those embraced by the persecuting groups.

Opponents of identity politics are not wrong, however, when they associate minority identity with suffering. They are wrong because they do not accept that pain and suffering may sometimes be resources for the epistemological insights of minority identity. This issue will arise whenever we consider disability identity, since it is the identity most associated with pain, and a great deal of discrimination against people with disabilities derives from the irrational fear of pain. It is not uncommon for disabled people to be told by complete strangers that they would kill themselves if they had such a disability. Doctors often withhold treatment of minor illnesses from disabled people because they believe they are better off dead—the doctors want to end the suffering of their patients, but these disabled people do not necessarily think of themselves as in pain, although they must suffer discriminatory attitudes (Gill; Longmore 149–203). Nevertheless, people with disabilities are not the only people who suffer from prejudice. The epistemological claims of minority identity in general are often based on feelings of injustice that are painful. Wounds received in physical attacks may pale against the suffering experienced in the idea that one is being attacked because one is unjustly thought inferior—and yet suffering may have theoretical value for the person in pain. While there is a long history of describing pain and suffering as leading to egotism and narcissism—a metapsychology that plays, I argue in chapter 2, an ancillary role in the evolution of the ideology of ability—we might consider that the strong focus given to the self in pain has epistemological value.[1] Suffering is a signal to the self at risk, and this signal applies equally to physical and social situations. The body signals with pain when a person is engaged in an activity that may do that person physical harm. Similarly, consciousness feels pain when the individual is in social danger. Suffering has a theoretical component because it draws attention to situations that jeopardize the future of the individual, and when individuals who suffer from oppression gather together to share their experiences, this theoretical component may be directed toward political ends.

By suggesting that suffering is theory-laden—that is, a sensation evaluative of states of reality—I am trying to track how and why minority identity makes epistemological claims about society. All identity is social theory. Identities are the theories that we use to fit into and travel through the social world. Our identities have a content that makes knowledge claims about the society in which they have evolved, and we adjust our identities, when we can, to different situations to improve our chances of success. But because mainstream identities so robustly mimic existing social norms, it is difficult to abstract their claims about society. Identities in conflict with society, however, have the ability to expose its norms. Minority identity gains the status of social critique once its content has been sufficiently developed by groups that unite to protest their unjust treatment by the society in which they live.

5. In addition to the four qualities proposed by Dworkin and Dworkin, groups claiming minority identity need to meet an ethical test. Minority identities make epistemological claims about the societies in which they hold liminal positions, but not all theories are equal in ethical content, especially relative to minority identity, since it begins as a product of oppression and acquires the status of social critique. While matters ethical are notoriously difficult to sort out, it is nevertheless worth pausing briefly over how ethics relates to minority identity because ethical content may serve to check fraudulent claims of minority status. For example, in South Africa of recent date, the ideology of apartheid represented the majority position because it held power, identified the nature of minority identity, and dictated differential and pejorative treatment of those in the minority. Today in South Africa, however, the apartheidists are no longer in the majority. Applying the theory of Dworkin and Dworkin, they might be construed as having a minority identity: they are identifiable, they have differential power, they are treated pejoratively, and they possess group awareness—that is, they present a set of claims that actively and consciously criticize majority society. They also believe themselves to be persecuted, and no doubt they feel suffering about their marginal position.

Why are the apartheidists not deserving of minority status? The answer is that the theories contained in apartheidist identity do not pass an ethical test. The contrast between its ethical claims and those of the majority are sufficiently striking to recognize. The apartheidists propose a racist society as the norm to which all South African citizens should adhere. Relative to South African social beliefs and those of many other countries, apartheid ideology is unacceptable on ethical grounds because it is biased, violent, and oppressive. Consequently, the apartheidists fail to persuade us with their claims, and we judge them not a minority group subject to oppression but a fringe group trying to gain unlawful advantage over others.

To summarize, the definition embraced here—and used to theorize disability identity—does not understand minority identity as statistical, fixed in time, or exclusively biological but as a politicized identity possessing the ability to offer social critiques. There are those who attack minority identities precisely because they are politicized, as if only minorities made political arguments based on identity and politicized identity in itself were a species of defective attachment. But many other examples of politicized identity exist on the current scene—Democrats, Republicans, Socialists, the Christian Coalition, the American Nazi Party, and so on. In fact, any group that forms a coalition to make arguments on its own behalf and on the behalf of others in the public forum takes on a politicized identity. Arguments to outlaw minority political action groups merely because they encourage politicized identities would have to abolish other political groups as well.

## Disability and the Theory of Complex Embodiment

Feminist philosophers have long argued that all knowledge is situated, that it adheres in social locations, that it is embodied, with the consequence that they have been able to claim that people in marginal social positions enjoy an epistemological privilege that allows them to theorize society differently from those in dominant social locations (Haraway 183–201; Harding). Knowledge is situated, first of all, because it is based on perspective. There is a difference between the knowledge present in a view of the earth from the moon and a view of the earth from the perspective of an ant. We speak blandly of finding different perspectives on things, but different perspectives do in fact give varying conceptions of objects, especially social objects. Nevertheless, situated knowledge does not rely only on changing perspectives. Situated knowledge adheres in embodiment. The disposition of the body determines perspectives, but it also spices these perspectives with phenomenological knowledge—lifeworld experience—that affects the interpretation of perspective. To take a famous example from Iris Young, the fact that many women "throw like a girl" is not based on a physical difference. The female arm is as capable of throwing a baseball as the male arm. It is the representation of femininity in a given society that disables women, pressuring them to move their bodies in certain, similar ways, and once they become accustomed to moving in these certain, similar ways, it is difficult to retrain the body. "Women in sexist society are physically handicapped," Young explains. "Insofar as we learn to live out our existence in accordance with the definition that patriarchal culture assigns to us, we are physically inhibited, confined, positioned, and objectified" (171). It is possible to read the differential and pejorative treatment of women, as if it were a disability, on the surface of their skin, in muscle mass, in corporeal agility. This form of embodiment is also, however, a form of situated knowledge about the claims being made about and by women in a given society. To consider some positive examples, the particular embodiment of a woman means that she might, after experiencing childbirth, have a new and useful perception of physical pain. Women may also have, because of menstruation, a different knowledge of blood. Female gender identity is differently embodied because of women's role in reproductive labor. The presence of the body does not boil down only to perspective but to profound ideas and significant theories about the world.

Embodiment is, of course, central to the field of disability studies. In fact, a focus on disability makes it easier to understand that embodiment and social location are one and the same. Arguments for the specificity of disability identity tend to stress the critical nature of embodiment, and the tacit or embodied knowledge associated with particular disabilities often justifies their value to larger society. For example, George Lane's body, we will see in chapter 6, incorporates a set of theoretical claims about architecture that the Supreme Court interprets in its ruling against the State of Tennessee, finding that Lane's inability to enter the Polk County Courthouse reveals a pattern of discrimination against people with disabilities found throughout the American court system. Chapter 5 explores disability passing not as avoidance of social responsibility or manipulation for selfish interests but as a form of embodied knowledge—forced into usage by prejudices against disability—about the relationship between the social environment and human ability. The young deaf woman who tries to pass for hearing will succeed only if she possesses significant knowledge about the informational potential, manners, physical gestures, conversational rituals, and cultural activities that define hearing in her society. Disabled people who pass for able-bodied are neither cowards, cheats, nor con artists but skillful interpreters of the world from whom we all might learn.

---

Dossier No. 2
*New York Times Online*
November 15, 2006

Officials Clash over Mentally Ill in Florida Jails
By Abby Goodnough

MIAMI, Nov. 14—For years, circuit judges here have ordered state officials to obey Florida law and promptly transfer severely mentally ill inmates from jails to state hospitals. But with few hospital beds available, Gov. Jeb Bush's administration began flouting those court orders in August. . . .

"This type of arrogant activity cannot be tolerated in an orderly society," Judge Crockett Farnell of Pinellas-Pasco Circuit Court wrote in an Oct. 11 ruling.

State law requires that inmates found incompetent to stand trial be moved from county jails to psychiatric hospitals within 15 days of the state's receiving the commitment orders. Florida has broken that law for years, provoking some public defenders to seek court orders forcing swift compliance. . . .

Two mentally ill inmates in the Escambia County Jail in Pensacola died over the last year and a half after being subdued by guards, according to news reports. And in the Pinellas County Jail in Clearwater, a schizophrenic inmate gouged out his eye after waiting weeks for a hospital bed, his lawyer said. . . .

The problem is not unique to Florida, although it is especially severe in Miami-Dade County, which has one of the nation's largest percentages of mentally ill residents, according to the National Alliance for the Mentally Ill, an advocacy group. . . .

In Miami, an average of 25 to 40 acutely psychotic people live in a unit of the main county jail that a lawyer for Human Rights Watch, Jennifer Daskal, described as squalid after visiting last month.... Ms. Daskal said that some of the unit's 14 "suicide cells"—dim, bare and designed for one inmate—were holding two or three at a time, and that the inmates were kept in their cells 24 hours a day except to shower....

But embodiment also appears as a bone of contention in disability studies because it seems caught between competing models of disability. Briefly, the medical model defines disability as a property of the individual body that requires medical intervention. The medical model has a biological orientation, focusing almost exclusively on disability as embodiment. The social model opposes the medical model by defining disability relative to the social and built environment, arguing that disabling environments produce disability in bodies and require interventions at the level of social justice. Some scholars complain that the medical model pays too much attention to embodiment, while the social model leaves it out of the picture. Without returning to a medical model, which labels individuals as defective, the next step for disability studies is to develop a theory of complex embodiment that values disability as a form of human variation.

The theory of complex embodiment raises awareness of the effects of disabling environments on people's lived experience of the body, but it emphasizes as well that some factors affecting disability, such as chronic pain, secondary health effects, and aging, derive from the body. These last disabilities are neither less significant than disabilities caused by the environment nor to be considered defects or deviations merely because they are resistant to change. Rather, they belong to the spectrum of human variation, conceived both as variability between individuals and as variability within an individual's life cycle, and they need to be considered in tandem with social forces affecting disability.[2] The theory of complex embodiment views the economy between social representations and the body not as unidirectional as in the social model, or nonexistent as in the medical model, but as reciprocal. Complex embodiment theorizes the body and its representations as mutually transformative. Social representations obviously affect the experience of the body, as Young makes clear in her seminal essay, but the body possesses the ability to determine its social representation as well, and some situations exist where representation exerts no control over the life of the body.

As a living entity, the body is vital and chaotic, possessing complexity in equal share to that claimed today by critical and cultural theorists for linguistic systems. The association of the body with human mortality and fragility, however, forces a general distrust of the knowledge embodied in it. It is easier to imagine the body as a garment, vehicle, or burden than as a complex system that defines our humanity, any knowledge that we might possess, and our individual and collective futures. Disability gives even greater urgency to the fears and limitations associated with the body, tempting us to believe that the body can be changed as easily as changing clothes. The ideology of ability stands ready to attack any desire to know and to accept the disabled body in its current state. The more likely response to disability is to try to erase any signs of change, to wish to return the body magically to a past era of supposed perfection, to insist that the body has no value as human variation if it is not flawless.

Ideology and prejudice, of course, abound in all circles of human existence, labeling some groups and individuals as inferior or less than human: people of color, women, the poor, people with different sexual orientations, and the disabled confront the intolerance of society on a daily basis. In nearly no other sphere of existence, however, do people risk waking up one morning having become the persons whom they hated the day before. Imagine the white racist suddenly transformed into a black man, the anti-Semite into a Jew, the misogynist into a woman, and one might begin to approach the change in mental landscape demanded by the onset of disability. We require the stuff of science fiction to describe these scenarios, most often for comic effect or paltry moralizing. But no recourse to fiction is required to imagine an able-bodied person becoming disabled. It happens every minute of every day.

The young soldier who loses his arm on an Iraqi battlefield wakes up in bed having become the kind of person whom he has always feared and whom society names as contemptible (Corbett). Given these circumstances, how might we expect him to embrace and to value his new identity? He is living his worst nightmare. He cannot sleep. He hates what he has become. He distances himself from his wife and family. He begins to drink too much. He tries to use a functional prosthetic, but he loathes being seen with a hook. The natural prosthetic offered to him by Army doctors does not really work, and he prefers to master tasks with his one good arm. He cannot stand the stares of those around him, the looks of pity and contempt as he tries to perform simple tasks in public, and he begins to look upon himself with disdain.

The soldier has little chance, despite the promise of prosthetic science, to return to his former state. What he is going through is completely understandable, but he needs to come to a different conception of himself, one based not on the past but on the present and the future. His body will continue to change with age, and he may have greater disabling conditions in the future. He is no different in this regard from any other human being. Some disabilities can be approached by demanding changes in how people with disabilities are perceived, others by changes in the built environment. Some can be treated through medical care. Other disabilities cannot be approached by changes in either the environment or the body. In almost every case, however, people with disabilities have a better chance of future happiness and health if they accept their disability as a positive identity and benefit from the knowledge embodied in it. The value of people with disabilities to themselves does not lie in finding a way to return through medical intervention to a former physical perfection, since that perfection is a myth, nor in trying to conceal from others and themselves that they are disabled. Rather, embodiment seen complexly understands disability as an epistemology that rejects the temptation to value the body as anything other than what it was and that embraces what the body has become and will become relative to the demands on it, whether environmental, representational, or corporeal.

## Intersectional Identity Complexly Embodied

The ultimate purpose of complex embodiment as theory is to give disabled people greater knowledge of and control over their bodies in situations where increased knowledge and control are possible. But the theory has side benefits for at least two crucial debates raging on the current scene as well. First, complex embodiment makes a contribution to influential arguments about intersectionality—the idea that analyses of social oppression take account of overlapping identities based on race, gender, sexuality, class, and disability.[3] While theorists of intersectionality have never argued for a simple additive model in which oppressed identities are stacked one upon another, a notion of disability embodiment helps to resist the temptation of seeing some identities as more pathological than others, and it offers valuable advice about how to conceive the standpoint of others for the purpose of understanding the prejudices against them. This is not to suggest that the intersection of various identities produces the same results for all oppressed groups, since differences in the hierarchical organization of race, gender, sexuality, class, and disability do exist (Collins 2003, 212). Rather, it is to emphasize, first, that intersectionality as a theory references the tendency of identities to construct one another reciprocally (Collins 2003, 208); second, that identities are not merely standpoints where one may stand or try to stand but also complex embodiments; and, third, that the ideology of ability uses the language of pathology to justify labeling some identities as inferior to others.[4]

For example, theorists of intersectional identity might find useful the arguments in disability studies against disability simulation because they offer a view of complex embodiment that enlarges standpoint theory. The applied fields of occupational therapy and rehabilitation science sometimes recommend the use of disability simulations to raise the consciousness of therapists who treat people with disabilities. Instructors ask students to spend a day in a wheelchair or to try navigating classroom buildings blindfolded to get a better sense of the challenges faced by their patients. The idea is that students may stand for a time in the places occupied by disabled people and come to grasp their perspectives. Disability theorists have attacked the use of simulations for a variety of reasons, the most important being that they fail to give the student pretenders a sense of the embodied knowledge contained in disability identities. Disability simulations of this kind fail because they place students in a time-one position of disability, before knowledge about disability is acquired, usually resulting in emotions of loss, shock, and pity at how dreadful it is to be disabled. Students experience their body relative to their usual embodiment, and they become so preoccupied with sensations of bodily inadequacy that they cannot perceive the extent to which their "disability" results from social rather than physical causes. Notice that such games focus almost entirely on the phenomenology of the individual body. The pretender asks how his or her body would be changed, how his or her personhood would be changed, by disability. It is an act of individual imagination, then, not an act of cultural imagination. Moreover, simulations tempt students to play the game of "What is Worse?" as they experiment with different simulations. Is it worse to be blind or deaf, worse to lose a leg or an arm, worse to be paralyzed or deaf, mute, and blind? The result is a thoroughly negative and unrealistic impression of disability.

The critique of disability simulation has applications in several areas of intersectional theory. First, the practice of peeling off minority identities from people to determine their place in the hierarchy of oppression is revealed to degrade all minority identities by giving a one-dimensional view of them. It also fails to understand the ways in which different identities constitute one another. Identities may trump one another in the hierarchy of oppression, but intersectional identity, because embodied complexly, produces not competition between minority identities but "outsider" theories about the lived experience of oppression (see Collins 1998). Additionally, coming to an understanding of intersecting minority identities demands that one imagine social location not only as perspective but also as complex embodiment, and complex embodiment combines social and corporeal factors. Rather than blindfolding students for a hour, then, it is preferable to send them off wearing sunglasses and carrying a white cane, in the company of a friend, to restaurants and department stores, where they may observe firsthand the spectacle of discrimination against blind people as passersby avoid and gawk at them, clerks refuse to wait on them or condescend to ask the friend what the student is looking for, and waiters request, usually at the top of their lungs and very slowly (since blind people must also be deaf and cognitively disabled), what the student would like to eat.[5]

It is crucial to resist playing the game of "What Is Worse?" when conceiving of intersectional identity, just as it is when imagining different disabilities. Asking whether it is worse to be a woman or a Latina, worse to be black or blind, worse to be gay or poor registers each identity as a form of ability that has greater or lesser powers to overcome social intolerance and prejudice. Although one may try to keep the focus on society and the question of whether it oppresses one identity more than another, the debate devolves all too soon and often to discussions of the comparative costs of changing society and making accommodations, comparisons about quality of life, and speculations about whether social disadvantages are intrinsic or extrinsic to the group. The compelling issue for minority identity does not turn on the question of whether one group has the more arduous existence but on the fact that every minority group faces social discrimination, violence, and intolerance that exert toxic and unfair influence on the ability to live life to the fullest (see Asch 406–7).


## Social Construction Complexly Embodied

Second, the theory of complex embodiment makes it possible to move forward arguments raging currently about social construction, identity, and the body. Aside from proposing a theory better suited to the experi- ences of disabled people, the goal is to advance questions in identity and body theory unresponsive to the social construction model. Chapters 3, 4, and 6 make an explicit adjustment in social construction theory by focus- ing on the realism of identities and bodies. By "realism" I understand nei- ther a positivistic claim about reality unmediated by social representa- tions, nor a linguistic claim about reality unmediated by objects of representation, but a theory that describes reality as a mediation, no less real for being such, between representation and its social objects.[6] Rather than viewing representation as a pale shadow of the world or the world as a shadow world of representation, my claim is that both sides push back in the construction of reality. The hope is to advance discourse theory to the next stage by defining construction in a radical way, one that reveals con- structions as possessing both social and physical form. While identities are socially constructed, they are nevertheless meaningful and real precisely because they are complexly embodied. The complex embodiment appar- ent in disability is an especially strong example to contemplate because the disabled body compels one to give concrete form to the theory of so- cial construction and to take its metaphors literally.

Consider an introductory example of the way in which disability complexly embodied extends the social construction argument in the di- rection of realism. In August 2000 a controversy about access at the Gale- head hut in the Appalachian Mountains came to a climax (Goldberg). The Appalachian Mountain Club of New Hampshire had just constructed a rustic thirty-eight bed lodge at an elevation of thirty-eight hundred feet. The United States Forest Service required that the hut comply with the

Americans with Disabilities Act (ADA) and be accessible to people with disabilities, that it have a wheelchair ramp and grab bars in larger toilet stalls. The Appalachian Mountain Club had to pay an extra $30,000 to $50,000 for a building already costing $400,000 because the accessible features were late design changes. Its members ridiculed the idea that the building, which could be reached only by a super-rugged 4.6 mile trail, would ever be visited by wheelchair users, and the media tended to take their side.

At this point a group from Northeast Passage, a program at the University of New Hampshire that works with people with disabilities, decided to make a visit to the Galehead hut. Jill Gravink, the director of Northeast Passage, led a group of three hikers in wheelchairs and two on crutches on a twelve-hour climb to the lodge, at the end of which they rolled happily up the ramp to its front door. A local television reporter on the scene asked why, if people in wheelchairs could drag themselves up the trail, they could not drag themselves up the steps into the hut, implying that the ramp was a waste of money. Gravink responded, "Why bother putting steps on the hut at all? Why not drag yourself in through a window?"

The design environment, Gravink suggests pointedly, determines who is able-bodied at the Galehead lodge. The distinction between the disabled and nondisabled is socially constructed, and it is a rather fine distinction at that. Those who are willing and able to climb stairs are considered able-bodied, while those who are not willing and able to climb stairs are disabled. However, those who do climb stairs but are not willing and able to enter the building through a window are not considered disabled. It is taken for granted that nondisabled people may choose when to be able-bodied. In fact, the built environment is full of technologies that make life easier for those people who possess the physical power to perform tasks without these technologies. Stairs, elevators, escalators, washing machines, leaf and snow blowers, eggbeaters, chainsaws, and other tools help to relax physical standards for performing certain tasks. These tools are nevertheless viewed as natural extensions of the body, and no one thinks twice about using them. The moment that individuals are marked as disabled or diseased, however, the expectation is that they will maintain the maximum standard of physical performance at every moment, and the technologies designed to make their life easier are viewed as expensive additions, unnecessary accommodations, and a burden on society.

The example of the Galehead hut exposes the ideology of ability—the ideology that uses ability to determine human status, demands that people with disabilities always present as able-bodied as possible, and measures the value of disabled people in dollars and cents. It reveals how constructed are our attitudes about identity and the body. This is a familiar point, and usually social analysis comes to a conclusion here, no doubt because the idea of construction is more metaphorical than real. The implication seems to be that knowledge of an object as socially constructed is sufficient to undo any of its negative effects. How many books and essays have been written in the last ten years, whose authors are content with the conclusion that x, y, or z is socially constructed, as if the conclusion itself were a victory over oppression?

Far from being satisfied with this conclusion, my analysis here will always take it as a point of departure from which to move directly to the elucidation of embodied causes and effects. Oppression is driven not by individual, unconscious syndromes but by social ideologies that are embodied, and precisely because ideologies are embodied, their effects are readable, and must be read, in the construction and history of societies. When a Down syndrome citizen tries to enter a polling place and is turned away, a social construction is revealed and must be read. When wheelchair users are called selfish if they complain about the inaccessibility of public toilets, a social construction is revealed and must be read (Shapiro 1994, 126–27). When handicapped entrances to buildings are located in the rear, next to garbage cans, a social construction is revealed and must be read. When a cosmetic surgeon removes the thumb on a little boy's right hand because he was born with no thumb on his left hand, a social construction is revealed and must be read (Marks 67). What if we were to embrace the metaphor implied by social construction, if we required that the "construction" in social construction be understood as a building, as the Galehead hut for example, and that its blueprint be made available? Not only would this requirement stipulate that we elaborate claims about social construction in concrete terms, it would insist that we locate the construction in time and place as a form of complex embodiment.

Whenever anyone mentions the idea of social construction, we should ask on principle to see the blueprint—not to challenge the value of the idea but to put it to practical use—to map as many details about the construction as possible and to track its political, epistemological, and real effects in the world of human beings. To encourage this new requirement, I cite three familiar ideas about social construction, as currently theorized, from which flow—or at least should—three methodological principles. These three principles underlie the arguments to follow, suggesting how to look for blueprints and how to begin reading them:

- Knowledge is socially situated—which means that knowledge has an objective and verifiable relation to its social location.
- Identities are socially constructed—which means that identities contain complex theories about social reality.
- Some bodies are excluded by dominant social ideologies—which means that these bodies display the workings of ideology and expose it to critique and the demand for political change.

## Chapter Two

# Tender Organs, Narcissism, and Identity Politics

We of the tender organs are narcissists. Tender of the eye—closeted in a dark little world. Tender of the ear—imprisoned within a soundless castle. Tender of the limb—the radius of our associations short and incestuous. Tender of the brain—thrown down into a well of private imaginings.

To theorize disability requires that we understand not only the history by which the accusation of narcissism is leveled against people with disabilities but the centrality of disability to the concept of narcissism itself. This is because narcissism represents perhaps the dominant psychological model used today to maintain the superiority of ability over disability, and there may be no more authoritative example of the logic of blaming victims for their own pain.[1] Narcissism is a psychological concept that defines social withdrawal, suffering, and demands for attention as the direct result of the psychopathology of the victim. Its structure allows no room for the idea that the accuser might be an interested party in the process of accusation. Narcissists, the theory goes, cease to love everyone but themselves. They turn away from society in favor of self-gratification, suffer the consequences, and then require others to take the blame for sorrows they have themselves created. Positive and negative attention alike contributes to a sense of their grandiose self, while indifference only increases feelings of narcissistic injury. In fact, injury is said to augment the feelings of self-importance felt by narcissists. This is even more powerfully the case for the narcissist than for the masochist, since masochism as a psychological concept relies on the more foundational theory of narcissism. (In theory there is no masochist who is not already a narcissist.) A critique of narcissism is vital to disability studies, then, because narcissism summons the metapsychology by which the isolation, suffering, and claims to attention of people with disabilities are turned against them and by which their reaction to their own disability becomes the proof of defects even greater than physical ones.

My primary goal here is to probe the metapsychology supporting the accusation of narcissism and to show how it relies on the idea of disability itself, but the politics of the moment obliges me to comment briefly on how the accusation of narcissism has been used to attack the emerging discipline of disability studies. In a culture said to be increasingly narcissistic, pockets of self-interest seem to be thriving, and disability studies is apparently the newest one—at least this is the position of its opponents. The most egregious attacks summon the specter of identity politics— those centers of hyperindividuality, supposedly bent on greater self-awareness and self-esteem, that have produced black studies, women's studies, and now disability studies. "Disability studies," Norah Vincent pronounces, is a form of "self-righteous goodspeak" and "the newest branch of social theory and its ignominious bedfellow, identity politics" (40). Camille Paglia calls disability studies "the ultimate self-sanctifying boondoggle for victim-obsessed academic-careerists" (cited by Vincent 40). "You can't win," complains Walter Olson, a conservative commentator who blames the Americans with Disabilities Act (ADA) for paralyzing the workplace in the United States: "Call attention to disability and you're oppressing them, ignore the disability and you're making them invisible" (cited by Vincent 40).

People with disabilities have forgotten how to suffer and be still. They want to raise the consciousness of others to their plight, to have their oppression recognized and brought to an end, and to feel good about themselves, even though other people do not feel good about disability.

For critics of disability studies, these goals are without merit. They prove merely that American society is suffering a breakdown, since people are more interested in pursuing self-gratification than in contributing to a common cause. That identity politics is thriving is supposedly proof that American society is a culture of narcissism.

Dossier No. 3
*Inside Higher Ed*
June 24, 2005

Unique Learners
By Scott Jaschik

The "last bastion of prejudice in higher education," according to
Cynthia Johnson, is the belief that developmentally disabled students don't have a place in colleges.

These students, many of whom would have been called mentally
retarded in an earlier era, have a range of skills. And while a growing
number of colleges have created a few programs or certificates for
such students, Johnson is running a program that is moving to another level.

Johnson directs the Venture Program at Bellevue Community
College, which offers a range of courses for developmentally disabled students. This fall, the program will offer an associate degree
curriculum, which Johnson and other experts believe is the first college degree program for this group.

"This is a population that has been ignored. No one had thought
of them having a college degree before. There is a desire by the students, but no one pushed the envelope to do this," Johnson says. . . .

It is wrong to study what you are. This allegation is familiar after more
than thirty years of attack against black studies and women's studies.[2] In
this light, disability studies appears to be only the latest example of "moi
criticism" because it privileges the special needs of a small group.[3] The
most urgent objection is supposedly to the politics of advocacy. Critics, especially in the sphere of higher education, object that identity politics
substitutes political advocacy for intellectual substance. The introduction
of black studies, women's studies, disability studies, and other forms of
consciousness-raising, they claim, has diluted the content of higher education, bringing about the current state of decline in the American university system.[4]

And yet politics is not really the problem. "Identity," not "politics," is
the vexed term in identity politics. For the ultimate purpose of any mi-

nority politics is self-identification. There can be nothing like an identity politics without a strong sense of identity because individuals would not be motivated by political action if they did not want to be in control of their own identities and if they did not feel that this opportunity had been denied them by groups more powerful than theirs. In this sense, identity politics is no different from any other form of political representation, since politics always implies the existence of a coalition whose membership is defined by ideological, historical, geographical, or temporal borders.[5] The objection that identity politics differs from other forms of politics, because it derives identity from a singular subjectivity or organizes itself single-mindedly around suffering, only carries negative connotations because suffering has been linked so successfully to narcissism. But if limited ideas of identity are properties of all forms of political representation—and if suffering and disability have been inappropriately linked to the psychology of narcissism—then we should distance ourselves from such objections to identity politics. The political psychology applied in current debates about identity politics is deeply flawed, and we need a more enlightened discussion about how questions of identity, oppression, and suffering contribute to the political as such.

If critics of identity politics value the capacity to generalize from experience, the necessity of representing the individual experiences of unique human kinds is clearly the goal of black studies, women's studies, and disability studies. An enlightened concept of the political cannot exist in the absence of either of these alternatives, which is why the choice between them is hardly clear-cut and why arguments for and against them have relied on misinformation and debilitating accusations. It would be worth tracking how the preference for general over individual experience—or disinterestedness over self-consciousness—achieved prominence and then lost its persuasive power, but this history is too complex to recount here. My goal is to interrogate the metapsychology that associates minority discourses with narcissism and to show that disability is a major component of this metapsychology, for it is precisely this metapsychology that represents acts of self-consciousness as negative by definition. My point is that the accusation of narcissism is one of the strongest weapons used against people with disabilities (and other minorities who pray that consciousness-raising will bring an end to their oppression). In fact, the psychological character attributed to people with disabilities and narcissists is more often than not one and the same.

## The Narcissism of Disability

The introduction of narcissism into the literature of psychoanalysis is also the concept's first major link to disability, although the association between excessive egotism and pain appears earlier and so plays a significant part in Freud's metapsychology. The "study of organic disease," Freud argues in "On Narcissism: An Introduction," may help launch a "better knowledge of narcissism" (14:82). Disability and the state of sleep are the two analogies used by Freud to introduce the idea of narcissism, and disability is more primary and enduring. "It is universally known," he explains, "and we take it as a matter of course, that a person who is tormented by organic pain and discomfort gives up his interest in the things of the external world, in so far as they do not concern his suffering. Closer observation teaches us that he also withdraws *libidinal* interest from his love-objects: so long as he suffers, he ceases to love" (14:82). In short, we of the tender organs are narcissists. Freud's prototype of the "painfully tender" organ is, of course, the penis, which is "the seat of a multiplicity of sensations" when "congested with blood, swollen and humected" (14:84). He coins the term *erotogenicity* to name this tenderness but recognizes it as a general characteristic of all organs and not only of the male member. For the tendency to erotogenicity produces a damming-up of libido in any tender organ. More important, it induces a parallel change of libidinal investment in the ego. The greater the attention given to a tender organ, the more energy flows to the ego. This parallel effect accounts for "the familiar egoism of the sick person" (14:82). A tender organ makes for a touchy ego—an equation that represents people with physical disabilities as the model for the narcissistic, selfish, and self-centered personality.

*Beyond the Pleasure Principle* broadens Freud's theory of tender organs. Here the primary concern is the relation between neurosis and the general anxieties produced by living in human society. Generalizing from his experience of soldiers suffering from battle fatigue, Freud asks why patients continue to relive painful traumas, even though the entire psyche is supposed by his theories to be organized around pleasure. He discovers that soldiers wounded in battle adjust to psychic trauma better than those who are merely frightened: a "wound or injury inflicted," he states, "works as a rule *against* the development of a neurosis" (18:12). This is the case because any injury strikes at both the body and the ego. The defenses of the body and mind are penetrated, and large amounts of energy are invested in repairing the intrusion. When only the psyche is wounded, the trauma is repressed, and the patient must relive it whenever it fights its way back to consciousness. When the body is wounded, however, the injury remains in the conscious mind; the trauma is not repressed but symbolized by the damaged body. Consequently, not only do injured people not develop a neurotic symptom as a result of trauma, they are protected by their wounds against neurosis in general. This is because neurosis in Freud's conception arises as a result of the ambiguity of social existence. We grow anxious because life is full of uncertainties, and we blame ourselves for our failure to adjust, but we blame ourselves for a thousand and one reasons. The inability to manage many reasons is neurosis. People with disabilities, according to this theory, have one good reason for all their failures—the tender organ—and so the radical uncertainty of human existence disappears or at least becomes more manageable.[6] Freud gives a hint of this process in his case study of Dora, although it precedes by a decade his work on neurosis and disability:

> Let us imagine a workman, a bricklayer, let us say, who has fallen off a house and been crippled, and now earns his livelihood by begging at the street-corner. Let us then suppose that a miracle-worker comes along and promises him to make his crooked leg straight and capable of walking. It would be unwise, I think, to look forward to seeing an expression of peculiar bliss upon the man's features. No doubt at the time of the accident he felt he was extremely unlucky, when he realized that he would never be able to do any more work and would have to starve or live upon charity. But since then the very thing which in the first instance threw him out of employment has become his source of income: he lives by his disablement. If that is taken from him he may become totally helpless. (7:44)

The fortunate fall of people with disabilities does not really guarantee a healthy mental existence. There are worse things in life than neurosis, according to Freud, and these are the narcissistic disorders. Bodily scars may serve as a protection against neurosis, but the sufferer's extreme investment in the body produces a parallel exaltation of the ego. The self inhabits the disabled body like an armored fortress. It is protected but alone, and its own dear self becomes its most cherished prize.

Freud conceived of the ego as a body ego. It exists on the surface of the skin. It may be more accurate to say that he thought of the self as a scar, as a wound healed over. As scar tissue accumulates, the self becomes less and less flexible. The initial mending of pain provided by scarification gives way to a rigidity more disabling than the original wound. We of the tender organs apparently have a guaranteed protection against the sorrows of social existence, but we pay for it with the tendency to narcissism, which is the more serious disorder because it has no cure.[7] Narcissists are beyond the reach of therapy because they refuse to invest energy in other people. So long as they suffer—and they suffer always—they cease to love.

If narcissism seems an extreme model for thinking about people with disabilities, the model nevertheless dominates the psychological literature.[8] Like narcissists, people with disabilities are said to be beyond the reach of therapy. It would seem impossible at this moment in history that such prejudice would exist, but it is widespread. "Much psychoanalytic literature on disability," Asch and Rousso show, "supports the contention that the disabled are inherently unanalyzable" (4). Any number of case studies try to prove this conclusion. Bornstein argues that the intense involvement of a congenitally blind musician with his art mobilizes "a grandiose self in the self-centered repetitive material having to do with his music and trumpet," placing him beyond the reach of therapy (33). Niederland associates "compensatory narcissistic self-inflation" with even "minor physical anomalies or imperfections" (519, 522). Some of the features accompanying narcissistic injuries, he explains, are self-aggrandizement, heightened aggressiveness, bisexuality, sadomasochism, and "florid birth-rebirth fantasies" (523). According to Niederland, people with disabilities convert "defectiveness into a mark of distinction and a seat of power" (526). People with disabilities, it seems, demonstrate a conspicuous resistance to reality, taking flight into an active fantasy life where their disabilities justify special privileges.[9] As one analyst sums it up, "the clinical problems presented during the psychoanalytic treatment of patients with disabilities are legion" (Yorke 187). Psychoanalysis treats disability almost exclusively as a symbol of narcissistic injury; disability has little meaning beyond this symptomology.[10]

---

Dossier No. 4
*New York Times Online*
March 30, 2003

Lifetime Affliction Leads to a U. S. Bias Suit
By Steven Greenhouse

ORTHPORT, Ala.—Samantha Robichaud was born with a dark purple birth mark covering her face, and she has felt the sharp sting of discrimination ever since.

"As a child, I was always exiled," Ms. Robichaud said. "No one wanted to play with me. Kids were scared that if they touched me it would rub off."

In school, Ms. Robichaud (pronounced ROW-buh-shaw) remained an outcast because of her birthmark, known as a port wine stain. . . .

Ms. Robichaud is 32 now, married and the mother of two, and well past worrying about schoolyard cruelty. Her struggle now is to obtain a measure of justice in a lawsuit that charges her former employer, a McDonald's restaurant, with treating her as shabbily as some grade-school children did.

In early March, the Equal Employment Opportunity Commission filed a federal lawsuit in Birmingham, 60 miles away, accusing the McDonald's franchisee of violating the Americans With Disabilities Act by refusing to promote Ms. Robichaud to manager because of how she looks. The franchisee, R.P.H. Management, denies the accusation. . . .

In August 2000, Ms. Robichaud took a job at a McDonald's restaurant here, down Highway 43 from her high school. "I let them know when I was hired that I would be seeking a management position, that I would not want to be on the bottom of the totem pole forever," she said. . . .

In her five months at McDonald's, she said she grew frustrated when some workers hired after her were promoted to manager. . . . One day, in January 2001, she said, opening the restaurant with the shift manager, the manager complained of health problems and voiced concern that there was no one suitable to replace her if she was out sick.

"I asked her, 'Why don't you train me to be a shift leader?' " Ms. Robichaud said. "She said: 'I'm tired of telling you a bunch of lies and coming up with a bunch of different excuses. You will never be in management here because I was told you would either make the babies cry or scare the customers off. . . .' "

---

The ordinary rules of life apparently do not apply to people with disabilities. Nor do the rules of psychoanalysis. The narcissism of patients with disabilities supposedly inhibits the transference, and thus the efficacy of therapy.[11] They seek revenge for their disabilities or demand compensation, it is said, and they refuse to place trust in their therapists.

A closer look, however, suggests that countertransference may be the real cause of therapeutic failures. A recent essay by Kenneth R. Thomas makes the absurd but telling case that "physical disabilities, largely because of the close developmental connection between the body and the ego, will tend to evoke specific types of countertransference responses from therapists" (151). In other words, analysts cannot bear to work with patients with disabilities. The sight of disability apparently evokes the threat of castration—the classic example of narcissistic injury—and the training of the analyst unravels: "therapists may experience a variety of reactions" to patients with disabilities, Thomas explains, "including 'imaginary' pangs of pain in the genital area, headaches, dizziness, or other physical symptoms" (152). Nevertheless, he counsels therapists not to ignore or to evade these symptoms. Rather, they should use them to formulate hypotheses concerning what the patient is feeling about the loss of bodily integrity. The "therapist has identified with the patient," Thomas concludes, and these "reactions are accurately mirroring what the patient is feeling" (153). In short, the threat to the therapist's self-integration becomes an analytic tool used to think about the patient's disability. These threats do not belong to the psychology of the therapist; they spring from the patient. For the patient's narcissism contaminates the therapist. A clearer case of concealing the role of the accuser could not be imagined. It is simply assumed that the therapist cannot resist the psychopathological condition of the patient, who bears the responsibility for the therapist's reactions—and this despite the enormous gulf supposedly existing between the psychological states of the expert doctor and the narcissistic patient.

‹ On the one hand, people with disabilities are supposedly unable to extend themselves emotionally to others. On the other hand, the sight of a person with a tender organ disables able-bodied people. Nor are people with disabilities acceptable as therapists, according to this logic. A number of experts have made the case over the years that narcissistic people should not work as therapists. A 1964 study of candidates rejected for psychoanalytic training reports that people with constricted patterns of defense and those considered narcissistic, controlling, isolated, and withdrawn are not suitable as analysts (Fox et al.). Asch and Rousso argue that psychoanalytic literature often maintains that disability itself causes such undesirable characteristics (4–11). Studies of face-to-face interaction between nondisabled and disabled individuals tend to support these findings. They show that able-bodied people focus in face-to-face encounters more on their own anxiety than on the feelings of the person with the disability, and that their acceptance of disability lessens as narcissistic regression increases.[12] These studies give some indication of the potential problems faced by therapists with disabilities.[13]

While this material gives us a clear view of the prejudices in psychology against people with disabilities, it is actually more revealing about American culture at large. Psychoanalytic theory and practice may have formalized the association between narcissism and disability, but the connection exerts a powerful and terrible influence well beyond that sphere. The same arguments demonstrating that people with disabilities make bad patients and analysts suggest that they make bad citizens. The narcissism of small differences supposedly obsesses disabled people, forcing them into separatist political action groups that accentuate their suffering. This last argument about citizenship is actually being made in attacks against disability studies and the ADA. The accusation of narcissism rages just below the surface in current debates about disability in higher education and in American culture. Most important, this accusation is a major impediment to reform in healthcare and other areas of concern crucial to the lives of people with disabilities. It represents the marginalization of disabled people as their own choice, one made for perverse and selfish rea-

sons, seemingly relieving society at large of any responsibility for antidis-
ability discrimination, the inaccessible built environment, and the long
history of confining disabled people in medical institutions.


## The Narcissism of Small Differences

Identity politics are supposedly plagued by what Freud calls the narcissism of small differences, a term describing his idea that minor distinctions between people summon the greatest amounts of narcissistic rage.
The smaller the difference from other people, the stronger the attempt to
define our difference and the greater the aggression generated. The more
we resemble the people from whom we want to differ, the angrier, the
more resentful, and the more violent we apparently become. Identity politics promote a narcissistic rage that threatens the social order, critics
complain, because the privileging of identity places too great an emphasis
on one group's differences, especially differences resulting from oppression. These differences derive, however, merely from psychopathological
causes, with no apparent basis in reality, and so embracing identity politics encourages only more violence and sickness—or so the argument
goes.

Despite the use of narcissism to attack identity politics, narcissism is
in fact incompatible with group psychology. Freud establishes in *Group
Psychology and the Analysis of the Ego* that solitary leaders are more likely
than groups to have narcissistic attributes. Group psychology requires the
suppression of individual narcissistic urges, he maintains, but for this reason people in groups tend to be fascinated by individuals whose narcissism sets them apart. Freud is also aware that this fascination may turn
into violence. The murder of the primal father by the primal horde provides the classic example of collective attack against the solitary narcissistic figure.

What Freud and the entire tradition surrounding narcissism miss,
however, are the similarities between his description of group psychology
and the history of collective violence. Narcissism is a collective accusation
that isolates one member of a community as completely different from
everyone else. Whether this difference represents excessive ability or disability counts for little in the final analysis because negative and positive

valences of difference shift suddenly whenever group psychology is involved. The only constant is the fact that the community turns against one individual and holds special properties of that individual responsible for its own actions. In short, this is the logic: we killed him but he made us do it. Narcissism promotes a structure of blame where collective violence is concealed and victims are described as people divided against themselves. Narcissists bring themselves down, and we know nothing and can know nothing about it. A more sinister form of violence could not be imagined.

Narcissism is a form of violent hyperindividualization imposed upon victims by political bodies and other groups. That people with disabilities are automatically assumed to be narcissistic reveals not only that they are being victimized but that the perception of their individuality is itself a form of violence. The major interpretations in this country relentlessly individualize disability. This applies to healthcare reform and rehabilitation, special education, the struggle for civil rights, as well as to attacks against disability studies and the ADA (Linton 134). The disability of individuals is always represented as their personal misfortune. Treatment isolates what is individual about the disability, only rarely relating it to the conditions of other people in a way that identifies a political problem such as the denial of constitutional rights guaranteed to every citizen (Hahn 192). Instead, the disability symbolizes not a suffering group but one person in his or her entirety: the crippled senior citizen in the park, the deaf boy on the bus, the blind student in the hall. This means, of course, that the deaf boy on the bus may be entitled to individualized educational planning and medical services, but this special treatment, since it is based on "special rights" and not "civil rights," exposes him to great isolation and suffering because it ends by symbolizing his individuality as such.

The narcissism of people with disabilities, then, is a political formation that inhibits their ability to act politically. It isolates them in their individuality, making a common purpose difficult to recognize and advance as a political agenda. Disability activists have made the case that prejudices against people with disabilities and discrimination based on race and gender are analogous. But this analogy almost always fails because racism and sexism lead easily to political action based on the recognition of a particular advocacy group, while discrimination against a person with a disability seeks the same kind of solution used in healthcare and rehabilitation. It designs an individual remedy that addresses one person's particular problem or a small subclass of problems (Funk 26). If a wheelchair user cannot enter a restaurant, the restaurant need not be made accessible; two waiters can lift the chair through the door, providing individual attention and an individual solution. A local street sign may designate the presence of a deaf child in the neighborhood, supposedly protecting the child but also eliminating the need to develop universal forms of accessibility. In short, political action against discrimination is based more often than not on the individualization of disability. Indeed, the association between narcissism and disability makes it almost impossible to view people with disabilities as anything other than absolutely different from one another. Prejudices against physical and mental disability are more difficult to overcome at the moment than prejudices against race and gender not only because people are less likely to identify with a blind person, for example, but because the perception of the individual with a disability is antithetical to the formation of political identity as such—which is to say that "individuality" itself is disabled for political use in the case of people with disabilities.

Identity politics in the United States emerged over the last few decades in the struggle for rights. Particular rhetorical points were scored by coining the phrase *special rights*. This rhetoric drew attention to the groups using it, made their individual agendas more visible, and gave them additional political currency. But it also separated them from a broader definition of rights, which is precisely why they have been attacked as special interest groups too preoccupied with self-gratification, self-esteem, and separatist agendas. It is ironic that the word *special* has particular usage in the representation of mental and physical disability because people with disabilities are the one group that does not need to individualize itself. People with disabilities need, if they are ever to form political coalitions, to reverse the general perception that they are unique or so special that they can expect neither to serve as citizens nor to possess the rights that come with citizenship.

The argument that individualization victimizes people with disabilities is crucial to the theorization of disability because it unravels the accusation of narcissism and exposes it as a component part of the ideology of ability. This ideology always works to diminish and contain the effects of disability, isolating it as a condition affecting only some individuals rather than as a property belonging to all human beings. But if disability is intrinsic to the human condition, it cannot be treated individually. Nor can it be described as an evil that sets off peculiar psychological syndromes such as narcissism in some people. It requires attention and action by the entire political society. The narcissism of small differences does not apply to disability because "small differences" is the excuse used to defeat general claims for the rights of the disabled. We need to challenge the reigning idea that rights of the disabled are not possible because each person with a disability is different. My point has been that this idea has taken hold in large part because of the association between narcissism and disability, with the consequence that individuality itself, a foundational concept in American politics, has been transformed from a principle enabling political action into an impediment.

## A Personal Conclusion, However Narcissistic

Disability studies, like black studies and women's studies before it, has relied in its first phase on a literature of witnessing. The autobiographical account has been the preferred method of representing disability to a wider public. But if disabled people are susceptible, beyond other minority identities, to the accusation of narcissism, it is to be expected that this strategy will backfire. Personal accounts of suffering and injury will only convince the opponents of disability rights that "the person who is tormented by organic pain and discomfort," in Freud's words, "gives up his interest in the things of the external world, in so far as they do not concern his suffering" (14:82). Disability activists have made the case that we need to move beyond the narcissism of first-person narratives to other paradigms if we are to be successful in revising the cultural misunderstanding of disability. Mitchell and Snyder, for example, argue that personal narratives invite reactions of pity and sympathy from readers rather than educating them about the social and political meanings of disability (1997, 11). This is an important argument, especially for the future of disability studies, because the lives of people with disabilities will never be improved if we do not change the current political landscape. But I also think that people with disabilities need to resist the suggestion that their personal stories are somehow more narcissistic than those of nondisabled people. If we cannot tell our stories because they reflect badly on our personalities or make other people queasy, the end result will be greater isolation. For human beings make lives together by sharing their stories with each other. There is no other way of being together for our kind.

More pragmatically, we of the tender organs need to think about ways of telling our stories that will communicate the truth of our existence as a group facing prejudices and other barriers, often physical, put in place by society at large. Disability has served throughout history to symbolize other problems in human society. Oedipus's clubfoot signifies his hubris and political overreaching. Tiresias's blindness symbolizes his gift of prophecy. No one ever sees Sophocles' play as a drama about a cripple and a blindman fighting over the future of Thebes. The *Iliad* shows the crippled Hephaestus being cast out of Olympus, but no one asks whether Achilles' isolation from his Greek brothers relates to his vulnerable heel. The heel merely symbolizes his mortality. But isn't every warrior in the *Iliad* mortal? Why, then, is Achilles so different? Shakespeare's Richard III is a hunchback, but his disability represents deceitfulness and lust for power, not a condition of his physical and complex embodiment.

Disability is the other other that helps make otherness imaginable. Throughout history, it has been attached to other representations of otherness to grant them supplementary meaning, sharper focus, and additional weight.[14] In providing this service, however, disability has lost the power of its own symbolism, and it is now time for disability activists to recapture it. By "symbolism," I understand a political process through which private emotions and thoughts are made compelling to the public imagination.[15] The political cannot exist in the absence of such symbolism because it describes the dynamic by which individuals are recognized by others and gather together into communities. Disability has provided the public imagination with one of its most powerful symbols for the understanding of individuality, but it always symbolizes something other than itself. Now disabled people need to introduce the reality of disability identity into the public imagination. And the only way to accomplish this task is to tell stories in a way that allows people without disabilities to recognize our reality and theirs as a common one. For only in this way will we be recognized politically.

And so I tell one of my stories (see also Siebers 1998b). The first time my legs buckled under me as an adult, I experienced a shock of recognition. I suppose a psychoanalyst would say that I was reliving the trauma of falling to polio at age two. But I remember distinctly that my thoughts were drifting in another direction. I could not believe it was the first time my legs had failed me because my memories were saturated with the experience. This was obviously as bewildering to me as the fact that I found myself hugging a lamppost to hold myself up. Suddenly, I remembered a recurring nightmare that has plagued me all my life. I am walking on my way home at night when an overwhelming sense of fatigue strikes my legs. I am forced to the ground, and I crawl through the darkness on my hands and knees—and once my knees fail, flat on my belly—until I reach my house. Then I drag myself up the stairs—there are always stairs, even though I have lived most of my life in one-story houses—and throw myself into bed. I wake up the next morning amazed that I have so quickly recovered the ability to walk.

Now the strange thing is that I realized that this dream was not part of my reality only when I was hugging that lamppost. It existed as part of my experience, but I had no understanding that it was experience given by nightmares rather than reality. The dream occurred so often and with such vividness that I had always assumed, until the moment I lost the ability to walk beyond short distances, that I had already lost that ability a long time ago.

I have tried to understand this dream since I first realized that I have been having it. My current interpretation is that it is a screen memory composed of many fragments of the experience of coping as a person with a disability with my physical and social environment. I cannot walk very far anymore, so I spend a lot of time counting blocks and gauging distances, trying to think about easier routes, avoiding stairways, spacing out tasks throughout the day and the week to conserve energy. But now that I am doing this so consciously, I have come to realize that I have always done it, because I have been disabled since I was two years old. I was always compensating for my disability, just like I was always dreaming that dream. I just never knew it.

But I knew it when I was having the nightmare. That is what my nightmare is: the knowledge that it is difficult for me to take one step after another. It is also the knowledge that I am totally alone in my dilemma and pretty much in the dark about what to do about it. The nightmare is also about the fact that, despite all this, I am going to get out of bed every morning and go through it all over again. But I am not going to think too much about it, at least with my conscious mind. The nightmare collects all my fears about my environment and serves them up to me, and now that I am more conscious of what those experiences are, I can describe them to myself and to you.

Here are some day fragments that just might be the stuff that dreams are made of. During my freshman year in high school, I joined the other boys in my gym class in a mandatory physical fitness campaign based on running. We spent a week at the track being timed by the track coach in the 60- and 100-yard dashes, the 220 and 440 runs. My most vivid recollection is of the 440 run because it lasted the longest. The slowest boy ran across the finish line about 220 yards ahead of me. The coach signed up the fastest boys for the track team. He asked me to be the team manager.

---

Dossier No. 5
*Los Angeles Times*
September 4, 2004

Public Defenders Decry Aid Recipients' Arrests
Critics call U. S. agents' roundup of mostly disabled people an abuse of authority. Some raise questions of possible racial discrimination.
By David Rosenzweig

Dessie Robinson, a 55-year-old welfare recipient who suffers from a heart ailment, diabetes and ulcers, had just finished showering in her room at a downtown homeless shelter early one morning in July when she heard a loud knock at the door.

Throwing on some clothes, she opened the door and was confronted by half a dozen armed federal agents who proceeded to arrest her on a misdemeanor charge of cheating the government out of $746.10, the monthly payment she receives under the federal program to aid the blind, disabled or elderly poor.

Robinson was among 21 people arrested at gunpoint that week during a sweep targeting individuals who said they hadn't received their monthly Supplemental Security Income checks, but who allegedly cashed the original and the duplicate checks, according to prosecutors. Most of those taken into custody were physically or mentally disabled and frightened out of their wits as they were handcuffed and hauled off to court, according to lawyers from the federal public defender's office. Several were schizophrenic. One was blind and in a wheelchair. Another had given birth the previous week. One man was taken to court dressed only in his undershorts. All those arrested, with one exception, were freed several hours later after being arraigned by a magistrate judge. . . .

The arrests were a departure from standard procedure at the U. S. attorney's office. Normally, prosecutors send a summons to a defendant accused of a nonviolent misdemeanor, but that practice was scrapped during this operation.

More puzzling, many of those arrested had previously reached accommodations with the Social Security Administration and were making restitution by having money deducted from future SSI checks, according to court papers.

All were African Americans, a fact that public defenders cited as an indication of possible racial discrimination. . . .

---

I approach a building for the first time. From my car, I try to scout out the location of the handicapped entrance. I spot a little blue sign with a wheelchair on it. I circle the block for twenty minutes, passing many other parking spaces while waiting for a parking place to open up near that little blue sign. I park and walk over to the door. But under that wheelchair is a tiny arrow, pointing to the left. No other writing. It seems that this is a sign telling me that this is not the handicapped entrance. The real handicapped entrance is somewhere to the left of me.

I am going to lunch with some friends. We are in animated conversation. We come to the stairs, and my friends, all fitness buffs, instinctively head for them. The elevator is in view. I fight my way up the stairs because I am too embarrassed to ask the others to take the elevator with me and too much in love with good conversation to take it alone.

Let it be recognized that physical barriers are each and every one of them psychic barriers as well. That is because people with disabilities travel in groups, although not necessarily always, and these groups are composed mostly of the nondisabled. When we come to a barrier, we realize that our perception of the world does not conform to theirs, although they rarely have this realization. This difference in perception is a social barrier equal to or greater than any physical barrier—which introduces my final point about the accusation of narcissism. Narcissism is profoundly incompatible with the reality of disability because disabled people have to rely so often on other people. Studies show, for example, that blind people are terrified of their own aggressive impulses because they are afraid that able-bodied people will also get angry and abandon them (Burlingham 131–32). People who rely on caregivers have to be diplomats. They also need a form of identity politics unlike any other.[16] To rewrite Freud, "the person who is tormented by organic pain knows that all things of the external world concern his suffering. So long as he suffers, he needs the love of others." This is why is it is so alarming when we see the solitary woman in a wheelchair in the middle of town fighting repeatedly to get her chair to jump a curb. This is why we wonder at the common sense of a blind man who goes to the shopping mall alone on a busy weekend. The sighting of these creatures is the equivalent of seeing a giraffe in a parking garage. People with disabilities do not often put themselves in such situations because they are at risk when they are alone. We of the tender organs need to be in groups. We need a community to support us.

Some of you have disabilities. Some of you do not. Most of you will someday. That is the reality of the human mind and body. Remember what you already know about people with disabilities, so the knowledge will be useful to you when you join us. The blind do not lead the blind. The lame do not want to walk alone. We do not love only our own kind or ourselves. You others are our caregivers—and we can be yours, if you let us. We of the tender organs are not narcissists.

## Chapter Three
# Body Theory
*From Social Construction to the*
*New Realism of the Body*

## Prologue

In the hall of mirrors that is world mythology, there is none more ghastly, more disturbing to the eye, than the three Graiae, sisters of Medusa— whose own ghastliness turns onlookers to stone. Possessed of a single eye and six empty eyesockets, the three hags pass their eyeball from greedy hand to greedy hand in order to catch a glimpse of the world around them. Is the lone eyeball of the Graiae blind while in transit from eye- socket to eyesocket? Or does it stare at the world as it moves from hand to hand? If so, the eye is more than a metaphor for the experience of the dis- abled body. It is its reality and therefore should tell us something about the construction of reality. The hand is the socket of seeing for the Graiae, just as it is for every other blind person. The blind alone do not live this way. All disabled bodies create this confusion of tongues—and eyes and hands and other body parts. For the deaf, the hand is the mouth of speech, the eye, its ear. Deaf hands speak. Deaf eyes listen.

Disability offers a challenge to the representation of the body—this is often said. Usually, it means that the disabled body provides insight into the fact that all bodies are socially constructed—that social attitudes and institutions determine, far greater than biological fact, the representation of the body's reality. The idea that representation changes the body has had enormous influence on cultural and critical theory, especially in gender studies, because it frees the body from the tyranny of anatomy.[1] The women's movement radicalized interpretation theory to the point where repressive constructions of the female form are more universally recognized, and recent work by gay and lesbian activists has identified the ways that heterosexual models map the physique of the erotic body to the exclusion of nonnormative sexualities. These theories have had an immediate impact on disability studies because they provide a powerful alternative to the medical model of disability. The medical model situates disability exclusively in individual bodies and strives to cure them by particular treatment, isolating the patient as diseased or defective, while social constructionism makes it possible to see disability as the effect of an environment hostile to some bodies and not to others, requiring advances in social justice rather than medicine. Thanks to the insight that the body is socially constructed, it is now more difficult to justify prejudices based on physical and mental ability, permitting a more flexible definition of human beings in general.

But what I have in mind—perhaps I should say "in hand"—is another kind of insight: the disabled body changes the process of representation itself. Blind hands envision the faces of old acquaintances. Deaf eyes listen to public television. Tongues touch-type letters home to Mom and Dad. Feet wash the breakfast dishes. Mouths sign autographs.[2] Different bodies require and create new modes of representation. What would it mean for disability studies to take this insight seriously? Could it change body theory as usual if it did?

## Social Construction

Let us step back from our places, as if we have put our hands on something prickly, and rearrange the objects of discourse on the usual table of thought. We have a theory of the body called "social constructionism." It exists in weak and strong senses, but its correctness and theoretical power are very nearly unchallenged on the current academic scene. In its weak sense, it posits that the dominant ideas, attitudes, and customs of a society influence the perception of bodies. In a racist society, for example, black people may feel uncomfortable seeing themselves in the mirror, while in an ableist society passing civil rights legislation to permit greater access for people with disabilities is thought unnecessary because the reigning myth explains that they neither understand nor desire to enter "normal" society. Social constructionism in the weak sense tries to advance a commonsense approach to thinking about how people victimize individuals unlike them. This is not to say that this commonsense approach is so very common, as many persons with a disability will explain at great length: people easily perceive when someone is different from them but rarely acknowledge the violence of their perceptions.

Unlike weak constructionism, the strong version does not rely on human ignorance or misunderstanding to account for prejudices of sex, gender, race, and ability but on a linguistic model that describes representation itself as a primary ideological force. Strong constructionism posits that the body does not determine its own representation in any way because the sign precedes the body in the hierarchy of signification. In fact, political ideologies and cultural mores exert the greatest power, social constructionists claim, when they anchor their authority in natural objects such as the body. Michel Foucault defined "biopower" as the force that constitutes the materiality of any human subject; it forms, secures, and normalizes human subjects through a process of "subjection" (1980, 140–41, 143–44). The techniques of biopower—statistics, demographics, eugenics, medicalization, sterilization—are all familiar to scholars of disability studies. They create the political alliance between knowledge and power in the modern state, but biopower is not merely a political force, controlled by one or two institutions. Biopower determines for Foucault the way that human subjects experience the materiality of their bodies. The human subject has no body, nor does the subject exist, prior to its subjection as representation. Bodies are linguistic effects driven, first, by the order of representation itself and, second, by the entire array of social ideologies dependent on this order.

If it is true that bodies matter to people with disabilities, it may be worth thinking at greater length about the limits of social construction. Judith Butler makes the case that constructionism is inadequate to the task of understanding material bodies, especially suffering bodies (1993, xi). Indeed, she isolates bodies in pain and abject bodies as resources for rethinking the representation of physicality. The "exclusionary matrix by

which subjects are formed," she explains, "requires the simultaneous production of a domain of abject beings, those who are not yet 'subjects,' but
who form the constitutive outside to the domain of the subject" (1993, 3).
Abject beings have bodies and desires that cannot be incorporated into social norms, Butler argues, and so they inhabit the border between the acceptable and unacceptable, marking it for the benefit of mainstream society. In short, people with disabilities are not yet "subjects" in Foucault's
disciplinary sense: their bodies appear uncontrolled by the ideological
forces of society. It is as if Butler has caught a glimpse of a badly turned
ankle under the petticoats of the "normal" world, and this vision of disability refuses normalization. Disabled bodies come to represent what
Rosemarie Garland-Thomson calls the "freak show." "Disability is the un-
orthodox made flesh," she writes, "refusing to be normalized, neutralized,
or homogenized" (1997, 23).

---

### Dossier No. 6
*New York Times Online*
March 27, 2001

Disabled Gaining on Access to Vote
By Katherine Q. Seelye

Paul Schroeder of the American Foundation for the Blind was recently shown how to use a voting machine that communicates by
sound. Jim Dickson has been blind since he was 7. Now 55, he has
never been able to vote by himself. Usually, he takes his wife into the
voting booth with him, an act that has cemented their relationship in
ways unforeseen.

As he asked her to mark his ballot in a recent mayoral race here,
his wife said to him: "Jim, I know you've always loved me. Now I
know you trust me because you think I'm marking this ballot for
that idiot."

So it goes with the blind and people with other disabilities as they
try to participate in American democracy. Often, they cannot, at
least not in the privacy that most citizens expect. Many do not have
access to voting places. And if they can get in, the machines are not
easy to use. Polling places tend not to offer ballots in Braille or large
print or voting machines with special knobs for those with physical
disabilities. And until recently, no one much cared.

But last fall's Florida election fiasco is changing all that.

As Paul W. Schroeder, a spokesman for the American Foundation for the Blind, put it, "The rest of the nation finally experienced what blind people have been experiencing all along: you never know if your vote actually counted. . . ."

---

Disability exposes with great force the constraints imposed on bodies by social codes and norms. In a society of wheelchair users, stairs would be nonexistent, and the fact that they are everywhere in our society seems an indication only that most of our architects are able-bodied people who think unseriously about access. Obviously, in this sense, disability looks socially constructed. It is tempting, in fact, to see disability exclusively as the product of a bad match between social design and some human bodies, since this is so often the case. But disability may also trouble the theory of social construction. Disability scholars have begun to insist that strong constructionism either fails to account for the difficult physical realities faced by people with disabilities or presents their body in ways that are conventional, conformist, and unrecognizable to them. These include the habits of privileging performativity over corporeality, favoring pleasure to pain, and describing social success in terms of intellectual achievement, bodily adaptability, and active political participation. The disabled body seems difficult for the theory of social construction to absorb: disability is at once its best example and a significant counterexample.

According to Foucault, "madness," "criminality," and "sexuality" are modern constructions, and his major writings are dedicated to tracking their involvement with social repression and exclusion.[3] Not surprisingly, these topics involve him with the representation of disability, but his treatment of it reveals tangles in the social construction argument not always visible elsewhere in his work. The chapter on "docile bodies" in *Discipline and Punish* begins by describing the ideal figure of the soldier before the modern age took control of it: "the soldier was someone who could be recognized from afar; he bore certain signs: the natural signs of his strength and his courage, the marks, too, of his pride; his body was the blazon of his strength and valour" (1995, 135). Foucault also emphasizes a long description of the soldier's body in which health dominates: "an erect head, a taut stomach, broad shoulders, long arms, strong fingers, a small belly, thick thighs, slender legs and dry feet" (135). His point is to contrast this soldier with the soldier of the modern age: "By the late eighteenth century," he writes, "the soldier has become something that can be made; out of a formless clay, an inapt body, the machine required can be constructed; posture is gradually corrected; a calculated constraint runs slowly through each part of the body, mastering it, making it pliable" (135). The contrast between the two ideas of the body could not be more strident. Foucault uses natural metaphors to describe the health and vigor of the premodern soldier, while deliberately representing the modern one as malleable, weak, and machinelike. Docility begins to resemble disability, and it is not meant as a term of celebration. The docile body is a bad invention—a body "that may be subjected, used, transformed and improved" (136).

Hidden underneath the docile body—the body invented by the modern age and now recognized as the only body—is the able body. Foucault's account is a not so subtle retelling of the Fall in which well-being and ability are sacrificed to enter the modern age. The new docile body replaces the able body. Health and naturalness disappear. Human beings seem more machinelike. The docile body requires supports and constraints, its every movement based on a calculation. This narrative, incidentally, is not limited to Foucault's account of the docile or disabled body. It dominates his observations on madness, sexuality, and criminality as well. Underneath each lies a freer and less compromised version—madness more mad than unreasonable, sex more polymorphously perverse than any plurality of modern sexualities, criminality more outrageous and unsociable than the criminal code imagines. The point is often made that Foucault reveals with great force the structure of exclusion at the core of modern history; it has never been remarked that he describes what has been excluded as purer and fitter conceptions of the body and mind.

This picture is wrong, of course, and many disability scholars know it. They understand that recent body theory, whatever its claims, has never confronted the disabled body. Most obviously, it represents the docile body as an evil to be eradicated. If the docile body is disabled, however, it means that recent body theory has reproduced the most abhorrent prejudices of ableist society. Lennard Davis argues that disability is as much a nightmare for the discourse of theory as for ableist society, and he provides a succinct description of the ways in which current body theory avoids the harsh realities of the body:

the body is seen as a site of *jouissance,* a native ground of pleasure, the scene of an excess that defies reason, that takes dominant culture and its rigid, powerladen vision of the body to task. . . . The nightmare of that body is the one that is deformed, maimed, mutilated, broken, diseased. . . . Rather than face this ragged image, the critic turns to the fluids of sexuality, the gloss of lubrication, the glossary of the body as text, the heteroglossia of the intertext, the glossolalia of the schizophrenic. But almost never the body of the differently abled. (1995, 5)

Many social constructionists assume that it is extremely difficult to see through the repressive apparatus of modern society to any given body, but when they do manage to spot one, it is rarely disabled. It is usually a body that feels good and looks good—a body on the brink of discovering new kinds of pleasure, new uses for itself, and more and more power.

The central issue for the politics of representation is not whether bodies are infinitely interpretable but whether certain bodies should be marked as defective and how the people who have these bodies may properly represent their interests in the public sphere. More and more people now believe that disabled bodies should not be labeled as defective, although we have a long way to go, but we have not even begun to think about how these bodies might represent their interests in the public sphere for the simple reason that our theories of representation do not take account of them. Only by beginning to conceive of the ways that disabled bodies change the process of representation, both politically and otherwise, might we begin to tackle the difficult issues of how access bears on voting rights, how current theories of political subjectivity limit citizenship for the mentally disabled, and why economic theories cast people with disabilities exclusively as burdens.

## Pain and More Pain

Only 15 percent of people with disabilities are born with their impairments. Most people become disabled over the course of their life. This truth has been accepted only with difficulty by mainstream society; it prefers to think of people with disabilities as a small population, a stable population, that nevertheless makes enormous and selfish claims on the resources of everyone else. Most people do not want to consider that life's passage will lead them from ability to disability. The prospect is too frightening, the disabled body, too disturbing. In fact, even this picture is overly optimistic. The cycle of life runs in actuality from disability to temporary ability back to disability, and that only if you are among the most fortunate, among those who do not fall ill or suffer a severe accident. The human ego does not easily accept the disabled body. It prefers pleasure. Perhaps, this is because, as Freud explained, the ego exists on the surface of the body like skin. It thrives on surface phenomena and superficial glimmers of enjoyment. No doubt, this explains why the body posited by social constructionism is a body built for pleasure, a body infinitely teachable and adaptable. It has often been claimed that the disabled body represents the image of the Other. In fact, the able body is the true image of the Other. It is a prop for the ego, a myth we all accept for the sake of enjoyment, for we all learn early on, as Lacan explains, to see the clumsiness and ineptitude of the body in the mirror as a picture of health—at least for a little while.

Pain is a subjective phenomenon, perhaps the most subjective of phenomena. It is therefore tempting to see it as a site for describing individuality. This temptation is troublesome for two reasons. First, individuality, whatever its meaning, is a social object, which means that it must be communicable as a concept. Individuality derived from the incommunicability of pain easily enforces a myth of hyperindividuality, a sense that each individual is locked in solitary confinement where suffering is an object of narcissistic contemplation. People with disabilities are already too politically isolated for this myth to be attractive. Second, both medical science and rehabilitation represent the pain of the disabled body as individual, which has also had dire consequences for the political struggles of people with disabilities. The first response to disability is to treat it, and this almost always involves cataloging what is most distinctive about it. Treatment programs regard each disability as completely individual, with the end result that people with disabilities are robbed of a sense of political community by those whom they need to address their pain. No two blind people appear to have the same medical problem or political interests. The paraplegic and the elderly have even less basis in the current climate to gather together for political purposes. The struggle for civil rights is different from the usual process for people with disabilities because they must fight against their individuality rather than to establish it—unlike political action groups based on race and gender. The point here, however, is not to separate the struggles against discrimination of people of color, women, queer people, and disabled people but to recognize that once pain becomes a justification for discrimination, intersecting identities may be compromised.

Consequently, the greatest stake in disability studies at the present moment is to find ways to represent pain and to resist models of the body that blunt the political effectiveness of these representations. I stress the importance of pain not because pain and disability are synonymous but to offer a challenge to current body theory and to expose to what extent its dependence on social constructionism collaborates with the misrepresentation of the disabled body in the political sphere.[4] There are only a few images of pain acceptable to current body theory, and none of them is realistic from the standpoint of people who suffer pain daily. The dominant model defines pain as either regulatory or resistant, and both individualize pain in ways that blunt its power to mobilize group identity. In the first case, pain is the tool used by society to enforce its norms. The second case usually spins off from the first, describing pain as a repressive effect that nevertheless produces an unmanageable supplement of suffering that marks out the individual as a site of resistance to social regulation. Despite the dominant principle that individuality is only an ideological construction, many body theorists turn to pain to represent a form of individuality that escapes the forces of social domination. Indeed, pain often comes to represent individuality as such, whether individuality is a part of the theory or not.

Judith Butler's argument in *Bodies That Matter* provides a clear example of the dominant model of pain. She claims that society uses the pain of guilt to produce conformity with what she calls the "morphology" of the heterosexual body. This morphology relies on ideas of a proper body strictly enforced by social taboo:

> To the extent that such supporting "ideas" are regulated by prohibition and pain, they can be understood as the forcible and materialized effects of regulatory power. But precisely because prohibitions do not always "work," that is, do not always produce the docile body

that fully conforms to the social ideal, they may delineate body sur-
faces that do not signify conventional heterosexual polarities. (1993,
64)

For Butler, pain has a delineating effect on our awareness of our bodies; it "may be one way," she explains, "in which we come to have an idea
of our body at all" (65). But the painful prohibitions against homosexuality also mold human desire and the body in an artificial way, constructing
heterosexuality at a grave cost—a fusion of fantasy and fetishism that al-
lies love with illness. In effect, pain forces the body to conform, but the
construction of this conformity is too burdensome to support, and it creates as a by-product another kind of pain from which a less repressive individuality may spring, in Butler's specific case, the individuality of the
lesbian body.

Notice that pain in current body theory is rarely physical. It is more
likely to be based on the pain of guilt or social repression. Society creates
pain, but this creation backfires, producing an individual who struggles
against society—this is the dominant theoretical conception of pain. I do
not want to underestimate the amount of psychic pain produced by society; nor do I want to deny that psychic pain translates into physical pain.
Clearly, the pain of disability is less bearable because people with disabilities suffer intolerance and loneliness every day. They hurt because the
nondisabled often refuse to accept them as members of the human community. And yet many people with disabilities understand that physical
pain is an enemy. It hovers over innumerable daily actions, whether the
disability is painful in itself or only the occasion for pain because of the
difficulty of navigating one's environment. The great challenge every day
is to manage the body's pain, to get out of bed in the morning, to overcome the well of pain that rises in the evening, to meet the hundred daily
obstacles that are not merely inconveniences but occasions for physical
suffering.

When body theorists do represent pain as physical—infrequent as
this is—the conventional model still dominates their descriptions. They
present suffering and disability either as a way of reconfiguring the physical resources of the body or of opening up new possibilities of pleasure.[5]
Pain is most often soothed by the joy of conceiving the body differently
from the norm. Frequently, the objects that people with disabilities live

with—prostheses, wheelchairs, braces, and other devices—are viewed not as potential sources of pain but as marvelous examples of the plasticity of the human form or as devices of empowerment. Some theorists, for example Leo Bersani, have gone so far as to argue that pain remaps the body's erotic sites, redistributing the erogenous zones, breaking up the monopoly of the genitals, and smashing the repressive and aggressive edifice of the ego. Rare is the theoretical account where physical suffering remains harmful for very long.[6] The ideology of ability requires that any sign of disability be viewed exclusively as awakening new and magical opportunities for ability.

Consider Donna Haraway's justly famous theory of the cyborg, "a hybrid of machine and organism" (149).[7] Haraway embraces hybridization to defeat social conformity and to awaken new possibilities for women's empowerment. She represents the cyborg as a world-changing fiction for women and a resource for escaping the myths of progress and organic history. Haraway's cyborgs are spunky, irreverent, and sexy; they accept with glee the ability to transgress old boundaries between machine and animal, male and female, and mind and body. They supposedly make up a future, fortunate race, but in fact they exist everywhere today. Our cyborgs are people with disabilities, and Haraway does not shy away from the comparison. Severe disability is her strongest example of cyborg hybridization: "Perhaps paraplegics and other severely-handicapped people can (and sometimes do) have the most intense experiences of complex hybridization with other communication devices" (178). Moreover, she views the prosthetic device as a fundamental category for preparing the self and body to meet the demands of the information age. "Prosthesis is semiosis," she explains, "the making of meanings and bodies, not for transcendence but for power-charged communication" (244 n. 7). Haraway is so preoccupied with power and ability that she forgets what disability is. Prostheses always increase the cyborg's abilities; they are a source only of new powers, never of problems.[8] The cyborg is always more than human—and never risks to be seen as subhuman. To put it simply, the cyborg is not disabled.

It is easy to mythologize disability as an advantage. Disabled bodies are so unusual and bend the rules of representation to such extremes that they must mean something extraordinary. They quickly become sources of fear and fascination for nondisabled people, who cannot bear to look at the unruly sight before them but also cannot bear not to look. Many people with disabilities can recount the stories. Here is one of mine. I wore a steel leg brace throughout my childhood, and one early summer evening, an angry neighborhood boy challenged me to a fistfight, but he had one proviso: he wanted me to remove my steel brace because he thought it would give me unfair advantage. He was afraid I would kick him. I refused to remove my brace, but not because I wanted an additional weapon. I had hardly the strength to lift my leg into a kick, let alone the ability to do him harm. I refused to remove the brace because I knew that at some point in the fight this angry boy or someone else would steal my brace from the ground and run away with it, and I would be left both helpless and an object of ridicule for the surrounding mob of children. I know the truth about the myth of the cyborg, about how nondisabled people try to represent disability as a marvelous advantage, because I am a cyborg myself.

Physical pain is highly unpredictable and raw as reality. It pits the mind against the body in ways that make the opposition between thought and ideology in most current body theory seem trivial. It offers few resources for resisting ideological constructions of masculinity and femininity, the erotic monopoly of the genitals, the violence of ego, or the power of capital. Pain is not a friend to humanity. It is not a secret resource for political change. It is not a well of delight for the individual. Theories that encourage these interpretations are not only unrealistic about pain; they contribute to the ideology of ability, marginalizing people with disabilities and making their stories of suffering and victimization both politically impotent and difficult to believe.

## These Blunt, Crude Realities

I have been using, deliberately, the words *reality, realism,* and *real* to describe the disabled body, but we all know that the real has fallen on hard times. The German idealists disabled the concept once and for all in the eighteenth century. More recently, the theory of social construction has made it impossible to refer to "reality" without the scare quotes we all use so often. Advocates of reality risk to appear philosophically naive or politically reactionary. This is as true for disability studies as for other areas of cultural and critical theory.

And yet the word is creeping back into usage in disability studies, even among the most careful thinkers. Disability activists are prone to refer to the difficult physical realities faced by people with disabilities. Artworks concerning disability or created by artists with disabilities do not hesitate to represent the ragged edges and blunt angles of the disabled body in a matter of fact way (see, for example, Ferris; Hevey). Their methods are deliberate and detailed, as if they are trying to get people to see something that is right before their eyes and yet invisible to most. The testimony of disabled people includes gritty accounts of their pain and daily humiliations—a sure sign of the rhetoric of realism. Cheryl Marie Wade provides a powerful but not untypical example of the new realism of the body:

> To put it bluntly—because this need is blunt as it gets—we must have our asses cleaned after we shit and pee. Or we have others' fingers inserted into our rectums to assist shitting. Or we have tubes of plastic inserted inside us to assist peeing or we have re-routed anuses and pissers so we do it all into bags attached to our bodies. These blunt, crude realities. Our daily lives. . . . We rarely talk about these things, and when we do the realities are usually disguised in generic language or gimp humor. Because, let's face it: we have great shame about this need. This need that only babies and the "broken" have. . . . If we are ever to be really at home in the world and in ourselves, then we must say these things out loud. And we must say them with real language. (88–89)

Wade experiences a corporeality rarely imagined by the able-bodied. Her account of complex embodiment ruptures the dominant model of pain found in body theory today, projects a highly individual dimension of feeling, and yet speaks in the political first-person plural. She describes the reality, both physical and political, of those people with disabilities who need care, and risk to pay for it with their independence and personal self-esteem as they struggle to maintain some portion of equality with their caregivers. The inequality threatening people with these kinds of disabilities at every instant derives from a body politic—the real physical expectation that all people beyond a certain age will perform their own bodily hygiene. What sea change in social attitudes about the body could bring an end to this expectation? Crudely put, unless all adults have their ass wiped by someone else, unless the caregiver cannot wipe his or her own ass, the people who alone require this service will be represented as weak or inferior.

A renewed acceptance of bodily reality has specific benefits for disability studies, and few of the risks associated with realism, as far as I can tell. It is difficult to think of disability activists as being philosophically naive or politically conservative, given the radical demands they have been making on society and its institutions. First, people with disabilities build communities through a more transparently political process than other groups; since they cannot rely on seemingly more "natural" associations, such as family history, race, age, gender, or geographical point of origin, they tend to organize themselves according to healthcare needs, information sharing, and political advocacy. Second, their commitment to political struggle is so obvious and urgent that their ideas are difficult to dismiss on philosophical grounds, especially given that ours is an age of political interpretation. Third, the views associated with disability studies turn many of the burning moral and political issues of our times on their head. Consider some disability perspectives on assisted suicide, abortion, and genetic research. Assisted suicide takes on an entirely different meaning for the disabled, and often in contradictory ways. On the one hand, whether you consider suicide a personal right or not, it is still the case that the majority of people may choose to end their own life, but some people with disabilities are deprived of this choice because they do not have the physical means to act by themselves. On the other hand, many disability activists view assisted suicide as a device to guilt-trip people with disabilities into ending their life for the "good" of society. The abortion of fetuses who will have physical or mental impairments does not mean the same thing to people with disabilities as it does to the able-bodied who view health as an essential human trait. Some disability activists have asked whether the wish to have a healthy baby is not as prejudicial as the wish to have a light-skinned baby. The vast sums of money being spent today on genetic research strike many in the disability community as a drain on resources that could be spent to support the needs of people who require immediate assistance with their impairments. It looks as if the government would rather eradicate people with disabilities than assist them.

None of these arguments is easily described as conservative or politically reactionary. Finally, disability activists have no reverence for conventional economic policy, which represents people with disabilities as a small but needy group that requires more resources than it deserves, and they have a radical view of political autonomy and freedom because their notion of independence allows for a great deal of support to encourage people with disabilities to practice their civil rights. An acceptance of the physical realities of the disabled body simply makes it impossible to view our society in the same light.

Restoring a sense of the realism of the disabled body, however, does have some risks. One worth stressing is the temptation to view disability and pain as more real than their opposites. The perception already exists that broken bodies and things are more real than anything else. The discourse of literary realism began in the nineteenth century to privilege representations of trash, fragments, and imperfect bodies, while modern art turned to the representation of human difference and defect, changing the sense of aesthetic beauty to a rawer conception. These discourses soon penetrated society at large. Somehow, today, a photograph of a daisy in a garden seems less real than a photograph of garbage blowing down a dirty alley. Incidentally, literary and cultural theorists often obey the same rules. A closer look at many of the major concepts of current body theory—hybridity, heterogeneity, difference, performativity—would reveal that each conceals a desire for what one might call "the more real than real," countering the illusion that "reality" is sound, smooth, and simple with the claim that it is in fact sick, ragged, and complex.

The disabled body is no more real than the able body—and no less real. In fact, serious consideration of the disabled body exposes that our current theories of reality are not as sophisticated as we would like to think. They prefer complexity to simplicity, but they lop off a great deal of reality in the process, most notably, the hard simple realism of the body. More often than not, these theories are driven by ethical concerns rather than the desire to represent what happens to bodies in the world. They are part of a rhetoric that exists less to explain how the body works than to make claims about how it "ought" to work in the society we all apparently desire.

Notice I am not claiming either that the body exists apart from social forces or that it represents something more "real," "natural," or "authentic" than things of culture. I am claiming that the body has its own forces and that we need to recognize them if we are to get a less one-sided picture of how bodies and their representations affect each other for good and for bad. The body is, first and foremost, a biological agent teeming with vital and often unruly forces. It is not inert matter subject to easy manipulation by social representations. The body is alive, which means that it is as capable of influencing and transforming social languages as they are capable of influencing and transforming it.[9]

---

### Dossier No. 7
*New York Times Online*
August 10, 2000

2 Babies, 1 Heart and 1 Chance at Survival
By Denise Grady

When Sandra and Ramón Soto, a couple in their 20's from Puerto Rico, called Children's Hospital in Boston last year, it was to seek help for a desperate accident of nature. Mrs. Soto, special-education teacher, was pregnant with twins. But the two tiny girls were fused at the chest and abdomen, locked in the classic embrace of Siamese twins. And only one had a heart.

---

The most urgent issue for disability studies is the political struggle of people with disabilities, and this struggle requires a realistic conception of the disabled body. In practice, this means resisting the temptation to describe the disabled body as either power-laden or as a weapon of resistance useful only to pierce the false armor of reality erected by modern ideologies. It means overturning the dominant image of people with disabilities as isolated victims of disease or misfortune who have nothing in common with each other or the nondisabled. Finally, it means opposing the belief that people with disabilities are needy, narcissistic, and resentful—and will consequently take more than their fair share of resources from society as a whole.

People with disabilities usually realize that they must learn to live with their disability, if they are to live life as a human being. The challenge is not to adapt their disability into an extraordinary power or an alternative image of ability. The challenge is to function. I use this word advisedly and am prepared to find another if it offends. People with disabilities want to be able to function: to live with their disability, to come to know their body, to accept what it can do, and to keep doing what they can for as long as they can. They do not want to feel dominated by the people on whom they depend for help, and they want to be able to imagine themselves in the world without feeling ashamed.

Sooner or later, whatever we think an object is, we come to esteem it not for what we think it is but for what it really is—if we are lucky. We still lack the means to represent what disabled bodies are because there are false notions everywhere and these bodies change what representation is. But people with disabilities are working on it, and they hope to be lucky. What would it mean to esteem the disabled body for what it really is?

## Epilogue

In April 1999, the Supreme Court began grappling with the purposely vague wording of the ADA of 1990, raising the question whether a person who can restore normal functioning by wearing glasses or taking a pill for hypertension can be considered disabled. One high-profile example for the Court concerned a law suit brought against United Airlines by two nearsighted women who were not accepted for jobs as pilots. At one point in the hearing, Justice Antonin Scalia removed his glasses and waved them in the air, proclaiming "I couldn't do my current job without them."[10] Shortly afterward, the Court handed down a decision much in the style of Justice Scalia's gesture, gutting the ADA and ruling to restrict the definition of disability to a narrow meaning.

Although justice is blind, Judge Scalia put his glasses back on after making his dramatic gesture. But I imagine a different scenario, one that touches upon the reality of those disabled people for whom remedies are not so easily available and resources are scarce. When Justice Scalia waved his glasses in the air, the greedy hands of Justice Souter stole them and moved them to his eyes—"Now I can do my job!" he exclaimed—after which the greedy hands of Justice O'Connor filched the glasses from him—"Now I can do my job!" she exclaimed—and on and on.

*Chapter Four*

# Disability Studies and the Future of Identity Politics

Nobody wants to be in the minority. People angle not to be left alone in a dispute, and those who risk to be seek the protection of those like them to lend greater weight to their social power. We all seem to share a basic intuition about what it means to be human and to face a community of others created by our exclusion. But the fear of being in the minority exerts pressure beyond the influence of social conformity. It carries tremendous weight in political and social theory as well, where minority identity appears as a category that will not go away, even though many political theorists give only a minor place to it. Liberal political theory, for example, is based on the expectation that minorities will eventually disappear as they become fully integrated into a single polity. For liberals, a utopian society with a minority population is inconceivable. If it is the case, however, that minority identity is not destined for extinction, it may be worth considering it as a factor in all political representation. Identity politics is often associated by its critics with minority groups, but it is crucial to a vision of democratic society in its complex entirety. For identity politics makes it possible to conceive of democratic society as comprising significant communities of interest, representing minor affiliations and different points of view, that need to be heard and included if democratic society is to continue.

At nearly 20 percent, people with disabilities make up the largest minority population in the United States, unless one considers women at 51 percent as a structural minority. Moreover, only 15 percent of people with disabilities were born with their impairment. Most people become disabled over the course of their life. These statistics suggest why people with disabilities do not present immediately as either an identity or minority group—which makes it theoretically important, I insist, to include them in any discussion about the future of identity politics. On the one hand, people with disabilities are not often thought of as a single group, especially as a political group, because their identities are too different from each other. Which political interests do blind, elderly, and paralyzed people share? On what basis do we consider them as having an identity in common? Is a woman cognitively disabled from birth like a man who receives a head trauma in a farming accident? On the other hand, the nature of disability is such that every human being may be considered temporarily able-bodied. The number of disabled in any given society is constantly on the rise, as more and more people age, have accidents, and become ill, and this fact is obscured only by controlled accounting practices that refuse to admit some disabilities into the statistical record. There are, for example, nearly fifty million disabled in the United States, but this number does not include people who wear eyeglasses, those who take medication for hypertension, the learning disabled, or people with AIDS or HIV. Neither does it include the elderly, many of whom cannot climb stairs or open doors with ease, nor children, whose physical and mental abilities fit uncomfortably with the adult world. The disabled represent a minority that potentially includes anyone at anytime. Their numbers may be increased by natural disasters, warfare, epidemics, malnutrition, and industrial accidents—not to mention by simple acts of redefinition. By what logic, then, do we consider people with disabilities as a minority group?

Disability seems to provide an example of the extreme instability of identity as a political category, but it would not be easy, I think, to prove that disability is less significant in everyday life for being a category in flux. In fact, that disability may take so many forms increases both its impact on individuals and its significance in society. Here I consider the future of identity politics from the perspective of the many forms of disability—and with two related emphases in mind. First, I insist that disability studies requires one to think with greater flexibility about what constitutes both an identity and a minority group. People with disabilities build political coalitions not on the basis of natural identification but on the basis of healthcare needs, information sharing, and support groups. Most obviously, disability requires a broad consideration of identity politics beyond communities of interest based on race, nation, class, gender, and sex, and for this reason, it is crucial both ethically and theoretically to give a place to disability in the field of minority studies. Second, I want to engage disability studies with two theories important to identity politics: social constructionism and philosophical realism. Both are at bottom social theories—each one offers a different way of thinking about political representation dependent on identity—and yet it is not clear that either theory has yet found a way to incorporate the many forms of disability. My specific goal here is to use disability to put pressure on both theories in the hope that they might better represent the concerns of people with disabilities and fight prejudices against them. I begin by deepening my analysis of social construction because it has played a crucial role in the emergence of disability studies, especially in the humanities. I then turn to the less familiar arguments of philosophical realism. My conclusion will be that if social construction has influenced the past of disability studies, realism may well be in a position to define its future.

## The Psychology of Social Construction

The theory of social construction is fundamental to current thinking about the disabled body and mind—and with good reason—because it provides a major alternative to the medicalization of disability. The medical model lodges defect in the individual body and calls for individualized treatment. Medicalization has at least two unsettling effects as a result: it alienates the individual with a disability as a defective person, duplicating the history of discrimination and shame connected to disability in the social world, and it affects the ability of people with disabilities to organize politically. Since no two people with a disability apparently have the same problem, they have no basis for common complaint or political activism. Storied language mocks the idea of "the blind leading the blind," but the medicalization of disability really does create a situation where it is extremely unlikely that a blind person will be allowed to take a leadership position in the blind community, let alone in the sighted community. The world is divided, as Susan Sontag put it in *Illness as Metaphor,* into the kingdom of the well and the sick, and although we all possess dual citizenship, the disabled usually lose their civil rights in the kingdom of the well, especially once they enter the doctor's office (1).

The social model challenges the idea of defective citizenship by situating disability in the environment, not in the body. Disability seen from this point of view requires not individual medical treatment but changes in society. Social constructionism has changed the landscape of thinking about disability because it refuses to represent people with disabilities as defective citizens and because its focus on the built environment presents a common cause around which they may organize politically. More generally, social construction offers advantages for the political representation of the disabled because it demonstrates the falseness of any claim for political identity based on natural kind. It reveals that gender, race, sex, nationality, and ability are heterogeneous, indeterminate, and artificial categories represented as stable or natural by people who want to preserve their own political and social advantages. It is not surprising, then, that many of the major theorists of disability in recent years have adhered to the social model.

That identity is socially produced means in theory that minority groups like the disabled may challenge their own identities, allowing greater freedom and mobility in the social world. In practice, however, the social model does not seem to be as viable an option for the identity politics of people with disabilities as one might think because social constructionists remain in the end highly skeptical about any form of identity. Critics of identity politics remind, for example, that no two women are alike and that "woman" is not a coherent political category. They also remind that most of us have multiple identities not always served by the stricter identities required by membership in a minority group. Theorists of disability have also expressed hesitation about conceiving of people with disabilities as an identity or minority group. Lennard Davis, for example, explains that disability does not fit with the "totality of an identity," noting that "the universal sign for disability—the wheelchair—is the most profound example of the difficulty of categorizing disability because only a small minority of people with disabilities use that aid" (2001, 536, 544). Rosemarie Garland-Thomson believes that "identity is a little bit like nationalism"—"a very coercive category, leading to political fragmentation and division" (quoted in Potok 183–84). Critics of identity fear that the old identities used to repress people will come to define them in the future, or that claiming one strong identity will excuse injustices against people not in that identity group. Neither is a small concern given the history linking identity and oppression.

The attack on identity by social constructionists is designed to liberate individuals constrained by unjust stereotypes and social prejudices. The example of disability in particular reveals with great vividness the unjust stereotypes imposed on identity by cultural norms and languages as well as the violence exercised by them. It also provides compelling evidence for the veracity of the social model. Deafness was not, for instance, a disability on Martha's Vineyard for most of the eighteenth century because one in twenty-five residents was deaf and everyone in the community knew how to sign. Deaf villagers had the same occupations and incomes as hearing people (Shapiro 1993, 86). This example shows to what extent disability is socially produced. But disability also frustrates theorists of social construction because the disabled body and mind are not easily aligned with cultural norms and codes.

David Mitchell and Sharon Snyder have noticed that the push to link physical difference to cultural and social constructs, especially ideological ones, has actually made disability disappear from the social model. They cite a variety of recent studies of the body that use "corporeal aberrancies" to emblematize social differences, complaining that "physical difference" within common critical methodologies "exemplifies the evidence of social deviance even as the constructed nature of *physicality itself* fades from view" (1997, 5). Susan Bordo, although not referring directly to the disabled body, comes to a similar conclusion about the paradigm of "cultural plastic" embraced by many theorists of the social model (246). She argues that the widespread notion of the body as "malleable plastic"—"free to change its shape and location at will"—obscures the physicality of the body in favor of a disembodied ideal of self-determination and self-transformation. This practice is most obvious in the case of theorists "who advocate 'heterogeneity' and 'indeterminacy' as principles" of interpretation. What kind of body, she asks, can become anyone and travel anywhere? Her response is "nobody," since this "body is no body at all" (38–39, 229). If we were to pose the same question to the disability community, we would receive an even simpler and more penetrating response—whatever this body is, it is rarely disabled.

Recent theoretical emphases on "performativity," "heterogeneity," and "indeterminacy" privilege a disembodied ideal of freedom, suggesting that emancipation from social codes and norms may be achieved by imagining the body as a subversive text. These emphases are not only incompatible with the experiences of people with disabilities; they mimic the fantasy, often found in the medical model, that disease and disability are immaterial as long as the imagination is free. Doctors and medical professionals have the habit of coaxing sick people to cure themselves by thinking positive thoughts, and when an individual's health does not improve, the failure is ascribed to mental weakness. Sontag was perhaps the first to understand the debilitating effect of describing illness as a defect of imagination or will power. She traces the notion that disease springs from individual mental weakness to Schopenhauer's claim that "recovery from a disease depends on the will assuming 'dictatorial power in order to subsume the rebellious forces' of the body" (43–44). She also heaps scorn on the idea that the disabled or sick are responsible for their disease, concluding that "theories that diseases are caused by mental states and can be cured by will power are always an index of how much is not understood about the physical terrain of a disease" (55). The rebellious forces of the body and the physical nature of disease represent a reality untouched by metaphor, Sontag insists, and "that reality has to be explained" (55).

Consider as one example of the psychology of the social model Judith Butler's writings on power. I choose the example deliberately because her work represents an extraordinarily nuanced version of social construction, offering a good idea of both its strengths and weaknesses on the subject of disability. A curious thing about Butler's work is that bodies, disabled or otherwise, rarely appear in it. This includes *Bodies That Matter*—a book that seems at first glance to describe how oppressed people are constrained to think about their bodies as deviant but that actually takes as its topic the psychological relation between guilt and subject formation. For Butler, psychic pain and guilt are the preconditions of subjectivity. Power puts the subject in place via a process of subjection that constitutes the materiality of the self. Subjection, however, is a psychological process rather than a physical or material one—a conclusion made apparent by the fact that Butler reserves the defining use of "materi-

ality" for the "materiality of the signifier" (1993, 30). Guilt not only regu-
lates the body, Butler insists, it projects specific morphologies of the body.
Consequently, political emancipation requires a revolutionary change in
the mental state of the subjected person—a throwing off of every feeling
prosaically referred to as guilt—but a change extremely difficult to achieve
because guilt is anchored by an apparatus of social power well beyond the
ken of the individual. Indeed, guilt predates the formation of subjectivity,
for the subject comes into being only as the self-inscription of guilt on the
body. Guilt is a regulatory idea that saturates the surface of the body and
appears as physical illness (1993, 64).

It is to Butler's credit that she is able to read so clearly what might be
called the tendency in the philosophy of mind to represent the body only
in terms of its encasement of the mind. In fact, another book, *The Psychic
Life of Power,* seems designed to apply her ideas about bodily subjection to
the philosophy of mind, where she demonstrates with considerable skill
the long tradition of philosophical misunderstanding of corporeality.
What is not obvious, however, is whether she offers an alternative to this
tradition because her main concern remains the *psychic* life of power. Butler's work refers most often to the mental pain created by power, almost
always referenced as guilt, and the ways that power subjects the body to fit
its ends. But if power changes the body to serve its perverse agenda, Butler seem to indicate, changing the body may also be an option for those in
search of a way to resist power. It is a matter, then, of finding a way to
imagine one's body differently. This last point bears repeating with an emphasis: to resist power, one imagines changing one's body, but one does
not imagine a different body, for example, a disabled body.

Butler's "psychoanalytic criticism" of Foucault provides an illustration of this last idea (1997, 87). For Foucault, according to Butler, the psyche oppresses the body, whereas Lacan permits a psychoanalytic reading
of the psyche as a site of resistance to bodily oppression. Butler identifies
this site as the Lacanian imaginary, arguing that it thwarts any effort by the
symbolic to constitute a coherent identity (97). Butler's reading of Lacan
is not particularly strong, since the relation between the imaginary and
the symbolic is not a simple binary, but my main point about her use of
the imagination to fight suffering is exemplified. Despite the Lacanian vocabulary, she is arguing that imagination can cure what ails the body.

The body supporting Butler's theories is an able body whose condition relies on its psychological powers, and therefore the solution to pain or disability is also psychological. The able or healthy body is, first, a body that the subject cannot feel. As Butler puts it, pain "may be one way in which we come to have an idea of our body at all" (1993, 65). The healthy subject is either disinterested in its body or in control of its feelings and sensations. Second, the health of a body is judged by the ability not only to surmount pain, illness, and disability but to translate by force of will their effects into benefits. It seems, to use the Foucauldian vocabulary often favored by Butler, that the body is "docile" only when the mind is docile, for her heady analyses intimate that the only way to save the body is by awakening the brain. It is almost as if the body is irrelevant to the subject's political life. The physical condition of the body is not a factor in political repression; only the inability of the mind to resist subjugation ultimately matters.

Butler's reading of Hegel replays the same logic and provides a final case in point. In Hegel the body is enslaved because it has fallen into "unhappy consciousness," and this unfortunate mental state either denies or sacrifices bodily life: "bodies are, in Hegel, always and only referred to indirectly as the encasement, location, or specificity of consciousness" (1997, 3, 34). Power involves forgetting that one is a body, while projecting one's body into the place of the subjected other. To use the familiar terms, the Master is thought, the Slave, body. Moreover, it is the fear of death, Butler explains, that causes the wholesale abandonment of the body and privileging of thought. The finite character of the body causes great terror, but this terror becomes the very condition by which self and other might recognize each other. The result is a dialectical process, Butler argues, in which "Hegel shows that if the suppression of the body requires an instrumental movement of and by the body, then the body is inadvertently *preserved* in and by the instrument of its suppression" (1997, 33). Butler's recognition of this dialectic would presumably lead her to give some representation to the body, perhaps with attention to how complex embodiment relates to oppression. It does not. She continues to describe the body, with Hegel, as the graveyard where the subject is buried. The body is deaf, dumb, blind, crippled, dead—described implicitly as impaired but never recognized explicitly as such, since disability for Butler refers ultimately to a mental, not a physical state.

Physicality is part of the reality of the disabled body, and if embodiment contributes to the experience of people with disabilities, then its misrepresentation as a mental condition will have a detrimental effect on their ability to organize themselves politically.[1] The tendency of the social model to refer physical states to mental ones, then, especially to those that privilege acts of the imagination, is a political act, and hardly a neutral one, because it often represents impairment as the product of mental weakness. There may be no more damning political gesture. Many are the obstacles placed before people with physical disabilities who want to participate fully as citizens in political process, but the majority of nondisabled people does not dispute that the disabled should have rights of citizenship. This belief does not extend to people with mental disabilities. The "feeble-minded" hold rights of citizenship nowhere, and few people in the mainstream believe this fact should be changed. Behind the idea that physical disability may be cured by acts of will or the imagination is a model of political rationality that oppresses people with mental disabilities. I turn to the problem of rationality and political representation in the second half of this chapter, but two ideas are worth stressing immediately. First, if the social model relies for its persuasive power on a shift from physical to mental disability, its claim to locate disability in the social environment rather than in the disabled person is less complete than it pretends, since the concept of individual defect returns to haunt its conclusions. Second, that one fails to throw off one's physical disability because of mental defect implies a caste system that ranks people with physical disabilities as superior to those with mental ones. This caste system, of course, encourages the vicious treatment of people with mental disabilities in most societies. Its influence is fully apparent in models of political citizenship, the history of civil and human rights, structures of legal practice, the politics of institutionalization, employment history, and the organization of the disability community itself.

---

Dossier No. 8
*New York Times Online*
August 7, 2000

Executing the Mentally Retarded Even as Laws Begin to Shift
By Raymond Bonner and Sara Rimer

LIVINGSTON Tex., Aug. 2—Oliver Cruz can barely read and write. He has an I.Q. of either 64 or 76, depending on the test. He flunked the seventh grade three times. He was rejected by the Army after failing the entry exam three times, and unable to decipher a job application, he did the menial work that came his way, cutting grass, cleaning houses and taking tickets for a traveling carnival.

Now, at 33, he has spent 12 years on death row in Livingston for the rape and murder of a 24-year-old woman, Kelly Donovan, who was stationed at the Air Force base in Mr. Cruz's hometown, San Antonio. Mr. Cruz, who in an interview this week took full responsibility for his crime and expressed anguished remorse, is scheduled to die by lethal injection on Wednesday at 6 p.m.

A defense psychologist testified at trial that tests, as well as a review of school records, showed Mr. Cruz to be mentally retarded. The state did not dispute this. Indeed, the prosecutor argued that the fact that Mr. Cruz "may not be very smart" made him "more dangerous," and so was a reason to sentence him to death....

---

A final point about the psychology of social construction and its inability to respond to the identity politics of people with disabilities: social construction, despite its preoccupation with political ideology, clings resolutely to a psychological model based on the autonomy of the individual rather than developing one designed to address political community. It seems to agree with liberal individualism that emancipation from repression relies on the intellectual and emotional resources of the individual but claims that individuals affected by pain and suffering are irrevocably impaired for political action. This is nowhere more apparent than in the contention that identity politics is invalid when linked to suffering. Wendy Brown, for example, argues that identity politics becomes "invested in its own subjection," feasts on "political impotence," and descends into a melancholy based on a "narcissistic wound" (70–72). She claims that identity politics are essentially a politics of resentment but defines resentment by applying Nietzsche's comments about an individual character, "the man of resentment," to political formation, as if the psychology of many people and a single mind were interchangeable.[2] Likewise, Butler comes to the conclusion that identity tied to injury—her formulation for identity politics—has little chance of freeing itself from oppression because once one is "called by an injurious name" and "a certain narcissism takes hold of any term that confers existence, I am led to embrace the terms that injure me because they constitute me socially" (1997, 104). In fact, the only chance of resisting oppression, she continues, occurs when the "attachment to an injurious interpellation," "by way of a necessarily alienated narcissism," supports "the condition by which resignifying that interpellation becomes possible" (104). It is revealing that Butler cannot critique identity politics without breaking into the first-person singular. Moreover, she hangs every form of political resistance and attachment on "narcissism"—an accusatory category with a long history of misapplication to people with disabilities.[3] Both gestures demonstrate her dependence on individual psychology—a dependence she shares with Brown and many other social constructionists.

What would it mean to imagine a model of political identity that does not rely on individual psychology—one that sees political psychology as greater than the sum of its parts? What would it mean to define political identity based not on self-interest or disinterest but on common interests? Finally, what would it mean to define physicality politically—not as the individual body supporting the political will or imagination but as a body beyond the individual? This body would be politically repressive because its form would be imprinted on the social and built environment, determining the exclusion of some people and the inclusion of others. But this body would also be politically enabling because its ideological form would belong not to one person but to the entire society. It would be a social body and therefore subject to transformation by direct political analysis and action.

## Realism and the Social Body

"Blackness" and "femaleness," to use typical examples, do not define individual bodies. It is true that some individual bodies are black, female, or both, but the social meaning of these words does not account for everything that these bodies are. Rather, these words denote large social categories having an interpretation, history, and politics well beyond the particularities of one human body. This fact is, of course, largely recognized, which is why the attempt to reduce a given body to one of these terms carries the pejorative label of "racist" or "sexist." We know a great deal more about racism and sexism than we did fifty years ago for the simple reason that they are now objects of knowledge for entire societies to consider, and their interpretation, history, and politics are growing ever more familiar as a result. We recognize the characteristics, experiences, emotions, and rationales that determine their usage. If discrimination is in decline—although it is not clear that it is—the result is due largely to the fact that categories such as "blackness" and "femaleness" have become objects of knowledge, ideological critique, and political interpretation for many people.

Disability does not yet have the advantage of a political interpretation because the ideology of ability remains largely unquestioned. A blind body, for example, is seen as one person's body. Blindness supposedly defines everything that this body is.[4] There is no term for the prejudicial reduction of a body to its disability. Disability activists have proposed the term *ableism* to name this prejudice, but it has not been accepted into general usage. Its use elicits scowls and smirks, even in progressive society. There is little sense either in the general population or among scholars that words like *blind, crippled, stupid, fat, deaf,* or *dumb* carry social meanings having an interpretation, history, and politics well beyond the particularities of one human body. The number-one objective for disability studies, then, is to make disability an object of general knowledge and thereby to awaken political consciousness to the distasteful prejudice called "ableism."

The theoretical resources required to satisfy this objective, however, are still in short supply. Social construction, we saw, has advanced the study of disability to the point where one may name the environment and not an individual body as the reason for disability. A reliance on individual psychology as well as the claim that causal connections between ideologies and physical bodies are relative, unstable, and unmappable have nevertheless obstructed the capacity of the social model to offer a strong and rational critique of ableism based on political ideals. If people with disabilities are to enjoy full access to society, they will need to find theories that will advance literacy about disability to the next stage and create a basis for political action. Acknowledging the philosophical limitations of the social model, Susan Wendell calls for an approach capable of recognizing the "hard physical realities" of disabled bodies:

In most postmodern cultural theorizing about the body, there is no recognition of—and, as far as I can see, no room for recognizing—the hard physical realities that are faced by people with disabilities. . . . We need to acknowledge that social justice and cultural change can eliminate a great deal of disability while recognizing that there may be much suffering and limitation that they cannot fix. (45)

Wendell's call to arms is compatible with a number of approaches being pursued in minority studies, most notably by scholars inspired by philosophical realism. Paula Moya, for example, also disagrees with recent critics of identity politics who dismiss the "physical realities" of existence. Her approach applies a philosophical realism, based on the work of Satya Mohanty, that links minority identity to the natural and social environment: "Theory, knowledge, and understanding," she writes, "can be linked to 'our skin color, the land or concrete we grew up on, our sexual longings' without being uniformly determined by them. Rather, those 'physical realities of our lives' will profoundly *inform* the contours and the context of both our theories and our knowledge" (2002, 37). Moya's point is that sex and race, while not definitive of a person's identity, arise from skin, color, land, and other physical realities that contribute to political knowledge and consciousness. More important, the links between physical states, social ideologies, and identities are open to scrutiny and criticism because they have a verifiable and rational character. This does not mean, of course, that social experience has absolute status as knowledge. We can be right, wrong, or beside the point, but experience remains intimately connected to political and social existence, and therefore individuals and societies are capable of learning from their experiences.

Realists, like social constructionists, believe that reality is socially produced. Unlike social constructionists, they believe that social reality, once made, takes on a shape, politics, and history that belong to the realm of human action, and as part of human action, it is available for rational analysis and political transformation. Realism entails a recognition of the significant causal factors of the social world by which the identities of groups and individuals are created.[5] Identities are not infinitely interpretable, then, because they obey the rules of their formation and have strong connections to other cultural representations. Their verification and analysis rely on a coordination with the real world and a coordination between interconnected hypotheses about and experiences with society, which means that identity is both pragmatic and epistemic. In short, cultural identities, because they respond to natural and cultural factors, make certain actions possible and present a resource for understanding society and its many meanings. Identities are complex theories about the social and moral world.[6]

---

### Dossier No. 9
*BBC News.com*
January 10, 2004

O'Neill Lashes 'Blind Man' Bush

A former US treasury secretary has given an unflattering account of his time under President George W Bush.

Paul O'Neill describes Mr Bush as being disengaged and says that at cabinet meetings the president was like a blind man in a room full of deaf people.

The remarks come as Democratic challengers prepare for the crucial Iowa and New Hampshire caucuses later this month. . . .

---

The politics of identity, then, are not about narrow personal claims, resentment, or narcissistic feelings. Rather, they are based on insights about how communities are organized. They also value cooperation as a moral good. Realists, in fact, make the case that there is no contradiction between identity politics and a certain moral universalism because both rely on the belief that human beings, regardless of culture or society, are capable of rational agency and therefore of cultural and political self-determination—an important claim that I will open to adjustment below. "No matter how different cultural Others are," Satya Mohanty argues, "they are never so different that they are—as typical members of their culture—incapable of acting purposefully, of evaluating their actions in light of their ideas and previous experiences, and of being 'rational' in a minimal way" (198). Realists celebrate diversity because it exposes dogmatic assumptions about a given culture's moral ideology (242); they embrace the hypothesis of moral universalism because it broadens the field of ethical inquiry beyond a given culture to recognize all human beings as rational agents. Identity, as both a specific cultural form and as a more abstract, rational principle, provides resources for human survival, welfare, justice, and happiness.

Consequently, realists affirm the positive value of identity for political representation. For them, identity politics creates points of contact between individuals, or identifications, some of which are embraced as common personality traits, physical characteristics, beliefs and traditions, moral values, aesthetic tastes, sexual orientations, geographic origins, kinship, and so on. These points of contact are social constructions insofar as they are constituted by a variety of experiences, but the political and cultural allegiances involved are often so powerful as to make the identity function as a social fact. Thus, people who identify themselves as members of a community have entered into cooperation for socially valid reasons, and their identities represent direct responses to distinct and often verifiable conditions of society, both positive and negative, whether shared customs, pleasures, and diets or the presence of racial prejudice, sexism, unequal distribution of resources, or an inaccessible built environment. Identities, then, actively expose the effects of ideology on individuals and provide a rational basis for acts of political emancipation. "Some identities," as Moya puts it, "can be more politically progressive than others *not* because they are 'transgressive' or 'indeterminate' but because they provide us with a critical perspective from which we can disclose the complicated workings of ideology and oppression" (2002, 27).

Disability studies has, of course, already developed a critical perspective that reveals the workings of ideology and oppression in the social and built environment. It claims that the ideology of ability favors one particular social body for which all spaces have been designed, and rarely is this body conceived as disabled. The body implied by social spaces, then, leaves no room for a conception of unaverage or less than perfect bodies, with the result that people with disabilities are not able to mix with other people in the very places designed for this purpose. The general population is not conscious of the features of the social body, even though they have remained remarkably consistent since the beginning of the modern architectural period, but this does not mean that the ideology of ability is unconscious—beyond analysis or correction—because the symptomology of an individual unconscious à la Freud does not determine it. Rather, we encounter something like the "political unconscious" described by Fredric Jameson—a social propensity to organize cultural representations and artifacts according to the symbolism of number and averaging rather than individualism.[7] In fact, this propensity is entirely open to scrutiny and theorization, as the briefest glance at modern architectural history reveals. For example, both Le Corbusier and Henry Dreyfuss developed a form language for architecture and industrial design based on the proportions of an ideal social body. Le Corbusier invented the modular scale of proportion, while Dreyfuss pioneered human factors engineering. The former favored a man six feet tall, possessing proportionate dimensions between his upraised hands, head, waist, and feet (see fig. 1). The latter created a series of charts representing "Joe," "Josephine," and "Joe Jr.," a typical American male, female, and child, whose proportions set the human factors needed to design the Bell telephone, Polaroid camera, and Honeywell thermostat as well as airplane interiors, tractors, vacuum cleaners, trains, and helicopters (see fig. 2). The efforts and principles of both men were entirely public and pursued with the best intentions in mind—to create objects and spaces more appropriate to human scale—but they also put in place what Rob Imrie calls a "design apartheid," a system that methodically excludes disabled bodies (19).[8]

When a disabled body moves into any space, it discloses the social body implied by that space. There is a one-to-one correspondence between the dimensions of the built environment and its preferred social body—the body invited inside as opposed to those bodies not issued an invitation. This social body determines the form of public and private buildings alike, exposing the truth that there are in fact no private bodies, only public ones, registered in the blueprints of architectural space. The social body is the standard—presupposed but invisible—until a nonstandard body makes an appearance. Then the standard becomes immediately apparent, as the inflexible structures of furniture, rooms, and streets reveal their intolerance for anyone unlike the people for whom they were built.

Permit me to take as an example the blueprint of my own house in Ann Arbor, Michigan. An analysis of a private dwelling is especially important because we usually think of access in terms of public buildings and functions, while the greatest cruelty of inaccessibility remains the fact that people with disabilities are excluded from the private spaces where most intimate gatherings occur—dinner parties, children's birthday parties and sleepovers, holiday meals, wakes, Shiva, and celebrations of births,

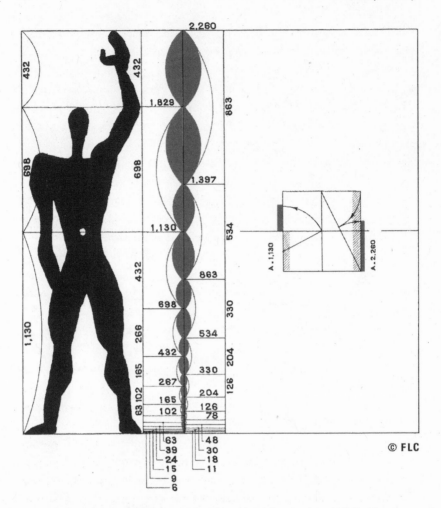

1. Le Corbusier, *Modulor*. (© 2007 Artist Rights Society (ARS), New
York / ADAGP, Paris / FLC.)

anniversaries, and weddings. My house is a frame, side-entry colonial
built in 1939. We constructed a major addition in 1990. It resembles many
other houses in the neighborhood, since most of them were built around
the same period. A one-car garage, long but narrow, stands at the back of
the lot. Poured concrete stairs, with three steps total, climb to the front
door, whose passage is 35 inches. A side door, at the driveway, also serves
the staircase to the basement and requires three steps to reach the main

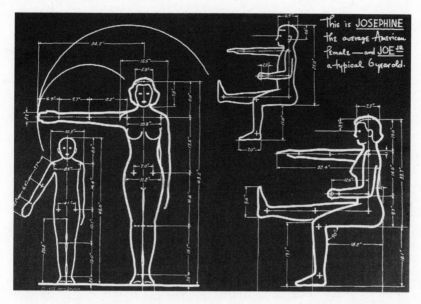

2. Henry Dreyfuss, *Josephine and Joe Jr. Designing for People*, 1955

floor. Its entry is extremely narrow and made more so by a coat rack. The kitchen door in the rear, off a patio, is the most accessible approach to the house, since it requires one step onto the patio and one step into the door, but the passage is 30 inches. Finally, another rear door, off the patio, requiring one step, enters the family room, but the door is blocked by furniture and never used. If I were to install a wheelchair ramp, the recommended ratio would mean that I would need fourteen feet of ramp to climb the two steps into the rear kitchen door. The front door would require a ramp significantly longer. Recommended standards for universal entry give 36 inches, and sometimes 42 are required, if the approach to the door is at an angle and narrow. All of my entry doors are too narrow, and they also have metal, unbeveled thresholds that a wheelchair user would need to "jump." Of course, if a wheelchair user were lucky enough to get into my house, it would still be impossible to use any of the bathrooms. The largest entry is the door to the master bedroom bath at 29 inches, but it is located on the second floor. The first floor half-bath has the smallest passage, 22.5 inches, and would not hold a wheelchair in any event. All of the toilets are too low for a wheelchair user, and there are no grab bars in any of the bathrooms. Nor could a wheelchair user sit easily at table in my house because the large table and small dining room leave little room to maneuver.

Other standard features in the house present difficulties for people with diverse body types. All of the door knobs are at the standard three-feet height, but none of them is graspable for people with arthritis or those missing hands or fingers. The light switches are set at four feet or higher. It is a curiosity that the ideal height for a door knob is supposedly three feet, but light switches are placed higher. One of the bathtubs is much deeper than the other and difficult to step in and out of. Mirrors are generally out of view for people below average height. My children perched dangerously on the toilet to comb their hair for years. The stairway to the second floor had only an ornamental banister on the initial run until we installed a more functional one on the second run. There are no banisters on the stairways at the side entry and descending to the basement. Until we remodeled, light switches were located in such a manner that one had to turn off the lights before leaving a room or a floor. We have never been able to get our doorbell to work, which makes it difficult to hear when someone is at the door. Finally, in our kitchen, top shelving is out of reach for my wife, and low shelving is beyond my capacity to squat, and deep, three-feet-high countertops keep items out of reach for children.

When we imagine differently abled bodies in a space, the social construction of the space is revealed to us by dint of the fact that it owes its existence and preservation to an application of political rationality that is entirely public. In sum, people in wheelchairs, people with diminished sight and hearing, those with difficulty climbing stairs, people uncomfortable reaching high or bending low, and those unable to grasp objects do not fit easily in my house. Nimble six-footers, with an intuitive sense of dark spaces, acute hearing, and a love of staircases do. These are social facts readable in the blueprint of my house, and when they appear in many other buildings—and they do—we may rightfully conclude that they are supported by an ideology—an ideology of ability open to scrutiny and correction because it belongs to the public domain. The availability of social facts, of course, does not immediately translate into political action. Some people will not admit facts even when they stare them in the face, and other factors, such as competing economic motives and existing structures of authority, may deter the correction of social injustices. The point remains, however, that oppression and injustice usually continue for political reasons, not because personal, psychological complexes render individuals incapable of action. It is to everyone's benefit, then, to develop a general theory for analyzing and critiquing different political rationales, but in the absence of a general theory, one may expect that individuals who have identified certain wrongs against them will gather together into groups for the purpose of better struggling against injustice. This is what we are witnessing currently with the rise of identity politics.

## Realism with a Human Face

Philosophical realists have a greater appreciation of rationalism than many literary and cultural critics writing today and therefore a more nuanced position on political rationality, both its value and dangers. Theirs is a flexible theoretical system adaptable to a variety of political analyses, sensitive to human diversity, and aware of past crimes committed in the name of objectivity, universalism, and rationalism. It is nevertheless the case that disability presents an obstacle to some of the basic tenets of philosophical realism.

One stubborn obstacle worth accenting here involves the connection in realism between rationalism and the concept of the human. Theories of rationality rely not only on the ability to perceive objective properties of things in the world; they configure rationality itself in terms of the objective properties and identifying characteristics of those agents whom Kant called rational beings, and these identifying characteristics do not always allow for the inclusion of people with disabilities, especially people with mental disabilities. I add two cautions immediately. First, neither ethics nor politics can survive without a concept of rationality, which is why realists have insisted that social construction needs to be integrated with rationalism. Second, the definition of human agency is a problem for the history of philosophy as much as for realists working and writing currently, which requires that we develop an adequate description of the ways that notions of moral personhood have evolved beyond the rigid eighteenth-century preoccupation with reason to attain the more flexible definitions of human beings and the respect due to them available today. Rationality theory, then, is not to be discarded—it is tied to human autonomy inextricably by the emancipatory ideals of the Enlightenment. But it needs to be pressured by disability studies because it is more exclusionary than necessary.

Juan Flores makes the point that the Enlightenment defines rationality by the creation of unenlightened others. Kant's idea of reason is suspicious of immature or underdeveloped thinking, he notes, and shuns "the inability to make use of one's reason without the direction of another" (cited by Flores 200). The moral and political capacity to be free, as described by both Rousseau and Kant, is loosely related to mature rationality as well, although it permits a great deal of flexibility in theory. Eighteenth-century ideals of rationality preserve a strong emphasis on human autonomy and self-reliance and a hatred of heteronomy. Mohanty makes it clear, we saw earlier, that philosophical realists accept this emphasis. "No matter how different cultural Others are," he notes, "they are never so different that they are—as typical members of their culture—incapable of acting purposefully, of evaluating their actions in light of their ideas and previous experiences, and of being 'rational' in a minimal way" (198). Moya in her response to Flores argues correctly that "any self only becomes a 'self' in relation to an 'other'" (n.d., 8). But the degree of interdependence ascribed by her to self and other stops short of recognizing people who are not capable of reflecting on their actions. She defines respect in part on the assumption that those with whom we disagree are not "confused or crazy or simple-minded" but comprehensible within their "world of sense," acknowledging that we have an obligation to listen to others because they might have something to teach us, not because they are "radically other" or "terribly smart" but because "they are related to us through interconnecting structures of power" (8–9). If respect depends on the possession of rationality, is there a minimal rationality below which no respect for human beings should be given? How do we preserve the ideal of rational agency and at the same time make Kant's kingdom of the ends accessible to differently abled people? This is not a rhetorical question but an interrogative that ought to be tied to our continuing aspiration to be human. I take it to be a very difficult question worthy of serious work.[9]

**Dossier No. 10**
*New York Times Online*
September 5, 2000

Ethical Dilemma with Siamese Twins
By The Associated Press

LONDON (AP)—Jodie may live, but only if Mary dies. Doctors want to operate, but the parents prefer to trust the will of God.

Thus, the fate of Siamese twins from Eastern Europe is in the hands of doctors and appeals court judges, who are struggling with the ethical issues.

Speaking of Mary, the twin whose less-developed body depends on her sister for oxygenated blood, Lord Justice Henry Brooke asked Tuesday: "What is this creature in the eyes of the law?"

A lawyer appointed to represent Jodie argued that "there are no best interests in preserving what is unfortunately a futile life."

Jodie and Mary—false names used by the court to preserve the girls' privacy—were born Aug. 8 at St. Mary's Hospital in Manchester and are joined at their lower abdomens. Mary's brain and body are less developed than Jodie's and the Manchester medical team says it is highly probable that if left unseparated, both twins will die within six months as Jodie's heart fails.

The parents, who have not been identified, are appealing the Aug. 25 decision by a High Court judge to allow surgeons to separate the twins. . . .

To treat one's personal maxim as if it were a categorical imperative, to summon Kant's famous formula for rational deliberation, is a narrative maneuver meant to help one imagine a position of autonomy, one free of partiality and private interest—a very difficult thing for a human being to do and thus a very valuable thing. The purpose of rational deliberation, however, is not to arrive at moral principles but to test them. Moral universals are only universals insofar as they are true in general and not in particular—by which I mean that they usually involve place-holding concepts, such as "human being," "freedom," "virtue," "vice," "cultural diversity," that require further narrativization to have a particular application. Using these concepts does not mark the end of the process of rational deliberation but its beginning, and such deliberation has to be without end as long as there is to be a kingdom of the ends.

The concept of the human, then, does not involve a fixed definition but must be a work in progress, just as human beings should always be works in progress. Oddly enough, the most flexible approach to the definition of the human today occurs in arguments for animal rights. The idea here is to treat animals with the respect due to them as equals to human beings, despite the fact that animals are not capable of extending respect as equals to us. This is an important gesture for ethical thinking, but I prefer, for political reasons, to make provisions for the accessibility of all members of the human species to the category of the human before we begin to provide access for other species. The simple fact remains that it is easier at the moment to make a case for animal rights than for disability rights, and at least one major philosopher has gone so far as to argue that we owe animals greater kindness than people with disabilities. Peter Singer concludes that we should outlaw animal cruelty and stop eating meat but that we should perform euthanasia on people with mental disabilities or difficult physical disabilities such as spina bifida:

> that a being is a human being . . . is not relevant to the wrongness of killing it; it is, rather, characteristics like rationality, autonomy and self-consciousness that make a difference. Defective infants lack these characteristics. Killing them, therefore, cannot be equated with killing normal human beings, or any other self-conscious beings. This conclusion is not limited to infants who, because of irreversible mental retardation will never be rational, self-conscious beings. . . . Some doctors closely connected with children suffering from severe spina bifida believe that the lives of some of these children are so miserable that it is wrong to resort to surgery to keep them alive. . . . If this is correct, utilitarian principles suggest that it is right to kill such children. (131–33)

This horrifying conclusion shows the limitations of eighteenth-century rationalism. My point is that another universal and metacritical concept of the human—one that moves beyond the eighteenth-century use of rationality as the determining factor for membership in the human community—is urgently required, if people with disabilities are to attain the respect due to them and if we are to make progress as a democratic society, and so I will try to provide one here. Humanness is defined by the aspiration to be human but in a paradoxical way that includes as part of that aspiration the requirement that one concede to other beings the status of human being in order to be recognized as human oneself. Conceding someone the status of human being, I note, is not so much a matter of giving them permission as just letting them be as human.

It is vital at the beginning of the twenty-first century to reconsider our philosophical ideas about humanness because democracy will have no legitimate basis for being the open society it claims itself to be without a generous and metacritical concept of the human, one that gives people with disabilities a place in the public forum. People with disabilities are not a political burden but a resource for thinking about fundamental democratic principles such as inclusiveness and participation.

## No Sin to Limp

Identity politics has been associated by both the Left and the Right with exclusion, injury, and weakness. Adherents of identity politics exist supposedly on the margins of society, on the outside, stung by a sense of injury at their exclusion. Thus, the Right condemns identity politics as narcissistic affect, shunning those people who feel too sorry for themselves or have a tasteless and exaggerated sense of their own pain, whereas the Left cannot stomach people who act like victims, whether they are really victims or not, because they are self-colonizers who set a bad example for everyone else. Both characterizations establish vital links to the politics of people with disabilities. For they, too, are said to live outside of society and to suffer for it. But people with disabilities have refused to accept these misconceptions, requiring different languages and theories of inclusion and pain. Perhaps, then, the perspective of disability studies may shed some light on current misconceptions about minorities and their identity politics.

How might disability studies revise, for instance, the concept of exclusion? It has been under assault since the eighteenth century, most obviously because the perceptional landscape of Enlightenment philosophy opposes most suggestions of externality. The Enlightenment depends famously on the position of the world spectator, and this position, responsible for promoting concepts as varied as empire, the United Nations, and reader-response criticism to name but a few, originates in part as a response to the moral problem of deciding between inclusion and exclusion. The value of world spectatorship lies in its conception of a world that has no outside, in its insistence that all notions of an outside are in fact false and destructive, whether one is discussing government secrecy or national borders.[10] Enlightenment philosophy was eager to right the wrong of exclusionary behavior, and its objective, inherited by every subsequent age, involves naming who is being excluded by whom and insisting on inclusion. We usually forget, however, that a reference to an outside determines inclusion as well. Here is where disability studies might effect a sea change by asking that the inclusion-exclusion binary be reconceived in terms of accessibility and inaccessibility, thereby taking power and momentum from those on the inside and stressing that societies should be open to everyone. In short, all worlds should be accessible to everyone, but it is up to individuals to decide whether they will enter these worlds. We live in a built environment that is inaccessible, so it is a stretch to think about a moral and political world that would be wholly accessible, but this is the challenge issued by disability studies. How will the language of universal access transform politics in the future?

Finally, how might disability studies begin to interpret the politics of injury attached to minority identity? The model of rationality most visible today, we have seen, defines political subjects as disinterested and unique selves capable of making choices in private and public life on the basis of their own individual being. One of the ramifications of this model is the fear that identity of any kind oppresses the self, and generally when identity fails, it is considered a good thing. All identity politics are, consequently, better off dead because they interfere with individual autonomy. This conclusion is a direct result of thinking about identity as a cultural construct that interferes with individual being, either constraining or misdirecting it. The rejection of identity politics, then, appears to aim solely at the emancipation of the self. But we might consider that the rejection of identity politics also derives from a certain psychology of injury supplemental to the ideology of ability. This psychology links injury to individual weakness, and it makes us afraid to associate with people who either claim to be injured or show signs of having been injured or disabled. We interpret injured identity as a social construction of personality that an individual should not put on, and since not everyone does, people with injuries are somehow inferior. People with disabilities are familiar with this psychological response to them, and greater dialogue between disability and minority studies might make it clear that attacks by the Right and Left against identity politics are motivated more by aversion than political rationality.

Identity politics is not a curse on minority individuals but a political boon. They do not gather together because of wounded attachments or narcissism. They are not trying to turn an injury to unfair advantage. Rather, they are involved in a political process. In fact, identity politics is no different from any other form of political representation, since politics always implies the existence of a coalition whose membership is defined by ideological, historical, geographical, or temporal borders. Limited ideas of identity, then, are properties of all forms of political representation, and there is no reason to reject identity politics either on this basis or because they have been inappropriately linked to exclusion or injury.

Disability studies has much to offer future discussions of minority identity and its politics. Other topics might include (1) considering why the poor have been unable to establish themselves as a minority or identity group and how this inability relates to the general poverty of people with disabilities, (2) providing further elaboration about the relation between citizenship rights, human rights, and mental disability and how this connection has influenced the representation of people of color and the GLBT community, or (3) asking how conceptions of disability determine different views of the marketplace, for example, images of health encouraged by genetic engineering and drug companies versus ideas about worker safety and health in heavy industry. We are just at the beginning of our inquiry, and the inquiry is difficult. But we may take comfort for the slow advance of our knowledge, to paraphrase Freud with irony intended, in the words of the poet:

What we cannot reach flying we must reach limping. . . .
The Book tells us it is no sin to limp.[11]

*Chapter Five*
# Disability as Masquerade

## To Pass or Not to Pass

My subject will be recognized as passing, although I plan to give it a few unexpected twists and turns. For I have been keeping secrets and telling lies. In December 1999 I had an altercation at the San Francisco airport with a gatekeeper for Northwest Airlines who demanded that I use a wheelchair if I wanted to claim the early-boarding option. He did not want to accept that I was disabled unless my status was validated by a highly visible prop like a wheelchair. My practice in the years since I have begun to feel the effects of post-polio is to board airplanes immediately after the first-class passengers, so that I do not have to navigate crowded aisles on wobbly legs. I answered the gatekeeper that I would be in a wheelchair soon enough, but that it was my decision, not his, when I began to use one. He eventually let me board and then chased me into the cabin on an afterthought to apologize. The incident was trivial in many ways, but I have now adopted the habit of exaggerating my limp whenever I board planes. My exaggeration is not always sufficient to render my disability visible—gatekeepers still question me on occasion—but I continue to use the strategy, despite the fact that it fills me with a sense of anxiety and bad faith, emotions that resonate with previous experiences in which doctors and nurses have accused me of false complaints, oversensitivity, and malingering.

In January 2001 I slipped on a small patch of ice and broke my knee. It was my right knee, the leg affected by polio when I was two years old. For the next few months, I used wooden crutches—a prosthetic device, unlike forearm crutches, that usually signifies temporary injury rather than long-term disability. Throughout my life I have spent long periods on crutches, and my return to them summoned a series of powerful emotions. For one thing, it was the first time I found myself on crutches since I had come out as disabled.[1] The crutches projected to the public world what I felt to be a profound symbol of my inner life as well as my present status as a person with a disability. They also gave me great hope for the future because I had begun to worry that I would not be able to get around as I grew older, and I soon realized to my relief that I could do very well on my crutches. I had been tutored in their use from such an early age that I felt as if a part of my body once lost to me had been restored as soon as I slipped them under my arms. Nevertheless, I found myself giving an entirely new answer to the question posed to me by people on the street. "What's wrong with you?" they always ask. My new answer: "I slipped on the ice and broke my knee."

To pass or not to pass—that is often the question. But do these two narratives about disability illustrate the conventional understanding of keeping secrets about identity? Erving Goffman defines passing as a strategy for managing the stigma of "spoiled identities"—those identities discredited by law, opinion, or social convention. When in the minority and powerless, Jews pass as Christians, blacks pass as whites, and gay, lesbian, and transgendered people pass as heterosexuals. Similarly, people with disabilities find ingenious ways to conceal their impairments and to pass as able-bodied. In *Epistemology of the Closet*, however, Eve Kosofsky Sedgwick suggests that secrets concerning identity are a more complicated affair than Goffman's definition allows, arguing persuasively that the historical specificity of the closet has marked indelibly the meaning of "secrecy" in twentieth-century Western culture (1990, 72). Closeting involves things not merely concealed but difficult to disclose—the inability to disclose is, in fact, one of the constitutive markers of oppression. The epistemology of the closet complicates the usual understanding of passing because it disrupts the structural binary that represents passing as an action taking place between knowing and unknowing subjects. The closet often holds secrets that either cannot be told or are being kept by those who do not want to know the truth about the closeted person. Some people keep secrets; other people are secrets. Some people hide in the closet, but others are locked in the closet. There is a long history, of course, of locking away people with disabilities in attics, basements, and backrooms—not to mention the many institutions created to keep secret the existence of disabled family members. Secrets about disability may appear mundane compared to those associated with the gay experience because the closet cannot be mapped according to the simple binary opposition between private and public existence. But if disability studies has anything to learn from queer theory, it is that secrecy rarely depends on simple binaries.

Sedgwick argues that an open secret compulsorily kept characterizes the epistemology of the closet, and she provides as an example the bewildering case of an eighth-grade schoolteacher named Acanfora who disclosed his homosexuality and was removed from the classroom. When he sued the local board of education, a federal court found that he could not be denied employment because of his homosexuality but supported the decision of the board to remove him because he had not disclosed his homosexuality on his job application (1990, 69–70). By a tortured logic, too much information suddenly became too little, and Acanfora was punished. It is increasingly apparent that a similar logic also plagues disability law, which is one reason why queer theory holds important lessons for disability studies. In a recent high-profile case, the United States Supreme Court found that two women pilots denied employment by United Airlines because they were nearsighted could not seek protection under the ADA due to the fact that they were not disabled. The social representation of impairment as negative or inferior, not the existence of physical and mental differences, defines disability discrimination. Yet the two pilots were not allowed to seek protection under the law, even though United Airlines denied them employment by deeming their bodies inferior and the Court ruled that this representation was false. For the purposes of the law, the women were given two bodies, one by the Court and another by United Airlines, as if doing so were the only way to sustain the impossible double standard being applied to them (Greenhouse 1999a; Tyjewski).

Dossier No. 11
*New York Times Online*
January 7, 2001

Frieda Pushnik, Turned Her Deformities Into a Career, Dies at 77
By Douglas Martin

Frieda Pushnik, who used being born without limbs to achieve a remunerative career, not to mention a quirky celebrity, by appearing in Ripley's and Barnum's sideshows as the "Armless and Legless Wonder," died of bladder cancer on Dec. 24 at her home in Costa Mesa, Calif. She was 77.

"At least they didn't call me brainless," she said with the wit that—when combined with demonstrations of skills including writing, typing and sewing—carried her sideshow performances beyond peculiarity to a lesson in adaptation and determination.

When asked in a CBS television interview in 1998 whether she thought it was all right to be stared at, she snapped back, "If you're paid for it, yeah. . . ."

The incoherent legal cases of Acanfora and the women pilots expose the closet at work, expose what Sedgwick calls "vectors of a disclosure at once compulsory and forbidden" (1990, 70). The closet is an oppressive structure because it controls the flow of information beyond individual desire for disclosure or secrecy and because it is able to convert either disclosure or secrecy into the opposite. Putting oneself in the closet is not as easy as closing the door. Coming out of the closet is not as simple as opening it. Parents and relatives do not want to hear about queer identity. "Don't ask, don't tell" is, of course, the motto of the military (Halley). Wheelchair users understand what it is to be overlooked by a sea of passersby, and people with birthmarks or facial deformities are often strategically ignored as well. The smallest facial deformity invites the furtive glance, stolen when you're not looking, looking away when you look back. Invite the stare you otherwise fear, and you may find yourself invisible, beyond staring. The disclosure of difference, as Patricia Williams explains in *The Alchemy of Race and Rights,* almost always involves a paradoxical conversion between being visible and being invisible. Williams notes that as a black woman she is highly marked and socially invisible at the same time. In fact, it is the heightened visibility of her blackness that produces her social invisibility (213–36). Passing is possible not only because people have sufficient genius to disguise their identity but also because society has a general tendency to repress the complex embodiment of difference. This is what queer theory teaches people with disabilities about the epistemology of the closet.

Nevertheless, the closet may not be entirely adequate to portray the experience of people with disabilities. Sedgwick makes the case that the image of the closet, as resonant as it may be for many modern oppressions, is "indicative for homophobia in a way it cannot be for other oppressions," including "physical handicap" (1990, 75). Oppressions based on race, gender, age, size, and disability, according to Sedgwick, focus on visible stigmas, while homophobia does not.[2] The concept of visible stigma provides no good reason, I will argue, to dissociate disability from the epistemology of the closet because it does not take into account invisible disabilities such as deafness, chronic fatigue, autism, diabetes, and dyslexia. More important, it makes no sense to link oppression to physical and mental characteristics of the body, visible or not, because the cause of oppression usually exists in the social or built environment and not in the body. Every inaccessible building is a closet representing the oppression of people with disabilities by able-bodied society. I do think, however, that Sedgwick is correct to hesitate about the wholesale equivalence of passing with regard to disability and homosexuality—not because people with disabilities are not closeted but because disability passing presents forms of legibility and illegibility that alter the logic of the closet.

Although people with disabilities may try to pass in the classic sense of the term by concealing their disability from discovery, they also engage in a little-discussed practice, structurally akin to passing but not identical to it, in which they disguise one kind of disability with another or display their disability by exaggerating it. This practice clouds the legibility of passing, and it is sufficiently different from traditional passing both to merit a closer look and to invite its own terminology. My strategy here is to reach out to queer theory and its prehistory for models to think about both passing and the politicization of identity in the disability community. Nevertheless, my argument is meant to be "second wave" insofar as it is concerned less with passing in the classic sense than with unconventional uses of disability identity that require a retheorization of passing.

My method is to gather as many narratives about alternative disability passing as possible to make up for the dearth of theory, since narrative is, according to Barbara Christian, where theory takes place.[3] I refer to these altered forms of disability passing as the "masquerade."

## Masquerading Disability

The concept of the masquerade, long a staple of feminist and queer theory, offers an opportunity to rethink passing from the point of view of disability studies because it claims disability as a version of itself rather than simply concealing it from view. Joan Riviere's 1929 essay, "Womanliness as a Masquerade," presents the case study of a gifted academic who flirts compulsively with the men in her audience after each successful intellectual performance, wearing the mask of womanliness to defend herself against both her own feelings of gender anxiety and reprisals by men. "I shall attempt to show," Riviere explains, "that women who wish for masculinity may put on a mask of womanliness to avert anxiety and retribution feared from men" (91). While this mask serves as a form of passing, it differs from the classic forms defined by queer theory and critical race studies. Gay, lesbian, bisexual, and transgendered people who closet themselves or people of color who pretend to be white usually wish to avoid social stigmatization and to gain the safety and advantages offered by dominant social roles. Only rarely do dominant groups try to pass as lesser ones. Adrian Piper, for example, notes that being black is a social condition that "no white person would voluntarily assume" (58).[4] Passing preserves social hierarchies because it assumes that individuals want to rise above their present social station and that the station to which they aspire belongs to a dominant social group. It stamps the dominant social position as simultaneously normative and desirable.

Riviere's "woman," however, puts on a socially stigmatized identity as her disguise. She mimics neither the normative nor the dominant social position. She displays her stigma to protect herself from her own anxiety and reprisals by men, but she does not pass. In fact, Riviere leaves behind very quickly specific reference to the closet. She comes to the famous conclusion that there is no difference between "genuine womanliness" and the "masquerade." "Whether radical or superficial," Riviere writes, "they are the same thing" (94). In other words, straight and gay women alike (and some men) put on the mask of womanliness, despite the fact that it represents a "spoiled identity" or "undesired differentness," to apply Goffman's understanding of social stigma (5). The behavior of Riviere's university woman is intriguing precisely because she exaggerates her "spoiled identity."[5] She outs herself as "woman," making herself into an undesirable stereotype. Riviere is describing both the ideological pressures on women to subject themselves to men by performing weakness, passivity, and erotic receptivity as well as the unequal gender conditions and accompanying feelings of oppression motivating the performance. The masquerade represents an alternative method of managing social stigma through disguise, one relying not on the imitation of a dominant social role but on the assumption of an identity marked as stigmatized, marginal, or inferior.

Joseph Grigely, a conceptual and visual artist, offers a parallel to the gender masquerade described by Riviere in his own desire at times to masquerade his deafness. He reacts to a recent experience at the Metropolitan Museum of Art where a guard struck him on the shoulder and berated him for not responding the first time to a command that he stop sitting on the floor: "I look into a mirror at myself, search for my deafness, yet fail to find it. For some reason we have been conditioned to presume difference to be a visual phenomenon, the body as the locus of race and gender. Perhaps I need a hearing aid, not a flesh-colored one but a red one . . . a signifier that ceremoniously announces itself" (27–28). Grigely compares his desire to announce himself as deaf to the oppressive practice of hanging a sign marked with the word BLIND around the neck of blind people. He feels compelled to out himself as disabled, so that nondisabled people will not be confused, while guaranteeing at the same time that he will be rendered invisible.

On analogy with Adrienne Rich's concept of compulsory heterosexuality, we may interpret Grigely's feelings as a response to "compulsory able-bodiedness," a logic presenting the able body as the norm that casts disability as the exception necessary to confirm that norm.[6] The ideology of ability makes able-bodiedness compulsory, enforcing it as the baseline of almost every perception of human intention, action, and condition and tolerating exceptions only with difficulty. Ability appears unmarked and invisible because it is the norm, while disability, as an affront to ability, feels the full and persistent force of an ideological impulse to erase from view any exception to ability. Whence the desire that people with disabilities sometimes experience to overcome their invisibility and its attendant violence by exhibiting their impairments, and the paradoxical consequence that they become even more invisible and vulnerable as a result. In fact, owing to the ideology of ability, the more visible the disability, the greater the chance that the disabled person will be repressed from public view and forgotten. The masquerade shows that disability exists at the same time that it, as masquerade, does not exist.

Although Riviere sometimes stresses the use of the masquerade as a response to injustice and oppression, she tries at the same time to resist this conclusion in favor of a narrower psychoanalytic explanation. She gives the classic psychoanalytic reading of oedipal rivalry in which unresolved personal conflicts torment the individual with anxiety, while providing a vivid picture of what it must have been like to be a woman competing with men in early-twentieth-century intellectual circles. She is acutely aware of the closed nature of these circles, of the daily parade of potentially hostile doctors and lawyers faced by any woman who dared enter there, because she had direct experience of it in her own life. Moreover, her patient tells her that she bitterly resents "any assumption" that she is "not equal" to the men around her and rejects "the idea of being subject to their judgement or criticism" (93). Riviere, however, does not allow that feelings of inequality and rejection of them should figure as part of her patient's social reality.[7] Womanliness is merely a symptom of internal psychic conflicts originating in early family life.

More important, when Riviere makes the famous leap generalizing the masquerade as a condition of femininity, she must also generalize the situation of the woman in the case study. The woman is one among many women with this problem, potentially one among all women, for she displays "well-known manifestations of the castration complex" (97). The reference to castration is crucial because it introduces a slippage between the categories of woman and disabled person. The castrated body, though imaginary, is read as a disabled body, with the result that all women are figured by psychoanalysis as disabled (see also Freud 14:315). Moreover, Riviere's description of her patient's underlying motives for the masquerade as "sadism," "rivalry," and the desire for "supremacy" (98–99) attributes her behavior to the psychological disability of narcissism rather than to political action or social protest.

"Rivalry" and the desire for "supremacy" are infelicitous formulations for the need to protest against inequality and subjugation. They remind one of phrases often used today to characterize minority groups as "schools of resentment" or bound by "wounded attachments."[8] The problem is especially aggravating in the case of people with disabilities because their calls for justice have so often been dismissed as special pleading by narcissistic, angry, or resentful individuals who claim to be the exception to every rule and care nothing for what is best for the majority. Better to use a political vocabulary, I insist, that attacks assumptions of inequality and rejects the idea that one should be categorically subjected to others because of individual psychology or ability.

## Six Political Fables

Successful political explanations avoid single and simple axioms in favor of respect for the complexity of human behavior. The world of politics will never be other than a messy place, no matter how much we think we know and how much experience we garner about it. If the reasons for disability masquerading are political, they cannot be reduced to simple laws but must be tracked through examples, descriptions, and narratives that establish greater awareness about the everyday existence of people with disabilities as well as attack the history of their misrepresentation. The task is not easy because there are few stories available told from the point of view of the disability community, and the desire to repress disability is powerful in our society. But if Tom Shakespeare is right, it is crucial to explore the range of possibilities defining disability identity. He argues that a qualitative difference exists between disability identities that claim disability and those that do not. Attempts to pass create temporary or compromised identities costly to individual happiness and safety, while positive disability identities, often linked to "coming out," reject oppression and seek to develop new narratives of the self and new political forms (Shakespeare 1996, 100; see also Linton; McRuer 2003).[9]

Greater awareness about disability identity requires both the ability to abstract general rules on the basis of one's experience and to recognize that one's experience differs from that of others. The challenge is to find a rhetorical form that satisfies theoretical, practical, and political requirements. Narratives about disability identity are theoretical because they posit a different experience that clashes with how social existence is usually constructed and recorded. They are practical because they often contain solutions to problems experienced by disabled and nondisabled people alike. They are political because they offer a basis for identity politics, allowing people with different disabilities to tell a story about their common cause. The story of this common cause is also the story of an outsider position that reveals what a given society contains. For example, when a disabled body moves into a social space, the lack of fit exposes the shape of the normative body for which the space was originally designed. Disabled identities make a difference, and in making this difference, they require a story that illuminates the society in which they are found.

Identities are a means of inserting persons into the social world. They are narrative responses to and creations of social reality, aiding cooperation between people, representing significant theories about the construction of the real, and containing useful information about how human beings should make their appearance in the world (Alcoff 2006; Siebers 1992, chaps. 2 and 4). Disability identities would seem to be the exception to this rule: they are perceived as a bad fit, their relation to society is largely negative, and so, it would seem, is their theoretical value. In fact, the reverse may be true. While people with disabilities have little power in the social world, their identities possess great theoretical power because they reflect perspectives capable of illuminating the ideological blueprints used to construct social reality. Disability identities, because of their lack of fit, serve as critical frameworks for identifying and questioning the complicated ideologies on which social injustice and oppression depend.

The problem, of course, is to move from theoretical to political power, to find a way to use critical knowledge about society to effect political transformation. The masquerade, I have been suggesting, claims disability as a way to manage the stigma of social difference, but I will now tell stories about the politics of this strategy. The six narratives that follow are designed to provide a fuller, though still admittedly incomplete, description of the theoretical and political implications of disability masquerade. Each narrative takes the form of a fable, with the political moral appended at the beginning rather than the end of the story. Narratives 1 through 4 explore the benefits of the masquerade for people with disabilities. The fifth and sixth narratives show the disadvantages of this practice.

**1. The masquerade may inflect private and public space, allowing expression of a public view of disability for political ends.** Consider the example of the Capitol protest for the ADA in the spring of 1990. Three dozen wheelchair users, representing ADAPT (American Disabled for Accessible Public Transit, a public transportation advocacy group for disabled people), abandoned their chairs to crawl up the marble steps of the Capitol building (see Shapiro 1993, 131–41). None of the protestors, I suspect, made a regular practice of crawling up the steps of public buildings. When they did, they participated in a masquerade for political ends. The network news cameras could not resist the sight of paraplegics dragging themselves up the Capitol steps. Some activists worried that the coverage pictured the image most people with disabilities want to avoid—that they are pitiable, weak, and childlike—and concluded that assuming this identity was not worth the publicity. Predictably, in fact, the cameras did pick out exhausted, eight-year-old Jennifer Keelan for special attention, twisting the emphasis from the concerns of adults to those of children and suggesting that ADAPT was taking advantage of children for its cause. At the end of the day, however, the major television networks stressed the important message that people with disabilities were demanding their civil rights.

**2. The masquerade may serve as a form of communication, either between people sharing the same disability or as a message to able-bodied people that a disabled person is in their midst.** "Stigma symbols have the character of being continuously available for perception," Goffman explains. "Fleeting offerings of evidence may be made—purposeful slips, as it were—as when a blind person voluntarily commits a clumsy act in the presence of newcomers as a way of informing them about his stigma" (101). Voluntary slips and disclosures always involve self-presentation, and when not an act of private communication between people with disabilities, they may serve a variety of purposes. They may send a sign to authority figures, who have a habit of swooping down violently without first asking questions, that the object of their attention requires a different mode of address. It is this strategy that tempts Joe Grigely when he ponders whether he should wear a red hearing aid to help manage the rudeness of people around him. Megan Jones details the strategy at greater length. Legally blind and hearing-impaired, she now uses a white cane in addition to a guide dog after having been assaulted many times by restaurant owners and other people for bringing her dog into forbidden places.

Most people do not recognize her dog as a guide dog because of its breed, but the addition of the white cane allows her blindness and the use of her dog to register. Of course, such tactics do not always have the desired effect. Voluntary disclosure and exaggerated self-presentation may not be sufficient to render disability visible, since the public is adept at ignoring people with disabilities. Authority figures will attack people for "faking" their disability, and if they are in fact exaggerating it, what stance can they take? The strategy is dangerous because it risks inflaming the anger of a public already irritated with disabled people.

3. **The masquerade may contravene an existing system of oppression.** Reasons for the masquerade can be as simple as preserving energy and as complicated as making a joke or protest at the expense of the nondisabled. "Piqued at continuing to inconvenience myself," Irving Zola reports, "I began to regularly use a wheelchair" for excursions to the airport. "I thought that the only surprise I'd encounter would be the dubious glances of other passengers, when after reaching my destination, I would rise unassisted and walk briskly away" (205). Zola is able to make his way through the airport at the beginning and end of trips, but the overuse of energy may mean that he will not have enough strength later in the day or the next day to meet his obligations. He turns to the wheelchair because traveling requires overcompensation, and people with disabilities are never more disabled than when they are overcompensating. "Just because an individual *can* do something physical," Zola argues, "does not mean that he *should*" (232). The wheelchair allows him to claim disability, refusing both overcompensation and the ideological requirement that everyone be as able-bodied as possible.

---

Dossier No. 12

*The Age*

August 13, 2004

Limbless Woman Sues Air France Over "Torso" Snub

(Reuters) A wheelchair-bound woman with no limbs has sued Air France for discrimination, alleging she was kept off a flight by a gate agent who told her a "torso cannot possibly fly on its own."

Adele Price, 42, a British citizen, sued the airline in Manhattan federal court seeking unspecified damages.

Price, who was born without limbs because her mother took the drug thalidomide during pregnancy, said in the suit she is able to manipulate a wheelchair and has traveled by air many times.

The suit states that she had bought a ticket in 2000 for travel between Manchester, England and New York. After Price had checked her luggage, she alleged that she was stopped by an Air France agent who told her that "a head, one bottom and a torso cannot possibly fly on its own."

Price said in the suit that Air France let her take another flight to New York but only after she was able to get a companion to go with her. However, Price said she had to pay for the companion's airfare and lodging.

She said the airline also made it difficult for her to return from John F. Kennedy Airport to Britain by requiring her to get opinions from four US doctors certifying she was able to fly alone.

A spokeswoman for Air France had no immediate comment.

---

Airports and other public places unfriendly to people with disabilities also present a host of emotional obstacles in addition to physical ones. Zola mentions the "angry glances" of fellow travelers when he climbs staircases "too slowly" or impedes "the rush to seats on a bus" (209). As a person with a disability, he attracts the anger and hatred of people around him. He becomes their "cripple," a disdainful blemish on society and disruptive to the normal way of life. His disability is the cause of his inability to be part of society and its hatred of him. By using the wheelchair, he disrupts the cause-and-effect logic used to humiliate him on a daily basis. He discovers a creative solution, one that adjusts his needs to his environment and bends the psychology of the situation to his advantage. The masquerade, of course, does not necessarily change how people respond to him— he is now a wheelchair user getting in the way—but it does introduce a disruption in the causal logic of humiliation because Zola's identity is masked prophylactically and therefore unavailable to public disdain. He is not who they think he is. He is not where they think he is. He is a target on wheels.

The reverse side of the demand that disabled people overcompensate in public, both to meet the expectations of nondisabled people and to save them from inconvenience, is the masquerade. It meets the demand for overcompensation with undercompensation.[10] Zola's use of the wheelchair improvises on his previous experience with the inaccessibility of public transportation and the reluctance of the general population to acknowledge the problem. His masquerade favors independence and self-preservation.

**4. The masquerade may put expectations and prejudices about disability in the service of disabled people.** Social prejudices about disability are rigid, and often people with disabilities are required to make their bodies conform to these expectations. As Goffman reports, the able-bodied "expect the cripple to be crippled; to be disabled and helpless: to be inferior to themselves, and they will become suspicious and insecure if the cripple falls short of these expectations" (110). Cal Montgomery provides examples of how actual behaviors contradict expectations about disability: "The person who uses a white cane when getting on the bus, but then pulls out a book to read while riding; the person who uses a wheelchair to get into the library stacks but then stands up to reach a book on a high shelf. . . . The person who challenges the particular expectations of disability that other people have is suspect. 'I can't see what's wrong with him,' people say, meaning, 'He's not acting the way I think he should.'" The masquerade may be used to expose false expectations, or it may use expectations to make life easier for the disabled person.

Prostheses play a crucial role in this process because they serve as indexes of disability. Indexical signs, being denotative rather than connotative, point to other meanings, thereby summoning the array of representations signifying any given social practice or object of knowledge. These representations often have an ideological content, existing outside the awareness of society and supporting clichés and stereotypes. Montgomery captures the relation between disability and the indexical property of prostheses with great simplicity and vividness: "When nondisabled people look at 'the disabled,'" she explains, "they see wheelchairs and picture-boards. They see helmets and hearing aids and white canes. With a few exceptions, they don't pick up on how individuals differ from one another; they notice the tools we use. And these tools, to the general public, equal 'disability.' Venture out without a well-known tool, and your disability is 'invisible' or 'hidden.'"

People with disabilities risk becoming their prosthesis, Montgomery worries, and this symbolism is demoralizing. But it also provides a resource for changing the meaning of disability. On the one hand, prosthetics tend to establish a law of substitution, diverting attention away from the disabled organ to its replacement. Kenny Fries reports that his crippled legs attract more attention than those of a friend who uses crutches. "I have noticed," he writes, "that although he walks with crutches his legs do not call the same kind of attention to him as mine do, as if the crutches serve as a satisfying explanation for the different way he walks" (110). People in the street ask Fries what is wrong with him and ignore his companion, suggesting that uninvited stares are diverted to prostheses, absorbed there, and satisfied, while disabled limbs spark endless curiosity and anxiety. On the other hand, the powerful symbolic connection between disability and prosthetics allows those who improvise on the use of their prosthesis to tinker with the social meaning of their disability. Anne Finger recounts her experience with a new kind of motorized wheelchair, as yet unfamiliar to most passersby: "People were forever stopping me on the street and saying, 'What is that?' When I said, 'a wheelchair,' they would invariably smile very broadly, say, 'I'm sorry,' and move backwards" (1990, 26). The instant the new machine is named as a "wheelchair," it assumes its indexical quality as a sign of disability, and people, who moments before approached its user with a sense of curiosity, back away with a sense of dread.

Of course, Finger could have represented her wheelchair in a way resistant to prejudices about disability. In fact, users may work the meaning of their disability by using different applications of their prosthesis. Jaclyn Stuart switches between prosthetic hands, depending on the effect she wants to achieve. She wears a nonfunctional, rubber cosmetic hand to avoid stares of revulsion in some intimate public situations: "I wear it when I go dancing because otherwise [if I wear my hook] the whole dance floor goes crazy!" But she views her hook prosthesis as a symbol of liberation from normalization: "when I see the hook, I say, boy, what a *bad* broad. And that's the look I like best" (quoted in Phillips 855). Wooden crutches rather than forearm crutches may allow their user to "fly under the radar," avoiding prejudices against people with long-term disabilities and assuming "visitor status" among the sick. People who require assistance walking participate at times in a complex semiotics of canes, using different types to mark themselves according to received ideas about age, gender, sex, and character types. The purposeful misapplication of prostheses introduces a temporary confusion in the public mind, allowing users a brief moment of freedom in which to assert their independence and individuality.

5. **Many representations of people with disabilities, however, use narrative structures that masquerade disability to benefit the able-bodied public and to reinforce the ideology of ability.** Human-interest stories display voyeuristically the physical or mental disability of their heroes, making the defect emphatically present, often exaggerating it, and then wiping it away by reporting how it has been overcome, how the heroes are "normal," despite the powerful odds against them. At other times, a story will work so hard to make its protagonist "normal" that it pictures the disabled person as possessing talents and abilities only dreamed about by able-bodied people. In other words, the hero is—simultaneously and incoherently—"cripple" and "supercripple." This image of disability belongs to the masquerade because it serves a larger ideology requiring the exaggeration of disability, although here it is for the benefit of the nondisabled audience, not the disabled heroes themselves, and this fact makes all the difference. Unlike the cases examined so far, this variety of the masquerade advantages able-bodied society more than disabled people because it affirms the ideology of ability. This ideology represses disability by representing the able body as normative in the definition of the human, and because human-interest stories usually require their hero to be human, they are obliged, when the focus is disability, to give an account of their protagonist's metamorphosis from nonhuman to human being.

Two typical human-interest stories about disabled heroes help to flesh out the ideology of ability informing this type of masquerade. The first gives an account of Herbert M. Greenberg, blind since the age of ten, who founded a human resources consulting firm, Caliper Management, that gives advice about the personality of job applicants to many famous companies, including the NBA (Brewer). A mutant strain of tuberculosis took Greenberg's sight in 1940. Public schools turned him away, and other boys beat him up at summer camp. But he was "motivated by adversity" and eventually earned a doctorate in social work from New York University. Nevertheless, most universities were not interested in hiring a blind professor, and after teaching stints in the 1950s and 1960s, while selling insurance on the side, he developed a psychological test that measures character traits like risk-taking, empathy, and resilience. He started Caliper with an associate, and today having administered 1.8 million tests, the firm has a stable of loyal clients.

The first lines of the story connect Greenberg's blindness directly to his ability to assess job applicants fairly: "Blind people can't easily tell if a job candidate is white or black, thin or obese, plain or pretty. So if they should happen to assess an applicant's professional qualifications, they might well focus on a more mundane matter: Is she actually suited for the job?" As the figure of blind justice, Greenberg shows the ability, through his disability, to do what sighted people cannot: he is blind to the prejudices that bias judgment. The figure of the blind judge, however, is merely a trope because it purposefully represses facts about blindness as well as about Greenberg's actual role in the narrative. On the one hand, the story misrepresents blindness as if it blocked all sensory perception. Sight loss, however, exists in different ranges, and blind people can gather a great deal of information about the people around them. Senses other than sight also provide information about the physical, gender, and racial characteristics of people. The story masquerades Greenberg as blinder than he is in order to establish him as the epitome of impartial judgment. On the other hand, Greenberg's other talents, ones able-bodied people do not always possess, make up for his blindness. The story must confirm that he has abilities that compensate for his disability if it is to privilege ability over disability as the ideological baseline of humanness. Despite his blindness, then, Greenberg is supposedly more perceptive than other people. John Gabriel, general manager of the Orlando Magic, introduces this idea when praising the scouting advice of his "blind consultant": "Sometimes analyzing a player involves what you can't see, the intangibles. They may be heart, hustle, drive, determination, leadership. Herb Greenberg can identify those for you." Of course, the fact that Greenberg assesses applicants by psychological test and not personal interview is ignored in order to establish the trope of the totally blind judge who nevertheless has extraordinary powers of perception about the moral and psychological character of other human beings. The story creates a persona for its protagonist that masquerades what disability is.

The second example is a human-interest story recounting the remarkable artistic success, "despite autism," of Jonathan Lerman, a fourteen-year-old charcoal artist, "retarded with an I. Q. of 53," who began to draw at age ten "in the way of savants" (R. Blumenthal). His specialty is portraits, although "most autistic artists don't show faces." Moreover, one authority has compared the work favorably to portraits by George Grosz and Francis Bacon, "without the horror and shame." "Raising him was heartbreaking," his mother reports, because of his uncontrollable and baffling behavior. At the lakeside he stepped on the bodies of sunbathers, as if they were part of the beach; he took food from other people's plates at restaurants without asking; and he refused to eat pizza with oregano and cheese bubbles. His artistic gifts are equally puzzling, the story continues, since "science is still struggling to understand what two Harvard neurologists have called 'the pathology of superiority,' the linkage of gift and disorder that explains how someone unable to communicate or perform simple tasks can at the same time calculate astronomical sums or produce striking music or art." In short, Lerman's disability and ability, the story asks the reader to believe, are well beyond the range of normal experience.

The general, descriptive phrase, "pathology of superiority," sums up nicely the paradox of human-interest stories about disability. The obligatory shift from disability to superability that characterizes the stories serves to conflate pathology with claims of exceptional talent. Each sentence in the story about Lerman carries the burden of this paradox. Here is, for example, an apparently simple and straightforward portrait of the artist as a young man with a disability: "Flowing from Jonathan's clutched charcoal, five and ten sheets at a sitting, came faces of throbbing immediacy, harrowing and comical." Lerman cannot hold his charcoal but clutches it. His works of art seem to flow not from his talent but from his disability. Words like "clutched" and "throbbing" lend pathology to his behavior, contaminating the more familiar language about artistic inspiration and talent. His ability is rendered dubious as a result, but not less dubious than his disability, because both rely on the masquerade.

Not surprisingly, what distinguishes Lerman's drawings from other works of art is what attracts and disturbs art lovers the most. The portraits, like many examples of Art Brut, are "uncooked by cultural influences." They pass the test of originality because they diverge from cliché, but since their origin is unfathomable, they also seem unnerving. John Thomson, chairman of the art department at Binghamton University, captures succinctly the contradictory impulse that this story attaches to Lerman—an impulse that marks him simultaneously as normal and abnormal. His work "would not be out of place in my classroom," Thomson explains, but it is also "really exceptional, characterized by an amazing lack of stereotypes common to drawings at all age levels." Similarly, the story takes pains to tell its readers that one of Lerman's idols is rock star Kurt Cobain, that his drawings are beginning to include references to sex and MTV, while stressing repeatedly how far removed he is from normal society. The punch line describes the young artist's happiness, despite his supposedly diminished capacity to be happy, with the fact that people love his art, suggesting some kind of breakthrough produced by his artistic abilities: "To what extent Jonathan knows the hit he has made is not clear. 'Jonathan's capacity to understand is not that great,' Mrs. Lerman said. 'I said, "People really love your art," and he was happy.'"

Human-interest stories do not focus as a rule on people with disabilities who fail to show some extraordinary ability. Blind women who run at Olympic pace, talented jazz musicians with Tourette's syndrome, deaf heart surgeons, or famous actors with a stutter are the usual stuff of these narratives. In each case, ability trumps disability, creating a morality tale about one person's journey from disease to cure, from inhumanity to humanity. These accounts fit with the masquerade because they exaggerate the disability of their heroes, suggesting that it is a mask that can be easily removed to uncover the real human being beneath. But they also exaggerate in the process the connection between humanness and ability, giving happy relief and assurance to those who consider themselves healthy.

Imagine if health were really the hallmark of humanity, if it were in fact possible to go through life without ever being sick. The result would be unbelievable and undesirable, and yet it is exactly what many stories about disability ask us to believe and to desire: "What would it be like for [a] person to go through life never being sick?" Anne Finger asks. "A man or woman of steel, a body impervious to disease, never facing those deaths of the old physical self that are a sort of skin-shedding" (1990, 43).

**6. A final variety of the masquerade, related to the type informing human-interest stories about people with disabilities, I call "disability drag." It, too, represses disability and affirms the ideology of ability.** Drag, of course, lines up oddly with passing, but the masquerade does as well, so it may be productive to consider the masquerade in the light of drag. The best cases of disability drag are found in those films in which an able-bodied actor plays disabled. I make reference to drag because the performance of the able-bodied actor is usually as bombastic as a drag performance. Esther Newton argues that drag queens represent the "stigma of the gay world" because they make the stigma most visible (3). While there are certain people with disabilities who embody the stigma of disability more visibly than others—and the masquerade permits the exaggeration of disability by people with disabilities—the most obvious markings of disability as a "spoiled identity" occur in the performances of able-bodied actors. The modern cinema often puts the stigma of disability on display, except that films exhibit the stigma not to insiders by insiders, as is the usual case with drag, but to a general public that does not realize it is attending a drag performance. In short, when we view an able-bodied actor playing disabled, we have the same experience of exaggeration and performance as when we view a man playing a woman.[11] Audiences, however, rarely recognize the symmetry. Dustin Hoffman does not pass as a woman in *Tootsie* (1982). Nor does he pass as disabled in *Rain Man* (1988). Audiences nevertheless have entirely different reactions to the two performances—they know the first performance is a fake but accept the second one as Oscar worthy—and yet Hoffman's performance in *Rain Man* is as much a drag performance as his work in *Tootsie*. In fact, the narrative structures of the two films are the same. In *Rain Man*, Hoffman's character Raymond may be an autistic savant, but it is his brother Charlie who cannot relate to other people. Among Raymond's many gifts is his ability to pull Charlie out of his "autism" and teach him how to love and trust other people. Similarly, Hoffman's character in *Tootsie* puts himself in touch with his feminine side by doing drag, but his real accomplishment is to teach the women of America to stand up for themselves and to embrace their femininity as ability, not disability.

*I Am Sam* (2002) provides another more recent use of disability drag. Some critics have praised the film as an accurate representation of "mental retardation." It has actors with disabilities in supporting roles, including one with Down syndrome. Sean Penn, however, plays Sam, a man with the intelligence of a seven-year-old trying to retain custody of his seven-year-old, able-bodied daughter, Lucy. Regardless of the power of his Oscar-nominated performance, it is difficult to agree that the film portrays disability accurately because accuracy does not lie only in the performance of actors but in the overall narrative structure and plot of films, and here the film fails miserably. Its use of music as a commentary on disability stigmatizes Sam, and the film creates scene after scene designed to set him apart as a freak. The final scene is paradigmatic of how the film treats him. It is a happy and triumphant scene staged at a soccer game at which the community is celebrating the fact that Sam has finally won custody of Lucy. Incomprehensibly, Sam appears as the referee of the soccer match. This plot twist places him in the action of the game but magnifies his disability by contrasting it with the duties usually performed by a referee. Instead of officiating the game and striving to be neutral in his calls, he cheers on Lucy, pursuing her all over the field, and when she scores a goal, he lifts her into his arms and runs in giddy circles, while an excited troop of children chase him and the adults whoop and cheer on the sidelines.

The advantage of disability drag is that it prompts audiences to embrace disability. Its disadvantage is that disability appears as a facade overlaying able-bodiedness. The use of able-bodied actors, whose bombastic performances represent their able-bodiedness as much as their pretense of disability, not only keeps disability out of public view but transforms its reality and its fundamental characteristics.[12] It renders disability invisible because able-bodied people substitute for people with disabilities, similar to white performers who put on blackface at minstrel shows or to straight actors who play "fag" to bad comic effect. As a result, the audience perceives the disabled body as a sign of the acting abilities of the performer—the more disabled the character, the greater the ability of the actor. Disability drag also transforms disability by insinuating ability into its reality and representation. When actors play disabled in one film and able-bodied in the next, the evolution of the roles presents them as cured of a previous disease or condition. The audience also knows that an actor will return to an able-bodied state as soon as the film ends.[13] Disability drag is a variety of the masquerade, then, providing an exaggerated exhibition of people with disabilities but questioning both the existence and permanence of disability. It acts as a lure for the fantasies and fears of able-bodied audiences and reassures them that the threat of disability is not real, that everything was only pretend—unlike the masquerade used by people with disabilities, where the mask, once removed, reveals the reality and depth of disability existing beneath it.

## Conclusion

Disability activists are fond of pointing out that there are a thousand ways to be disabled but that able-bodied people are all alike. This is true only metaphorically, of course, since variation thrives in every facet of human existence, but it is worth emphasizing because the ideology of ability makes a powerful call on everyone in society to embrace uniformity. The desire to pass is a symptom of this call. The hope of those who try to pass is that no one will have anything different to say about them. Passing compels one to blend in, to be the same, to be normal. Barry Adam asserts that passing supports the "general inequality" of society with the promise of opportunity but benefits very few people in the final analysis. Those who pass improve their own life, he argues, but they fail to change the existing system of social privilege and economic distribution. They may win greater acceptance and wealth but only by pretending to be someone they are not and supporting the continued oppression of the group to which they do belong.

A more complex consideration of passing, however, focuses on the psychological and physical price paid by those who pass as well as on the knowledge they have acquired about the organization of human society. On the one hand, to free themselves from curiosity, prejudice, economic disadvantage, and violence, disabled people develop sophisticated tactics designed to help them blend into society, but these tactics may also exact a heavy toll on individuals both mentally and physically, leading to psychological crises and secondary health problems. On the other hand, passing represents a vivid understanding of everyday life and its conventions. Those who pass treat social situations that others consider natural and normal as calculated, artificial, and subject to manipulation, thereby demonstrating their knowledge about social organization and human perception. Disability passing involves playing roles, but its essential character is less a matter of deception than of an intimate knowledge of human ability and its everyday definition. Those who pass understand better than others the relation between disability and ability in any given situation. As careful strategists of social interaction, they know what sightedness looks like, though they may be blind; they know what conversation sounds like, though they may be deaf. Passers are skillful interpreters of human society. They recognize that in most societies there exists no common experience or understanding of disability on which to base their identity. For where a common acceptance of disability exists, passing is unnecessary.

Temporary passing is empowering, producing brief moments of freedom from the prejudice and morbid curiosity often found to surround disability. Pretending to be able-bodied is one way of performing normalcy, of inserting oneself in society and escaping the alienating experience of being disabled. In the long term, however, disabled people who try to pass may feel guilty or become depressed about constructing their acceptance by society on the basis of pretense. They also internalize prejudices against disability, seeing their hidden identity as wrong, lacking, or shameful. For both the physically and mentally disabled, passing often requires overcompensation that exacerbates already existing conditions. A woman with chronic fatigue or post-polio syndrome may extend herself to the limits of endurance to maintain the appearance of able-bodiedness, but the result will be a worsening of her condition, sometimes permanently. The college student with a learning disability may discover that passing adds levels of unbearable stress to an already difficult classroom situation. Moreover, those who pass often find that keeping their secret requires solitude. Passing is a solo experience for most people. The feelings of relief that accompany coming out as disabled often derive from the discovery that one is no longer alone and that other disabled people exist on whom one may depend for acceptance, friendship, and love.

The masquerade counteracts passing, claiming disability rather than concealing it. Exaggerating or performing difference, when that difference is a stigma, marks one as a target, but it also exposes and resists the prejudices of society. The masquerade fulfills the desire to tell a story steeped in disability, often the very story that society does not want to hear, by refusing to obey the ideology of ability. It may stress undercompensation when overcompensation is required, or present a coming out of disability when invisibility is mandatory. As a consequence, the masquerade produces what Adam calls "overvisibility," a term of disparagement aimed at minority groups who appear to be "too much" for society to bear, but a phenomenon that nevertheless carries potential for political action (49). Women who make demands on men are "too pushy." African Americans are "too boisterous" and "too noisy" around white people. Gay men are "too flashy" and "too effeminate" for straight taste. People with disabilities should stay out of sight because able-bodied society finds them "too ugly." Overstated differences and feigned disabilities serve as small conspiracies against oppression and inequality. They subvert existing social conventions, and they contribute to the solidarity of marginal groups by seizing control of stereotypes and resisting the pressure to embrace norms of behavior and appearance.

Passing exists in two perspectives, the point of view of the disabled and the nondisabled. The first tells a story to the second, but each side expresses a desire, the desire to see disability as other than it is. The question is whether it is the same desire on both sides, whether there are resources for interfering with the desire to pass, whether other stories exist. The masquerade presents us with the opportunity to explore alternative narratives, to ask what happens when disability is claimed as some version of itself rather than simply concealed from view.

## Chapter Six
# Disability Experience on Trial

On May 17, 2004, the fiftieth anniversary of *Brown v. Board of Education*, the U.S. Supreme Court delivered in *Tennessee v. Lane* another ruling with far-reaching implications for civil rights. The Court ruled unexpectedly and by a narrow margin that states not making courtrooms and legal services physically accessible to people with disabilities could be sued for damages under Title II of the ADA. George Lane, the plaintiff and a wheelchair user, told how he was summoned to the Polk County Tennessee Courthouse on a minor traffic charge and had to crawl up two flights of stairs to the courtroom, as the judge and other court employees stood at the top of the stairs and laughed at him. "On a pain scale from 1 to 10," he later explained, "it was way past 10" (for details of the case, see Cohen). When his case was not heard in the morning session, Lane was told to return following lunch for the afternoon session. When he refused to crawl up the two flights of stairs a second time, he was arrested for failing to appear and jailed. A second plaintiff, Beverly Jones, who works as a court reporter, joined the suit, claiming that she had to turn down work in twenty-three Tennessee courthouses because they were not accessible to her wheelchair. Once in a courthouse without an accessible bathroom, the judge had to pick her up and place her on the toilet. Another time, a court employee carrying her to the next floor slipped and dropped her on the stairs.

Every indication was that the Supreme Court would find for the state of Tennessee, since the Court has favored states' rights in general and had ruled only three years before that states are immune from employment suits based on disability discrimination, regardless of the evidence in the case.[1] Why did the justices rule against the states in *Tennessee v. Lane*? Did the interest of the Court in the legal process give the case a different slant? Was it the compelling nature of the personal testimony? What did the justices learn from the experience of the disabled plaintiffs that they did not know before?

The focus on experience is not arbitrary to the ruling but required by the ADA itself. Any application of Title II of the ADA necessitates that it be "judged with reference to the historical experience which it reflects" (Syllabus, *Tennessee v. Lane* 2). The justices note at the beginning of the majority decision that "Congress enacted Title II against a backdrop of pervasive unequal treatment of persons with disabilities in the administration of state services and programs, including systematic deprivations of fundamental rights" (Syllabus, *Tennessee v. Lane* 3). More important, they affirm that Title II is "an appropriate response to this history and pattern of unequal treatment" and set out to demonstrate that the pattern of disability discrimination continues to this day (Syllabus, *Tennessee v. Lane* 3). *Tennessee v. Lane* itself takes as one of its primary tasks the documentation of disability experience required for the application of Title II; the ruling catalogs experience after experience of disability discrimination for the purpose of proving that the U.S. legal system excludes people with disabilities.

By attending to the testimony of disabled plaintiffs, however, the justices may be guilty of relying on an evidentiary notion of experience. Using experience as evidence, Joan Scott claims in an essay that now defines the dominant theoretical position on experience in historical and cultural studies, "weakens the critical thrust of histories of difference" by remaining within "the frame of orthodox history," naturalizes the "difference" and "identities" of those whose experience is being documented, and "reproduces rather than contests given ideological systems" (777–78).[2] Even when used to create alternative histories or to correct prevailing misinterpretations, according to Scott, experience becomes, if given the status of evidence, merely another brick in the foundationalist discourse of history; and she attacks feminist and cultural historians for backsliding into foundationalism when they argue for the need to rewrite history on the basis of the experiences of women, people of color, and victims of class discrimination. "It is not individuals who have experience," she concludes, "but subjects who are constituted through experience" (779). Apparently, because it is socially constructed, individual experience may serve neither as origin of explanation nor as authoritative evidence about what is known (780).

The value of experience is on trial for both Scott and the Supreme Court, but they have entirely different ideas about it. It may be worth asking for a moment about the political shape of this difference. The disability community was surprised and pleased when the conservative Court suspended its attack on the ADA in *Tennessee v. Lane* and recognized both the existence of disability discrimination and the judiciary's prior endorsement of it. We witnessed an orthodox Court apparently led out of orthodoxy by the power of disability experience. Scott's attack on the use of experience as evidence also stands against orthodoxy. She does not want to see historians of difference entangled in orthodox epistemologies to establish their emancipatory goals, although it is not clear that her critique of experience is ultimately compatible with these goals.

One of the legacies of poststructuralism is the desire for absolute critique, one in which the ability to turn critique against itself is valued above all others and critique as such is defined as a process of subtraction in which knowledge claims have fewer and fewer foundations on which to base themselves. The argument has always been that the more radical and absolute the critique, the greater its potential for emancipation, but the proof for this argument is less and less apparent. The question arises whether the desire for absolute critique always serves politically progressive goals. Is the banishment of experience, for example, radical or reactionary? I argue here that disability experience has the potential both to augment social critique and to advance emancipatory political goals. More important, it is my hope that the knowledge given by disability experience might renew the incentive to reclaim and to retheorize other experiences of minority identity, despite the argument by Scott and others that they have no critical value.[3]

We are at a curious moment in history. Is this the last moment when we might reduce emancipatory thinking to orthodoxy in the name of critique without being thought to serve orthodoxy?[4] From now on, it might be better to keep in mind the political implications of our arguments and to put them in the service of both critique and emancipation.

## Discrimination by Design

Jean-François Lyotard defines the *différend* as a situation in which victims are denied the means to demonstrate that they have been wronged. The wronged are doubly victimized because they have both suffered injustice and been deprived of the means to argue their case. It is ironic that Scott's critique of experience posits a *différend* that even the Supreme Court justices with their orthodox tendencies cannot accept. They interpret Lane's experience as evidence not about his life in isolation but as evidence establishing a pattern of injustice affecting many people, thereby giving these people the opportunity to demonstrate the wrongs against them and to give voice to their oppression. Perhaps more significant, Justice Souter indicted the U.S. legal system itself in the history of discrimination against people with disabilities, calling the decision in *Tennessee v. Lane* a "welcome step away from the judiciary's prior endorsement of blunt instruments imposing legal handicaps" and inviting the judiciary to critique its previous support of discriminatory behavior (Souter concurring 2).

It is nevertheless important to realize that Scott and the Court share some ideas about what experience is, even though they disagree about its evidentiary value. The justices take seriously, as does Scott, that experience is socially constructed. They trace the basis for Lane's discrimination, as Scott might, to a "history and pattern of unequal treatment" rather than attributing it to a natural cause such as the biological inferiority of disabled people. Unlike Scott, the justices do not believe that experience is threatened by its social construction as a basis for knowledge claims. In fact, they find that the built environment is socially constructed and reasonably conclude that it has been constructed in the wrong way for disabled bodies and minds. Notice that it is not Lane's personal suffering per se that sways the Court. The fact that the judge laughs when Lane crawls up the stairs to his hearing is reprehensible but not evidence for the rightness of his discrimination suit. Rather, it is the fact that Lane's experience is representative of discriminatory behavior writ large. Lane experiences discrimination on the basis of his identity as a disabled person, and this discrimination toward a member of a class is demonstrated most clearly by the blueprint of the Polk County Courthouse itself. The physical inaccessibility of the building is a social fact readable by everyone from the Supreme Court justices and Lane to those who made him an object of ridicule, and when this inaccessibility represents a widespread feature of many other buildings, as it does, then one may rightfully conclude that prejudices against disabled people are at work in the architecture of society itself. The majority decision and the amicus briefs strive to render obvious this blueprint of society's prejudice against people with disabilities, exposing what Justice Stevens calls the "pattern of disability discrimination" (*Tennessee v. Lane* 15). This pattern of discriminatory behavior includes "hearing impaired prisoners who normally express themselves by using sign language . . . shackled at their hearings making such communication impossible," "a blind witness . . . denied access to information at his hearings because he could not see the documents," "a double amputee forced to crawl around the floor of jail," "criminalizing the marriage of persons with mental disabilities," and deaf and blind persons "categorically excluded from jury service" (*American Bar Association as Amicus Curaie* 13 n. 16, 13 n. 11, 13 n. 8, 14 n. 1).

In a country of the blind, the architecture, technology, language use, and social organization would be other than ours. In a country of the mobility impaired, staircases would be nonexistent, and concepts of distance would not imitate our own. In a country of the deaf, technology would leave the hands free for signing, and there would be no need to shout across a noisy room. Disability provides a vivid illustration that experience is socially constructed, but it exposes just as vividly that the identities created by experience also contribute to a representational system whose examination may result in verifiable knowledge claims about our society. When a disabled body enters any construction, social or physical, a deconstruction occurs, a deconstruction that reveals the lines of force, the blueprint, of the social rendering of the building as surely as its physical rendering. Constructions are built with certain social bodies in mind, and when a different body appears, the lack of fit reveals the ideology of ability controlling the space. The presence of a wheelchair at the Polk County Courthouse exposes a set of social facts about the building. We may reduce these facts to an ideology, but this should not prevent us from understanding that what is revealed has an objective social location because we witness the situation of disability identity in a verifiable way. In general, the social construction of identity is displayed whenever forbidden bodies and minds enter spaces. When Rosa Parks sat in the front of the bus, for example, a social construction of African American identity in our society was displayed. "Identities are indexical entities," according to Linda Alcoff, and "real *within* a given location" (2000, 337). Social identities may be constructed, but they are also "real," and because they are real, they are entirely open to political critique and transformation, as *Tennessee v. Lane* demonstrates. The Court's opinion recognizes people with disabilities as a minority identity suffering from unequal treatment under the law and thereby empowers them to gather as a group both to force changes in the inaccessible environment and to increase their participation in public life.

---

## Dossier No. 13
*New York Times Online*
August 25, 2004

A Little Movement Toward More Taxis for Wheelchairs
By Michael Luo

Four years ago, taxi officials raised the possibility of making all the city's yellow cabs accessible to wheelchairs. But the idea never went anywhere, apparently fading into the ranks of other well-intentioned public accommodations that never seem to become reality in New York, like public toilets and direct train service to the airport.

Today, only three of the city's 12,487 yellow cabs are accessible, meaning that someone in a wheelchair has about one chance in 4,162 of hailing an accessible minivan.

In contrast, other major American cities, including Chicago, Boston and San Francisco, have significantly expanded the availability of the vehicles in recent years. In London, every cab has been wheelchair-accessible since 1989.

"New York is grossly behind," said Diane McGrath-McKechnie, a former chairwoman of the city's Taxi and Limousine Commission who has become a proponent of making cabs wheelchair-accessible since leaving office several years ago. "These other cities have been out there far in advance of New York. I think it's outrageous."

There is movement now, however hesitant, on a matter that to some New Yorkers is as basic as being able to get across town without a major ordeal.

"The issue with yellow cabs is spontaneity," said Edith Prentiss, an advocate for the disabled and a Manhattan resident who uses a motorized wheelchair. "I don't need to make a plan like I'm invading Europe, which is really what it often feels like."

The Taxi and Limousine Commission is expected to vote today to modify the rules of its next medallion auction to try to encourage the purchase of medallions specifically designated for wheelchair-accessible cabs, something it tried but failed to do in the last auction. . . .

---

Groups are constituted as minorities in two ways: by patterns of discriminatory treatment of them and by their awareness of these patterns. Minority groups must have, according to Dworkin and Dworkin, "identifiability, differential power, differential and pejorative treatment occasioned by the power differential, and group awareness facilitated by the differential treatment" (viii; see also Albrecht 79). Subjects are both formed by experience and have an awareness of the formative nature of their experience—and when this experience is both negative and different, the subject's identity takes on a minority cast. To refuse to recognize these aspects of identity formation is to fail to understand that experience is always socially constructed and that our most valuable knowledge concerns verification of a social construction's given features. The belief seems to be that oppression will end as soon as minority identities vanish, but without a theory that can verify how social identities are embodied complexly in lived experience, how they become real, it is not clear that we can understand what oppression actually is and how it works.[5]

Here is the primary difference between poststructuralist and realist accounts of minority identity. Poststructuralists discount for the most part the knowledge claims of minority identities because they hold that identities are little more than socially constructed fictions. Philosophical realists recognize both the social construction of identity and that identities constitute theories—sometimes right, sometimes wrong, sometimes indifferent—about the world in which we live. Realism defines objects of knowledge not as natural entities but as social facts that exist in human society as part of a causal network.[6] In other words, realists take the cognitive value of social constructions seriously, viewing them as points of departure for further research into the status of knowledge claims. They understand that social knowledge comprises a dense network of social facts where teasing out one fact summons others for the simple reason that each fact is mediated by others—and not always in predictable ways. Knowledge for realists defines precisely the verifiability of a social construction in meaning as referenced by other meanings. There are few cases that exemplify this epistemology better than the disability experience. It demonstrates both the social construction of experience and the political promise arising from the knowledge that experience is constructed. The experiences of people with disabilities help to clarify the fact that identities may contain legitimate claims to knowledge, and this knowledge, once verified, is a valuable weapon against the oppression of minority people.

## The Sex of Architecture

Poststructuralist theory has difficulty with both suffering and sex.[7] It often eschews suffering as a weakness of identity politics and uses sexual behavior as a prop to enrich its analysis of gender and sexual orientation. Scott's discussion of experience would seem to be a case in point. First, Scott has little patience with the idea that gays and lesbians might constitute themselves as a minority identity facing a history of painful discrimination. Second, sexual practices have no place in her discussion, even though Samuel Delany's *The Motion of Light in Water,* a book manifestly about sexual experience, provides the example at the heart of her argument. Sexual behavior is an important factor in the way that our identities and experiences in the world are constructed, but it is often set aside in favor of activities more easily associated with the public sphere. The bedroom does not seem as paradigmatic as the courtroom when one considers the social construction of experience and the ways in which this construction discriminates against various people. Disability law, for example, has had only minor success ensuring the accessibility of public buildings. *Tennessee v. Lane* is significant precisely because it makes such a crucial and unexpected intervention in the legislation of accessibility for public state buildings. This minor success looks like a major success, however, when considered in the context of private residences, since no law exists to compel individuals to make single-family dwellings accessible to differently abled people.[8] The chance of a law promoting accessibility for intimate sexual behavior is even more remote.

And yet there is such a thing as the sex of architecture, and it affects the sexual practices allowed by various spaces and the artifacts in them. Sex may seem a private activity, but it is wholly public insofar as it is subject to social prejudices and ideologies and takes place in a built environment designed according to public and ideal conceptions of the human body. Significantly, *Tennessee v. Lane* documents a variety of public and legal practices discriminating against the sexual practices and reproductive rights of disabled people. Justice Stevens emphasizes laws barring the marriage of people with disabilities in the majority opinion, and Justice Souter builds on the emphasis when concurring by attacking the involuntary sterilization of people with mental disabilities and citing some of the most egregious examples in the law, including Oliver Wendell Holmes's opinion: "It is better for all the world, if instead of waiting to execute degenerate offspring for crime, or to let them starve for their imbecility, society can prevent those who are manifestly unfit from continuing their kind. . . . Three generations of imbeciles are enough" (Souter concurring 1–2.). In short, the Court does not set aside sex in its consideration of disability discrimination but asserts the relevance of sexual experience as evidence of unequal treatment under the law.

---

Dossier No. 14

*New York Times Online*
January 22, 2004

Stuck in a Walk-Up, Only Steps Away From Life
By David W. Chen

Sometimes it is four or five flights that stand between them and the sunshine. Sometimes it is only 12 stairs—a physical barrier so daunting that it has virtually marooned many aged or ailing New Yorkers in apartments they cannot afford to give up, trapped high above the teeming street life they once enjoyed and took for granted.

Were it not for the stairs, people like Robert Fine, who has multiple sclerosis and uses a wheelchair, would not need to make appointments with friends to carry him down from his second-floor West

Village apartment so that he can enjoy some fresh air. And he would not need to ask strong-looking strangers on the street to carry him back up.

Were it not for the stairs, people like Sebastian Pernice would not have to wait for the world to come to him, in his airy fifth-floor apartment of almost 30 years in the West Village, 67 steps off the ground.

"Sometimes, you feel very trapped," said Mr. Pernice, who has a diagnosis of AIDS. "Everyone tells me that I should get out more, because I'm often depressed. The only thing is—the stairs."

New York City has thousands of people in walk-ups who, though not completely homebound, are still separated from the world by a finite number of vertical steps, bedeviled by what they might consider a conspiracy of fates. They do not fit the classic definition of a shut-in, those so bedridden or immobile that they could not leave any apartment. Many of the marooned would eagerly encounter the outside world if they lived on the ground floor or in an elevator building. . . .

---

The idea that sexuality is socially constructed usually refers to concepts of gender or sexual orientation rather than to sexual practices. Homophobia and sexism tend facilely to confuse identities with sexual practices, and maintaining a separation between identity and sexual practices has been one way to resist these prejudices. Consequently, sexual behavior seems marginal to the argument about social construction, and people with disabilities, of course, are often marginal to the way that experience—sexual or other—is conceived. Nancy Mairs makes this point with great clarity, reorienting at the same time the critical concept of the margin away from its ableist tendencies and insisting on the right of people with disabilities to assert the sexual component of their identities. She complains that modern theory always conceives of marginality in terms of power relations between one group of people and another. "It is never taken to mean," she claims, "that those on the margin occupy a physical space literally outside the field of vision of those in the center" (1996, 59).

The centrality of experience in arguments about social construction preserves the presupposition that individuals have access to the centers of social and public existence. Experience is nearly always described in spatial metaphors, referring either to how experience positions and encloses the subject or to how the subject acts as a receptacle for experiences, storing them in the mind or unconscious. Rarely, if ever, do these spatial metaphors include considerations of access. Similarly, many discussions of gender and sexual orientation assume that people have the opportunity and ability to explore sexual identities and emotions, but this is not the case for many disabled people. Samuel Delany's coming to consciousness about gay political identity, for example, takes place in a labyrinthine, badly lit building with multiple floors. Other notable episodes in his sexual education occur in subway lavatories and truck parks—not the most accessible venues.[9] Mairs stresses the fact that she and other disabled people live elsewhere: "over here, on the edge, out of bounds, beneath your notice" (1996, 59). There are people with disabilities who never enter the spaces that cultural theorists associate with the defining social experiences of modernity, and when they do manage to occupy these spaces, they fall outside the awareness of many people.

Disability activists and theorists are beginning slowly to take up the problem of sexual access. Their focus extends from public venues concerned with sexual and reproductive health, such as hospitals and doctors' offices, to private spaces where sex manuals, products, devices, and assistance are used to create new sexual environments better suited to people with disabilities. In "Sex and the Gimpy Girl," Mairs provides an unforgettable illustration of the reproductive care that women with disabilities are liable to receive:

> I had scheduled a Pap smear at a clinic new to me, on the eighth floor of the hospital at the center of the Arizona Health Sciences Center. In this building, I can't reach higher than "3" on the elevator buttons, so I must make sure someone else gets on with me. When I arrived at the clinic, the doors weren't automated: another wait till some other woman came along. The counter was too high for me to reach the sign-in sheet—so high, in fact, that I couldn't see the receptionist to ask for help. After a thirty-five minute wait, a nurse escorted me into a windowless cubicle with a standard examining table, although I had specified when booking the appointment that I required a model that can be lowered and tilted.
> "I can't use that," I said.
> "You can't?" She sounded skeptical and slightly aggrieved.

"No, my legs are too weak to climb up. That's why I use a wheelchair." (1999, 44)

Mairs goes on to recount a sexual history full of dismissals of her
erotic feelings and contradictory advice about her reproductive health.
Doctors do not want her to have sex or children, and she contrasts her experience with that of nondisabled women for whom doctors muster an
"arsenal of scopes and dyes and hormones and catheters" to increase sexual attractiveness and fertility (1999, 48). As a disabled woman, Mairs has
as much difficulty fitting into the medical conception of woman as she
does into her doctor's examining room. Disabled women supposedly have
no reason to reproduce and no reason to have sex:

> When it comes to sexuality in the disabled, dismissal is apt to turn
> into outright repression. Made uncomfortable, even to the point of
> excruciation, by the thought of maimed bodies (or, for that matter,
> minds) engaged in erotic fantasy or action, many deny the very pos-
> sibility by ascribing to them the "innocence" of the very young. . . .
> Perhaps this disgust and denial stem, as the sociobiologists would
> probably have it, from the fact that such bodies are clearly less than
> ideal vehicles for the propagation of the species. Whatever its origin,
> the repulsion lies buried so deeply in consciousness as to *seem* natural
> rather than constructed. As a result, even someone with the best in-
> tentions in the world may fail to see a disabled woman whole. The
> parents of a congenitally disabled daughter may rear her to believe
> that she will never enter into a sexually intimate relationship like the
> one that they enjoy themselves, withhold information about repro-
> ductive inevitabilities like menstruation, perhaps punish her for the
> sexual acting out that adolescence brings. Those responsible for her
> health may "forget" that she requires reproductive care or provide it
> in a manner so cursory that she is left baffled and ashamed. (1999, 50)

In contrast to the reception of disabled people at the center of the
modern experience is their experience on the margins where some of
them are trying to create a safe space for sexual activity and expression.
Mairs notes playfully in her memoir, *Waist-High in the World,* that she
considered calling the book *Cock-High in the World,* because she is not opposed to giving a nuzzle or two when the opportunity presents itself (1996,

54). A small shift in the ethics of personal assistantship may be moving in the direction of greater sexual access, as some personal attendants accept that part of their job includes helping their disabled employers make love and have sex. Education is paramount to understand what disabled bodies can and cannot do and how to overcome the feelings of disgust associated with the erotic body. Personal attendants, for example, are trained to overcome feelings of disgust when cleaning up excrement, but they are often repulsed by the idea of cleaning up semen or vaginal discharge. Specialized sexual aids may be designed for disabled bodies, explains Cory Silverberg, who retrofits sex toys with tongue toggles for people with limited use of their hands, "You have to look at what a person can do. If they don't have fine motor control, they may be able to press themselves against a vibrator. There are vibrators you can put on the hand, and they can masturbate that way, if they can press their hands against their body. If they can't use their hands at all, they may be able to lie beside a vibrator" (cited by Stoner). Significantly, as in universal design where innovations in architecture and product design for nondisabled society often evolve out of a disability context, some of the newest and most significant inventions in sexual products have been developed by people with disabilities. For example, Goswell Duncan, president of his local chapter of the National Spinal Cord Injury Foundation, invented and first put into production the silicone dildo (Kaufman et al. 271). It is a considerable improvement over other models because it is soft, pliable, easy to clean, and retains body heat.

Despite the fact that disabled people are usually assumed to be asexual, their sexual practices seem on first hearing outlandish or kinky, exposing that limited expectations about the relationship of bodies to other bodies determine the choreography of sexual life and its spaces. For example, the question that everyone wanted answered (and still does) about Chang and Eng, "the original Siamese twins," is how they had sex with their two wives. Did everyone do it together or did the twins take turns with each wife? Chang and Eng had custom chairs installed for their body in the parlor but nothing designed for the bedroom, and the bedroom today remains an inhospitable space for people with different bodies or for those who need help from personal attendants.[10] A recent study guide for a video about sexuality after spinal cord injury illustrates not only the physical obstacles to sexual fulfillment but also the social obstacles confronting the idea of disability sex. Here is a description of one scene: "Lynn is straddling Mark while he is undressing her. He takes off her panties with the use of his mouth and teeth" (Tepper 1997, 198). Lynn and Mark are having sex, so their actions are meant to be erotic, but removing your partner's panties with your teeth means something different when you are paralyzed and have no use of your arms. People who view the film need to be prepared, the study guide explains, about the meaning of the acts they will witness. Illiteracy about the minds and bodies of disabled people drapes their sexual practices in deviance and perversion. My point, however, is not to celebrate the presumption of deviance as a special resource for eroticism. Only a greater illiteracy about disability than what we have currently would assume that the marginality of disabled sexual practices is in itself a viable resource for pleasure.

A familiar idea of recent cultural theory describes excluded people and ideas as representing a constitutive outside—an uncanny space on the margins possessing the power either to determine the character of modern existence or to invert it, thereby serving as a resource for transgressive happiness. Michel Foucault, for instance, refers to these outside places as "heterotopias"—places external to all places, even though they may be possible to locate in reality (1984). Hospitals, prisons, cemeteries, fairgrounds, freak shows, vacation villages, brothels, imperial colonies, and cheap motels define some heterotopic spaces of free-flowing difference and desire. The heterotopia par excellence for Foucault is the ship—a floating piece of space, a place without a place, existing by itself, enclosed in itself, and yet given over to the infinity of the sea and unbounded freedom of movement—vying from port to port in quest of treasure and sexual delight. Heterotopias are spaces of sexual desire by virtue of their difference, marking places where those in power go to express forbidden desires or where the powerless are held and branded as deviant. The conception of these spaces, however, relies on the idea that a freewheeling mobility exists between the center and margin, that the center in fact requires for its very existence the others at the margin, and that in this sense the margin is the true center. People with disabilities living on the margins have a different experience. Their experience demonstrates that society is constructed without their access in mind and with little thought of visiting the places left to them. Theirs are not heteroclite and mobile spaces of transgression, fancy, or revolution but places with real-world qualities where human beings want to experience pleasure, creativity, knowledge, and recognition—basic needs often ignored and unsupported when it comes to the disability experience.[11]

Prejudices against disability are extremely difficult to overcome because they are built into the environment. Even if one could wave a magic wand and improve everyone's attitudes about disability, the built environment would still remain as a survival of discrimination and an impenetrable barrier to the participation of people with disabilities. For those who doubt the existence of disability discrimination, the built environment should stand as living proof of the social exclusion of the disabled, but attitudes sometimes prove to be as rigid to change as concrete walls, wooden staircases, and cobblestone walkways. When George Lane crawled up the stairs of the Polk County Courthouse the first time and refused to crawl up a second time, he sent a message to the highest court in the land—a courtroom that disabled people have not always been able to reach—about the value of disability experience as evidence, and the Court used that evidence to rewrite history, this time in favor of both critique and emancipation.

## Chapter Seven

# A Sexual Culture for Disabled People

Sexuality is not a right which must be earned or a possession that must be purchased, but a state of being accessible to all individuals, even those who sometimes have to fight for that access.
—LUCY GREALY

The emergence in recent decades of people who define their identities based on sexual preferences and practices is transforming the landscape of minority politics. Sexual minorities are fighting for the rights and privileges accorded to majority populations on many legal and political fronts. The fight over gay marriage is only the most public and contentious of current struggles for full and equal rights by a sexual minority. Proponents of minority sexual identity attack the neat division between the private and public spheres, the relevance of the traditional family and its institutions of marriage and child-rearing, and the moral certainty that sexuality is better controlled or repressed than set free. Claims that sexuality is a major part of a person's identity, that sexual liberation is a good in itself, and that sexual expression is a civil right crucial to human happiness have led to new conceptions of civic life linked to sex. Jeffrey Weeks argues that attention to sexual identity gives birth to the "sexual citizen." For him, sexual citizenship remedies "limitations of earlier notions of citizenship" (39), focuses attention on "sexualized identities" (38), and blunts "forces that inhibit" the "free, consensual development" of human relationships "in a democratic polity committed to full and equal citizenship" (38). Kenneth Plummer also represents the new sexual identities as a form of citizenship, defining "intimate citizenship" as "the *control (or not) over*

one's body, feelings, relationships: *access (or not) to* representations, relationships, public spaces, etc; and *socially grounded choices (or not) about*
identities, gender experiences" (14). Finally, Abby Wilkerson notes that oppressed groups tend to share the experience of sexual repression, explaining that sexual agency is central to political agency and that "sexual
democracy should be recognized as a key political struggle" (35).[1]

The emphasis on control over one's body, access to public spaces, and
political agency will sound familiar to disability-rights activists. Disabled
people have long struggled to take control of their bodies from medical
authorities and to gain access to built environments and public institutions apparently designed to exclude them. Like the sexual minorities described by Weeks, Plummer, and Wilkerson, disabled people experience
sexual repression, possess little or no sexual autonomy, and tolerate institutional and legal restrictions on their intimate conduct. Moreover, legal
and institutional forces inhibit their ability to express their sexuality freely
and to develop consensual relationships with sexual partners.

It would be an exaggeration to define the oppression of disabled
people exclusively in the sexual context; not many people with disabilities
consider themselves a sexual minority. Nevertheless, I want to argue that
disabled people do constitute a significant sexual minority and that recognizing their status as sexual citizens will advance the cause of other sexually oppressed groups. "Sexuality is often," Anne Finger explains about
people with disabilities, "the source of our deepest oppression; it is also often the source of our deepest pain. It's easier for us to talk about—and formulate strategies for changing—discrimination in employment, education, and housing than to talk about our exclusion from sexuality and
reproduction" (1992, 9). The facets of my argument are multiple, but most
of them rely on the power of disability as a critical concept to defamiliar-
ize how we think currently about sex. First, thinking about disabled sexuality broadens the definition of sexual behavior. Second, the sexual experiences of disabled people expose with great clarity both the fragile
separation between the private and public spheres, as well as the role
played by this separation in the history of regulating sex. Third, co-think-
ing sex and disability reveals unacknowledged assumptions about the
ability to have sex and how the ideology of ability determines the value of
some sexual practices and ideas over others. Finally, the sexual history of

disabled people makes it possible to theorize patterns of sexual abuse and victimization faced by other sexual minorities.

---

Dossier No. 15

*New York Times Online*

August 30, 2004

School Achievement Reports Often Exclude the Disabled

By Diana Jean Schemo

The first time Tyler Brenneise, a 10-year-old who is autistic and mildly retarded, took the same state achievement tests as California's nondisabled children, his mother, Allison, anxiously awaited the results, along with the state report card on his special education school, the Del Sol Academy, in San Diego. But when the California Department of Education issued its annual report on school performance several months later, Del Sol Academy was nowhere to be found. Ms. Brenneise wrote state officials asking why. "They wrote back," she said, "that the school doesn't exist."

That is because San Diego labels Del Sol a program, not a school, said Karen Bachoffer, spokeswoman for the San Diego schools. And like most other states, California does not provide report cards for programs that educate disabled children.

"He doesn't count," Ms. Brenneise said. "He's left behind."

The problem is not confined to California. Around the country, states and school districts are sidestepping the spirit, and sometimes the letter, of the federal No Child Left Behind Education Act when it comes to recording their successes and failures in teaching disabled youngsters. . . .

---

My argument will hinge on what I call the "sexual culture" of people with disabilities. This phrase is meant to set in motion a process of defamiliarization directed at experiences so intimate and unspoken, so familiar and yet mysterious, that few people will discuss them. These experiences are bundled under what is colloquially called a "sex life"—a term I contrast heuristically to "sexual culture." Sexual culture refers to neither gender assignation nor sexual preference, although obviously they are components of sexual being. Sexual culture references the experience of sex itself—pure, impure, and almost never simple. By sexual culture, I mean to suggest two ideas about how disabled sexuality disrupts the notion of a sex life: first, sexuality assumes a larger role in the quotidian life of people with disabilities than the usual phrase *sex life* indicates; second, the idea of a sex life is ableist, containing a discriminatory preference for ability over disability. Being able-bodied assumes the capacity to partition off sexuality as if it were a sector of private life: that an individual *has* sex or a sex life implies a form of private ownership based on the assumption that sexual activity occupies a particular and limited part of life determined by the measure of ability, control, or assertiveness exercised by that individual. People with disabilities do not always have this kind of sex life. On the one hand, the stigma of disability may interfere with having sex. On the other hand, the sexual activities of disabled people do not necessarily follow normative assumptions about what a sex life is. Neither fact means that people with disabilities do not exist as sexual beings. One of the chief stereotypes oppressing disabled people is the myth that they do not experience sexual feelings or that they do not have or want to have sex—in short, that they do not have a sexual culture.

Two cautions must be remarked before I undertake an extended argument about the sexual culture of disabled people. First, the distinction between sex life and sexual culture does not turn exclusively on the issue of privacy. While it is true that disabled people sometimes lack privacy for sex, their situation is not wholly unique. Gay, lesbian, bisexual, queer, and transgendered people also suffer from a lack of sexual privacy, and economic resources may determine whether people have sex in private or public. Crowded housing situations, for example, are as offensive to the conception of private sexual expression as healthcare facilities. The distinction between sex life and sexual culture relies not on privacy but on access as defined in a disability context: sexual culture increases access for disabled people not only by breaking down the barriers restricting them from sexual locations but also by bringing sexual rights to where they live. Second, the idea of sexual culture strips away what one might call the existential connotations of a sex life. Existentialism posits that identities are constructed by ourselves for ourselves, that all values are subjective, that we are responsible for our choices, and that we are condemned to be free. The notion of sexual culture relies on different presuppositions about identity. I define sexual identities as theory-laden constructions, combing both objective and subjective values, used by individuals to make choices, to test the consequences of their actions, and to explore the possibilities and responsibilities of their sexuality. Sexual culture is designed as a concept to provide a deeper, more sustained idea of how sex and identity interconnect by resisting the partitioning and privatization characteristic of a sex life. It means to liberate sex, allowing it to overflow the boundaries of secured places and to open up greater sexual access for people with disabilities.

## No Walks on the Beach

I am looking for an intelligent, literate woman for companionship and, perhaps, sexual play. I am, as you see, completely
paralyzed, so there will be no walks on the beach.
    —PERSONAL AD

Sex always happens somewhere. We go to certain places to fall in love or to have sex. A sex life, perhaps to our disappointment, tends to occur in the same places—the bedroom, hotels, automobiles, health clubs, baths, and so on. Sex will not happen if we do not have access to such places or if we cannot return to them once we discover that they permit sexual activity. If sex is walking together on the beach, if it is running across a field of flowers to meet in an embrace, what is the nature of sex apart from the ability to walk or to run? If a person's wheelchair gets stuck in the sand or if low vision makes it uncomfortable to dash across a field, does it mean that this person will have little chance of having sex? Clearly, people who do not do these things or go to these places manage to have sex, but that is not exactly the point. The point is to ask how the ideology of ability determines how we think about sex.

    The ideology of ability represents the able body as the baseline of humanness. Absence of ability or lesser ability, according to this ideology, marks a person as less than human. The preference for ability permeates nearly every value in human culture, including the ability to have sex. In fact, sex may be the privileged domain of ability. Sex is the action by which most people believe that ability is reproduced, by which humanity supposedly asserts its future, and ability remains the category by which sexual reproduction as such is evaluated. As a result, sex and human ability are both ideologically and inextricably linked. Mark O'Brien recounts a story about the belief that the inability to have sex robs the disabled person of human status:

> We watched a movie about disability and sexuality. The movie consisted of four or five able-bodied men joking and laughing about how they once lugged their crippled friend up a flight of stairs to a whorehouse. . . . After the movie, a doctor talked about disability and sexuality. . . . I will always remember his closing line: "You may think you'll never have sex again, but remember . . . some people do become people again." (O'Brien and Kendall 2003, 80)

The doctor is speaking loosely about sex and membership in the human community, but he employs a widespread prejudice used against those who have lost human status along with the ability to have sex. What is it about sex that bestows human status? Barbara Waxman Fiduccia argues that disability assumes the characteristic of a sexual perversion because disabled people are thought unable to produce "quality offspring" (168–69). It is reproduction, then, that marks sexuality as a privileged index of human ability. In fact, the ideology of ability underlies the imperative to reproduce at many levels, establishing whether an individual supposedly represents a quality human being. First, sex appeal determines the opportunity to have sex. The greater a person's capacity to attract partners, the more opportunities to have sex. Second, a person must be able physically and mentally to have sex. Third, a person must be able to reproduce, to be either virile or fertile. To fail to be able to reproduce is somehow to fail as a human being. Finally, successful reproduction is thought to pass our essential abilities and qualities to our children. The predominant assumption is that what we are will be visited upon our children. If a person does not measure up to society's ideas about ability, that person's opportunities to have sex will be limited. People with disabilities share with gay men and lesbians the suspicion by majority populations that they cannot, will not, or should not contribute to the future of the human race. They will not reproduce, but if they do, the expectation is that the results will be tainted. Social stigma would have little impact on sexual behavior if it were not for the fact that ability represents the supreme measure of human choices, actions, thoughts, and values.

Dossier No. 16

*New York Times Online*
September 19, 2004

When Gender Isn't a Given
By Mireya Navarro

The moment after labor when a mother hears whether her new child is a boy or a girl, Lisa Greene was told she had a son. She named her baby Ryan and went home. Ms. Greene learned five days after the birth that her baby was really a girl.

Doctors who ran tests diagnosed congenital adrenal hyperplasia, a condition that, put simply, can make baby girls' genitals look male. As the young mother struggled to get over her shock, to give explanations to relatives and put away the blue baby clothes, she also had to make a decision: whether to subject her daughter to surgery to reduce the enlarged clitoris that made her look like a boy, or leave it alone.

Thus Ms. Greene, a 26-year-old cashier in East Providence, R.I., was thrown into a raging debate over a rare but increasingly controversial type of cosmetic surgery.

For decades, parents and pediatricians have sought to offer children whose anatomy does not conform to strictly male or female standards a surgical fix. But the private quest for "normal" is now being challenged in a very public way by some adults who underwent genital surgery and speak of a high physical and emotional toll.

Some of them gave tearful testimony at a hearing last May before the San Francisco Human Rights Commission, which has taken up the surgeries as a human rights issue and is expected to announce recommendations before the end of the year. They spoke of lives burdened by secrecy, shame and medical complications: some said the surgeries robbed them of sexual sensation and likened the procedures to mutilation; others said they were made to feel like freaks when nothing was really wrong with them. . . .

---

The concept of a sex life encapsulates many of the ways in which the ideology of ability distorts current attitudes about sexuality. At the most superficial level, a sex life is described almost always in the context of health. A sex life must be, first and foremost, a healthy sex life, and the more healthy a person is, the better the sex life is supposed to be. Whence the imperative in today's culture to "work on" one's sex life, to "improve" or "better" it, to do special exercises or adopt a particular diet for it, "to spice it up"—all for the purpose of discovering "the ultimate pleasure." These and other catch-phrases attend the commodification of sex as healthy and satisfying, but the connection between a sex life and ability runs deeper than cliché expressions. When disability is linked to sex, it becomes a clinical matter in which each disability betrays a particular limitation of sexual opportunity, growth, or feeling. The literature on sex and disability recites a litany of limitations for each category of impairment. The blind have trouble with sex because it centers supposedly on a visualization of the body as integral whole, and lacking sight, they cannot visualize what a body is (Hamilton 239). The mobility impaired and paralyzed are apparently cut off from sources of information about sex from peers, and their sexual development remains stunted (Shuttleworth 265–66). Because of language delays, deaf people are believed to be emotionally and sexually immature, living without the language tools needed to meet the high standards of communication required for sex (Job 264, 266). Disabled women are said in the desire to be normal to tolerate sexism and objectification (Fine and Asch 29–30). In general, people with disabilities are thought to suffer from distorted body images, considering themselves ugly, and they do not feel at home with typical gender roles.

While many of these problems ring true, they also expose the difficulty of conceiving of sexuality in ways that do not reproduce the ideology of ability. Because a sex life depends on ability, any departure from sexual norms reads as a disability, disease, or defect. Moreover, the equation runs in the other direction as well: disability signifies sexual limitation, regardless of whether the physical and mental features of a given impairment affect the ability to have sex. The fusion between ability and sexuality appears foundational to the nature of humanity, so much so that any attempt to unfuse them is considered a threat to the human race itself. Eugenics and the human genome project design futures for humanity on the basis of the desire to eliminate transmissible traits linked to disability, but the fear of disability also stymies intimate romantic relations, even when reproduction is not an expectation in the relationship. Many people in the disability community are still waiting, as Corbett Joan O'Toole explains, to hear a story where a man or woman who chooses to be lovers with a disabled person is congratulated by family and friends for making a good choice (2000, 217). What sea change in current scientific, medical, political, and romantic attitudes would be necessary to represent disabled sexuality as a positive contribution to the future? To reconceive sexuality apart from ability, it would be necessary to imagine the sexual benefit of a given impairment, to claim and celebrate it as a sexual advantage—a paradoxical but necessary thought.

## Private Parts in Public Places

I was very shy before my accident. Dealing with lots of nurses
doing extremely personal things to you—sometimes in front of
other people—knocks off your shyness.
    —A QUADRIPLEGIC

If people with disabilities are to develop a sexual culture, they will need to access safe spaces where they may develop new erotic theories and modes of being. A major obstacle to this project is the separation between the private and public spheres and the history of this separation in regulating sexuality in general and disabled sexuality in particular. Feminists identify the private/public split as a source of gender and sexual oppression because it often reifies gender differences and disempowers women. First, men have more power than women to draw the lines between private and public life. Second, men often use this power to maintain or to increase their advantage over women, forcing them into dependency, using privacy to conceal sexual violence, and stifling any attempts by them at political protest. Because the state is reluctant to enter the private sphere, women are imprisoned there, made vulnerable to abuse by domestic partners and given the status of second-class citizens. Early feminists thought the solution to patriarchy was to destroy the separation between private and public life—whence the banner cry "The personal is political." More recently, they have argued that the private/public distinction is a double-edged sword: it gives political power to men, but it also maintains spheres of intimacy traditionally valued by women.

Disability studies supports the feminist argument that the private/ public split is responsible for political oppression, while deepening the perception that privacy is abandoned at a terrible cost. The experience of disabled people with the medical model has been key to this perception. At first glance, the doctor's office would seem to provide only one more example of patriarchy at work. No doubt it does. However, the medical establishment maintains the separation between men and women not by matter of difference but degree when compared to the separation between the disabled and nondisabled. The medical model thrives by sustaining an essential difference between nondisabled and disabled people, defining disability not as a flourishing of biological diversity but as an individual defect that medical professionals cure or eradicate in order to restore a person to the superior state of health required by the ideology of ability. For twenty-first-century medicine, then, it matters only a little whether you are a man or a woman when a surgeon reaches into your body and puts a hand on an internal organ. Nor does it matter a great deal whether the doctor is male or female. The organ will be removed if the doctor thinks it should, whether the procedure has been discussed or not. Male and female doctors alike have experimented on me, and I never knew that experimentation was happening until later, sometimes years later. Rare is the doctor who explains procedures, let alone allows patients to question them. There seems to be no protected realm, no private sphere, into which the medical establishment cannot reach.

If an urgent task is to protect privacy, while attacking its use in the oppression of women, minorities, and people with disabilities, there is no better place to begin than with the medicalization of the private sphere. My focus is on questions of sexuality, of course, but it should be noted that issues of power are never far away because the medical prohibition of disabled sexuality demonstrates that the private/public split uses sexuality as an adjunct to power. The medicalization of the private sphere produces, particularly when linked to sex, a set of exclusionary practices unlike any other, transforming the traditional division between private and public life in surprising ways and discarding practices valued and protected in almost all other cases. For this reason, the critique of the medical model in disability studies represents a genuine resource for rethinking the separation between private and public life. Disability studies may also offer explanations about why sexual minorities and their intimate practices threaten many people at this moment in time.

One way to retheorize the private/public split is to look at the impact of medicalization on economic class. Money buys privacy, and many practices, legal and other, follow the money. Clubs using private money need not obey antidiscrimination laws. Customers who pay more win the right to have their own private spaces carved out of the public domain. For example, first-class and business-class passengers on airlines routinely have bathrooms reserved only for their use and into which coach passengers may not go. Property rights based on economic advantage also determine privacy laws. Indeed, laws against trespassing are a primary support to the right to privacy. The spaces that one owns or rents define the places where private things are permitted; if one tries to do private things in public— that is, commonly owned places—police intervention and arrest are more likely to occur. Private dwellings are protected against forced entry and search, unless there is a warrant, while people who live on the street are almost always vulnerable to search and seizure. Public restrooms, rest stops, and community parks have enforced vagrancy and decency laws designed to control economically disadvantaged people and other populations thought marginal. Without the money to buy privacy, there is little protection against public exposure and its invasive extensions. Presumably, then, the economic basis of privacy should be hard to disrupt. If money maintains the separation between private and public life, those with economic means have a strong interest in preserving the hold of money over privacy.

Here the presence of disability exposes the fragility of the traditional separation between private and public because economic factors do not obtain for disabled people in expected ways. Medicalization opens privacy to assault, and while economic privilege may make this assault less intrusive, it does not eliminate it. A private room in a hospital, no matter how expensive, is not like a hotel room, although it is leased for a certain period. No "Do Not Disturb" sign, controlled by a patient, will ever hang on the doorknob. Doctors, nurses, aides, and janitorial staff enter and exit at will. Despite the persistent fantasy that doctors, nurses, and nurse assistants provide sexual services, hospital trysts and erotic sponge baths are not part of their job descriptions. In fact, their professionalization hinges on being able to invade privacy while divorcing that invasion from its sexual associations. It may be acceptable, Dominic Davies explains, for male patients to get an erection when having their penis washed, but "consensual, vigorous washing is seen as forbidden" (183–84). As long as medical staff *act* professionally, they do not consider themselves responsible for sexual side effects, and yet they cross erotic boundaries constantly, with little real regard for the consequences of their actions. Patients in medical institutions are simply not considered able-bodied, and they do not possess the same rights as nondisabled staff. It is as if sick or disabled individuals surrender the right to privacy in exchange for medical care, even though caregivers work for them. "The difference between those of us who need attendants and those who don't," Cheryl Wade claims, "is the difference between those who know privacy and those who don't" (88).

Group homes and long-term care facilities purposefully destroy opportunities for disabled people to find sexual partners or to express their sexuality. Even though inhabitants in group homes pay rent for their rooms, the money buys no functional privacy or right to use personal space (Stoner). The staff usually does not allow renters to be alone in their room with anyone of sexual interest. Renters are subjected to intense surveillance, their activities entered in the day log. In many care facilities, staff will not allow two people to sit together alone in the same room. Some facilities segregate men and women. Add to these restrictions the fact that many people with disabilities are involuntarily confined in institutions, with no hope of escape, and the enormity of their oppression becomes palpable. The intimate lives of disabled men and women, as O'Toole phrases it, are "monitored, documented and discussed by others" (2000, 220). Medical authorities make decisions about access to erotic literature, masturbation, and sexual partners.

The unequal power relations between staff and patients encourage sexual abuse. We are only beginning to gather data on the sexual abuse of people with disabilities, but initial statistics indicate that the incidence of abuse is high (Ward 1349), perhaps two to ten times more than the experience of the nondisabled population (Kaufman et al. 8; Shakespeare 1999, 63). It is puzzling that paralyzed women are especially vulnerable, given that disabled women are not considered sexually attractive by mainstream society, until a closer look is given to the conditions of abuse. A woman unable to leave her bed is a woman always in bed, and conventionally a bed is a sexual site. Paralysis is also pictured easily as sexual passivity or receptiveness—an invitation to sexual predictors, since the erotic imagination thrives on cliché positions and gestures. No wonder paralyzed women who cannot get out of bed worry about imagining themselves as rape victims, even when engaging in consensual sex (Westgren and Levi 311, 314).[2]

Not surprisingly, the depersonalizing effects of medicalization often wound the psyches of disabled people, inducing feelings of worthlessness and sexual shame. O'Brien recounts how nurses made jokes in front of him about his involuntary erections, saying things like "Looks like someone's having a good time" (O'Brien and Kendall 2003, 45). On numerous occasions, therapists engaged in sexual banter and teasing about intimate parts of his body (70–73). Medical staff place patients on bedpans in public, sometimes forgetting about them for long periods of time (O'Brien and Kendall 2003, 23; Johnson 60). Frequently, the abuse is premeditated, representing acts of discipline, payback, or sexual harassment. O'Toole reports that many disabled women experience unacceptable touching by male doctors during medical examinations; they are sometimes publicly stripped and displayed to medical students. These women recount feelings of fear, embarrassment, vulnerability, and shame; they often try to separate themselves from their body, pretending that nothing is happening to them (2000, 218–19). Regrettably, most disabled women and men possess no language to express or discuss these experiences, and little is known about the impact of public stripping and unacceptable touching on their sexual feelings.

Personal choice and autonomy are constitutive features of the private sphere, but once subjected to medicalization, individual preference and self-determination evaporate. When the right to privacy and the medical model come into conflict, a new public sphere, controlled by medical figures and supportive of their authority, appears on the horizon. This medical zone of publicness replaces for people with disabilities everything formerly considered private. It engulfs them in an invasive and discriminatory space where they are viewed exclusively as medical subjects and the most casual stranger feels empowered to touch them, to comment on their disability, and to offer medical advice or charity. The medical model too often makes of the world a hospital where the disabled are obliged to be perpetual patients and the nondisabled have the right to play doctor.

## The Erotics of Disability

Because I am so sensitive to touch, so acutely aware of a breeze on my neck, a ring on my finger, the rib of a sock pressing into

my ankle, when I choose to participate in sexual contact, my un-
usually heightened physicality works for and not against me.
     —AMY WILENSKY

When a people are oppressed, the tendency is to explore the depths of
their oppression rather than cataloging the inventiveness of their resistance. As a sexual minority, people with disabilities face many limitations
on their intimate behavior and erotic feelings. But, aware of their oppression and defiant of its injustice, they have begun to explore an alternative
sexual culture based on the artfulness of disability. The progress has been
slow because the fight for access has usually targeted the public sphere
where sexuality is not included as part of the agenda or the story. For
people with disabilities, "the fight to end discrimination in education, employment and other areas of life," Shakespeare explains, "was all about
making personal troubles into public issues. But the private lives of disabled women and men were not seen as being equally worthy of concern"
(2000, 159–60). Furthermore, the social construction model favored by
critics of the built environment tends to neglect physical aspects of disability related to sexuality (Shakespeare 2000, 162). Consequently, we
know much more about the public dimension of disability than about its
private dimension; we are at the beginning of a period of sexual investiga-
tion for disabled people, where information is scarce and ethnography
and sharing of practices need to be pursued.

     Nevertheless, there are signs that people with disabilities are claiming
a sexual culture based on different conceptions of the erotic body, new
sexual temporalities, and a variety of gender and sexed identities. These
emerging sexual identities have at least two significant characteristics.
First, they represent disability not as a defect that needs to be overcome to
have sex but as a complex embodiment that enhances sexual activities and
pleasure. Second, they give to sexuality a political dimension that
redefines people with disabilities as sexual citizens. It is crucial to understand that sexual citizenship does not translate merely into being able to
express sexuality in public—a charge always levied against sexual minorities—but to the right to break free of the unequal treatment of minority
sexualities and to create new modes of access for sex. In the case of disabled people, sexual citizenship has particular stakes. Some specific
agenda items include access to information about sexuality, freedom of

association in institutions and care facilities, demedicalization of disabled sexuality, addressing sexual needs and desires as part of healthcare, repro- fessionalization of caregivers to recognize, not deny, sexuality, and privacy on demand. The rights of sexual citizenship change the conditions of en- ablement for sexual expression, defying medicalization and redefining privacy according to the sexual needs and desires of dependent and inter- dependent people.

Sexuality represents, according to Steven Seidman, the last aspect of our humanness not recognized as "socially created" and "historically vari- able" (2). While certain aspects of the body are not open to transforma- tion, sexual desire and erotic sensation are remarkably flexible. The sexual responses of animals fire on cue instinctively, with few diversions, but hu- man desire, because it relies not on instinct but on symbols, invents new sexual cues all the time. For example, people with paralysis, who have lost feeling in traditional erogenous zones, have found ways to eroticize other parts of their body. They also develop new ways to please their partners by creating erotic environments adjustable to differently abled bodies. As feminists have made clear, normative sexuality requires a distinctive map- ping of the body into limited erogenous zones (Irigaray). A parallel geog- raphy exists between the places on the body marked for sex and the places where bodies have sex. It is as if the separation between the public and pri- vate spheres dictating where we may or may not have sex also maps the body according to zones where sexual feelings do or do not reside. Al- though it is considered kinky to have sex in out of the way places, it does not usually cross one's mind to summon sexual feelings in places on the body not already demarcated by them. Andrew Vahldieck adds a particu- larly vivid and thoughtful account to the literature on sex after spinal cord injury about the erotics of the disabled body:

> There's a bumper sticker that proclaims, "Quads Make Better Lovers" and perhaps it's true. One positive by-product of adapting to a disability is having to learn to go with the flow of experience, both mentally and physically. After severe spinal injury, one must begin again, and this includes developing alternate sense faculties. My erotic self need not be solely localized at the tip of my cock, where I've lost much sensation; I have learned that other areas of my body can be erotically sensitive and responsive. Sensation is mobile. My passion, desire and heat can be creatively restrained or refocused on

more sensitive areas: ears, lips, neck, shoulders. In doing so, I can transfer sensual feeling into areas where sensation is diminished.

Just as important has been learning to free myself from a preoccupation with my own pleasure. To give myself over to my partner. To slow down, not because I'm disabled and have to, but because I want to. This has proved crucial, paradoxically, to building up my own libidinous momentum. By relaxing into a quiet, tender space while stroking and touching my lover, I can engage vicariously in her enjoyment and stimulation so intensely as to share in her—and expand upon my own—felt pleasure. How curious that pleasing women orally has never been held as a form of manly sexual expression. Speaking as a man labeled "severely disabled," this may truly be considered a high and most subtle erotic art.

Disabled sexuality not only changes the erotics of the body, Vahldieck infers, it also transforms the temporality of lovemaking, leaving behind many expectations and myths found in normative sexuality. For example, in the same way that narrative temporality has a beginning, middle, and end, normative sexuality requires beginning, middle, and end points. This is especially true of penetrative sex. Penetration has a preparatory phase, a period of sustainment, and a climax—all designed to prop up the physiognomy of the penis. One gets it up, gets it in, and keeps it up for as long as possible, until one loses it. Penetrative sex figures as a race against fatigue—a performance with a beginning, middle, and end. It also smacks of the assembly or production line, where part after part is added until the product is finished. The dependence of sex on penetration, incidentally, represents one reason why people tend to partition their sex life from everyday existence. Because the temporal phases of penetrative sex are so indelible, its narrative seems relatively autonomous, and it is easy to think of it as an activity apart from all other facets of life.

Because disabled people sometimes require advanced planning to have sex, their sexual activity tends to be embedded in thinking about the day, not partitioned as a separate event. Among disabled people, the so-called sex act does not always qualify as an action or performance possessing distinct phases such as beginning, middle, and end. Moreover, the myth that sex must be spontaneous to be authentic does not always make sense for people who live with little privacy or whose sexual opportunities depend on making arrangements with personal attendants. Rather, disabled sexuality has an ebb and flow that spreads it out among other activities, and its physiognomy does not necessarily mimic conventional responses of arousal, penetration, or orgasm. "I used to get stuck, needing orgasm, needing penetration, etc.," one woman explains. "Now, my sexuality has matured. . . . For example, one of the greatest highs I get (full-body orgasms? or spiritual-like orgasms?) is from having my neck bit" (Kaufman et al. 126). Some people without bodily sensation report experiencing mental orgasms when engaged in kissing, verbal play, or sexual fantasy. Others remark that sexual pleasure grows more intense with the advent of disability, owing either to physical changes or to a greater awareness of their body: "Since I became paralyzed in both legs I have noticed that I have varying kinds of orgasms, depending upon the situation. For example, when I play with myself and rub my clit a certain way my orgasms are much more intense. Sometimes my leg will go into spasm and my crotch feels tingly" (Kaufman et al. 52).

A crucial consideration for people with disabilities is not to judge their sexuality by comparison to normative sexuality but to think expansively and experimentally about what defines sexual experience for them. Sex may have no noticeable physical signs of arousal or may not conclude with an orgasm. When touching is involved, the places being touched may not be recognizable to other people as erogenous zones, which makes sex in public possible and a lot of fun. Sex may extend beyond the limits of endurance for penetrative sex, resembling slow-dancing instead of the twist. It may seem kinky by comparison to what other people are doing. According to O'Toole, disabled sex often surprises a person's community, no matter how radical. For example, in Boston in the mid-1990s, Connie Panzarino marched in a Gay Pride parade with a placard reading, "Trached Dykes Eat Pussy All Night Without Coming Up for Air." That a woman with little movement below the neck could be the active partner in sex and use her disability to enhance her partner's pleasure stunned and shocked people. "This disabled woman," O'Toole notices, "was using her disability as an advertisement for a sexual partner. She was appealing to partners who like extended oral pleasure. She was turning her apparent severe disability into a distinct sexual advantage" (2000, 220–21). O'Toole also mentions an account given by a lesbian amputee about enhancing the pleasure of her partners: "Can I just say that my two leg stumps make fabulous sex toys. I really think my amputated body is tailor-made for lesbian sex: I can crawl on top of my lover and grind my leg into her cunt in ways that I couldn't if I had 'real' legs. Having my little stumps gives me much more freedom of motion and I can get closer, deeper into her that way. Plus, pushing myself into her and away from her and into her again, moving my hips and legs against/on her body is the closest I have come to slow-dancing in years and I love it" (2000, 215).

Disabled people may advance a different sexual geography both for the body and for the places where bodies express their sexuality. Just as disabled persons may change places on the body not usually associated with sexual feeling into erogenous zones, they reorganize places inhabited by bodies as locations for sexual culture. Citizenship rights tend to be practiced in certain locations—polling places, town centers, courtrooms, and so forth—and these locations are not always accessible to people with disabilities. Sexual citizenship suffers from the same restrictions, but here the goal is not necessarily to make the built environment more accessible, although it is an important goal, but to bring rights to the places where disabled people want to have sex. Privacy on demand, for example, could transform a hospital room into a safe space for sexual activity, avoiding the difficulties described by this disabled person: "Even though I am often by myself, I never know when someone will walk in on me. I may look back and think, 'I've just had half an hour to myself, I could have masturbated,' but the time wasn't guaranteed. It isn't really my time" (Kaufman et al. 114). Unfortunately, we are still at a stage where there are more negative illustrations of how rights of sexual citizenship fail than positive examples of how they might work. Nevertheless, people intent on having sex find fugitive places to commingle: "Accessible toilets are FAB. . . . One can get pushed in there by a lover and everyone thinks, 'Isn't that sad, someone needs to wipe their bum,' and you can shag away in private and then come out and no one has a clue as to what really went on! It's liberating and definitely one of the few perks of being a wheelchair user!" (Kaufman et al. 130–31). Embracing greater sexual diversity is key to the rights of disabled people, and it might have unanticipated benefits for thinking about sex in general. As one woman explains it, "if you are a sexually active disabled person, and comfortable with the sexual side of your life, it is remarkable how dull and unimaginative non-disabled people's sex lives appear" (Shakespeare 2000, 163).

New formations of gender and sexed identity may be the final frontier of sexual citizenship for people with disabilities. Although present currents on the Left and Right wish to abolish identity entirely, especially identities connected with sickness and perceived weakness, gender and sexed identities make sexuality present as a mode of being not easily closeted away or partitioned into isolated temporal and spatial segments. Claiming an identity based on sexual culture thrusts one's minority status into the foreground, politicizes it, and creates the opportunity to clarify sexual needs and desires. It also resists the closeting of gender and sexuality central to Western attitudes about sex. It may be especially valuable for people with disabilities to assert sexed identities, since Western attitudes seem married to the argument that "sex is sick," giving people perceived to be "sick" extra purchase in making counterarguments.

Apart from the urgency of political resistance, it may simply be the case that different identity formations suit people with disabilities better. They often complain that conventional notions of male and female or straight and gay do not apply to them (Shakespeare 2000, 163), and it is fairly obvious that their sexual practices depart from many of the founding myths of normative sexuality. Disabled people do not embody gender in "natural" ways because gender stereotypes do not allow it. "It's like I don't have any maleness," one disabled man complains (Shuttleworth 272). Certain disabilities appear to offer specific gender limitations. Men with cerebral palsy cannot touch or hug their female partners in the ways to which they are accustomed (Shuttleworth 269). Blindness changes sexual flirtation from afar between men. But another person puts a positive spin on flexible gender identity: "Why should men be dominant? Why should sex revolve around penetration? Why should sex only involve two people? Why can't disabled people be assisted to have sex by third parties?" (Shakespeare 2000, 163). O'Toole notes that no lesbian equivalent of the missionary position exists, and that partners are not obliged to have orgasms in the same position at the same time (2000, 213). Disabled sexuality embraces a similar flexibility. The sexed identities of disabled people are of value to all sexually active people, Shakespeare claims, because they allow for a continuum of sexual practices and encourage a greater willingness to embrace diversity, experimentation, and alternative sexual techniques (1999, 58).

## Conclusion

If we are to liberate disabled sexuality and give to disabled people a sexual culture of their own, their status as sexual minority requires the protection of citizenship rights similar to those being claimed by other sexual minorities. The challenge of sexual citizenship for people with disabilities is great because they remain one of the largest unrecognized minority populations, little awareness exists about the manner of their oppression, sex is a taboo subject for everyone in general and for disabled people in particular, and the unquestioned embrace in most societies of ability as an ideology denies participation in the public sphere to those not deemed quality human beings. Integral to sexual citizenship for people with disabilities is the creation of a safe space with different lines of communication about disabled sexuality; they need in effect to invent a new public sphere receptive to political protest, public discussion, erotic association, and the sharing of ideas about intimate practices and taboos, erotic techniques and restrictions, sexual innovation and mythologies.

An illustration of one space of exemplary safety and communication is found in the experience of disabled parents who adopt children with disabilities. It is exemplary both because it seems not to rely on a reproductive politics so difficult to untangle from the ideology of ability and because it establishes communication lines between the generations that do not obey the sexually repressive laws often obtaining between parent and child. How strange are the sanctions by which parents limit in children the very sexual behaviors that gave birth to them, as if parents wish secretly that their children had never been born and will produce no offspring. Better to develop lines of communication between parent and child and sibling and sibling that assist sexual expression and happiness. If one objective of disabled people is to build a new sexual culture, it is crucial for them to pass information from one generation to another about gender and sexed identities. Disabled children, then, are key to the future of disabled sexuality.

Disabled children, unlike nondisabled ones, cannot rely necessarily on peers for information about sex, since peer groups represent more likely sources of discrimination and intolerance. Disabled parents must be proactive about their disabled children's sexual concerns because the prejudices against disabled sexuality are so strong. O'Toole and Doe report that disabled mothers have come together to initiate a new sexual culture that teaches disabled children to love and to care for their bodies. The main strategy is to pass on positive sexual values to children and to teach them how to resist negative stereotypes about disabled sexuality. A consensus statement by 614 women from eighty countries captures the essence of their philosophy: "We want a disability sexual culture focused on our entitlement to pleasure and love, understanding the advantages of possessing bodies and functions different when compared to women's majority culture" (O'Toole and Doe 99). The result is a radical transformation of the parent-child relationship, creating a positive atmosphere for sexual expression, providing useful advice about gender identity and reproductive care, and promoting sexual self-esteem in children.

The project of educating disabled children about sexuality, however, is not without its dangers. Primary is the resistance to viewing the parent-child relationship in a sexual light, even an educational one. One mother, for example, was worried that her daughter was trying but failing to reach her genitals for masturbation; she wanted to "facilitate her daughter's sexual independence" without interfering with her sexual expression (O'Toole and Doe 98). But the mother found no sources of advice on the topic, and other parents cautioned her not to raise the issue with medical professionals, unless she wanted to be accused of sexual abuse. Disabled sexuality has long been closeted, and bringing it to light carries a serious threat, one often matched by the threat of violence. Until a fundamental change occurs, those who would seek to advance a sexual culture for disabled people will remain at risk, whether from outright violence or more subtle forms of aggression.

In the clash of the culture wars, some people have argued for a monoculture where we abandon all identities except nationality, while other people argue for a multiculture where we embrace many identities—racial, ethnic, gendered, national, and sexed. The call for a disability culture in general and a sexual disability culture in particular will arouse, no doubt, the anger of the first group and garner, with luck, the support of the second. But the stakes in the emergence of a sexual culture for disabled people are greater than the dispute between these two political factions. The stakes concern questions about fundamental rights expected by all citizens in a democratic society: freedom of association and intimate companionship, authority over their own body, protection from violence, abuse, and oppression, and the right to pursue a sexual future of their own choosing. Because every citizen will become sooner or later a disabled citizen, the struggle of people with disabilities for sexual rights belongs to everyone.

# Chapter Eight
# Sex, Shame, and Disability Identity

*With Reference to Mark O'Brien*

I began to feel that I was a bad, filthy thing that belonged to
the nurses.
— MARK O'BRIEN, *How I Became a Human Being*


My goal in this chapter is to use the discourse of gay shame as a jumping-
off point to investigate further both the sexual culture of disabled people
and the power that disability exercises as a critical concept for revising
theoretical paradigms. My strategy and pleasure are to pursue this goal
with constant reference to the writings of Mark O'Brien, the Berkeley
poet, now deceased, who spent all but six years of his life in an iron lung
due to polio and whose poetry and journalism represent a vivid testimony
to the fusion between the three key terms of this chapter: sex, shame, and
disability identity.

Eve Kosofsky Sedgwick, of course, argues that shame has ethical lever-
age because it manages the threshold between identity construction and
erasure (2003, 35–65). Shame promotes a kind of queer identity—an identity in which difference may metamorphose into shared dignity with and
ethical sympathy for victimized people. Nevertheless, Sedgwick does not
illustrate the capacity of shame to create a new ethics with examples from
the gay community. Rather, she uses disability to exemplify shame,
whether representing the shared humiliation felt before the "toothless
face" of New York's post–September 11 cityscape or her own identification
with Judith Scott, the fiber artist with Down syndrome portrayed on the
cover of *Touching Feeling*.[1] In fact, Sedgwick's principal technique for il-

lustrating the ethical power of shame is to ask her presumptively nondisabled audience to visualize an "unwashed, half-insane man" who might
wander "into the lecture hall mumbling loudly, his speech increasingly accusatory and disjointed, and publicly urinate in the front of the room,
then wander out again" (37). The example of this man, she explains, calls
the members of her audience into burning awareness of their own "individual skin," while being unable at the same time "to stanch the hemor-
rhage of painful identification with the misbehaving man" (37). The audience members feel alone with their shame, singular in the susceptibility to
being ashamed for a stigma that has now become their own.[2] For Sedgwick, shame is the queer emotion by which we put ourselves in the place
of others. It is ethically useful because it legitimates the question of identity without giving identity the status of an essence. And yet Sedgwick in-
terrogates neither the shame nor the identity of the disabled man.[3]

In contrast, Harriet McBryde Johnson, a disability-rights lawyer and
activist, recounts a story of public urination from the disabled person's
point of view, providing an experience missing from Sedgwick's narrative.
Johnson also explores shame as shared emotion, but what is most notable
about her story is that shame is denied where one would most expect it to
arise. After enjoying lunch with some disabled friends in an institution,
Johnson prepares to return home, but first she wants to go to the bathroom:

> Time to go home, but first I have to use the bathroom. Why did I sip
> that coffee in the conference room? Oh, well. At least this place has
> beds and bedpans and aides who handle them regularly. I ask for
> help.
>
> Aides scurry about to improvise a screen. "I'm sorry there's no
> privacy; we're just not set up for visitors to use bedpans."
>
> What about residents? Is privacy only for visitors . . . ?
>
> I can't ask; I'm begging a favor. In front of my friends, I can't de-
> mand special treatment. If they routinely show their nakedness and
> what falls into their bedpans, then I will, too. Despite my degree and
> job and long hair, I'm still one of them. I'm a crip. A bedpan crip.
> And for a bedpan crip in this place, private urination is not some-
> thing we have a right to expect. (60)[4]

This is one day in the life of Harriet McBryde Johnson, but for the more
than 1.7 million people locked up in what she calls "America's disability

gulag," this day is every day (60). The disability gulag represents control as care and protection and describes forced confinement as voluntary placement.

While I share with Sedgwick an interest in ethics, her use of the "unwashed, half-insane man" compels me to ask a basic political question about shame. Who gets to feel shame? The question may seem strange. Aren't all human beings ashamed of something? Isn't the human condition—social creatures that we are, living under the gaze of others, and subject to their judgments and scrutiny—predicated on the possibility of feeling ashamed? What would it mean to deny the feeling of shame to a class of human beings? Would they become less human as a result? Three categories dear to the critical and cultural theory of the last thirty years will shape my interrogation of shame and the sexual experiences of people with disabilities: agency, the split between the private and public spheres, and the sex/gender system. My emphasis throughout is on how these categories rely on the ideology of ability—the belief that the able body defines the baseline of humanness.

---

Dossier No. 17
*New York Times Online*
March 8, 2006

New York Puts Mental Patients in Homes Illegally, Groups Say
By Richard Pérez-Peña

New York State regularly sends patients from mental hospitals to nursing homes, where it illegally houses hundreds of them without the care they need and often under conditions that approach imprisonment, according to legal groups designated by the state to represent the disabled. . . .

The groups say that they have talked with the Pataki administration for years, seeking to end the practice, but that the problem has worsened. They say more than 1,000 former psychiatric patients could now be in nursing homes in New York and New Jersey. They charge that 500 to 600 are in two New Jersey homes alone, nearly twice as many as in 2002 when the practice first came to light.

The groups charge that the nursing homes do little more than medicate the mentally ill residents and do not adequately provide the services that the state is legally required to offer—treatment by psychiatrists and social workers, and training in everyday skills like shopping and cooking. The mentally ill residents, who have not been declared a threat to themselves or others, are generally not allowed to leave the nursing homes and in many cases are even restricted to their floors most of the day, the groups say. . . .

Under Gov. George E. Pataki, the state has cut the population of its psychiatric hospitals by more than half, to about 4,000, in part to save money. . . . The state, for instance, pays the entire cost of community housing for the mentally ill, but when those people are instead placed in nursing homes, the costs are paid by Medicaid, and thus split among the federal government, the state and local governments. . . .

---

## Agency

There is so much of it to wash,
"It" being me, a former person.
     —MARK O'BRIEN, "The Morning Routine"

Shame confers agency, according to Sedgwick. It floods the self, its heat pervading our physical and mental existence with a burning awareness of our own individual skin. The identity or being into which shame calls us, however, is not necessarily the one we desire. One of Sedgwick's formulations of shameful identity captures the problem succinctly: "one is *something* in experiencing shame" (2003, 37). Shame creates a form of identity in which one risks being some thing rather than some person. Shame is painful and isolating for this reason. Nevertheless, shame is so appealing because being something is better than being nothing. So what about nothingness? Do people to whom we ascribe no agency feel ashamed? Can one feel shame if one has no agency?

Disabled people are not often allowed to have agency, sexual or otherwise. Rather, they are pictured as abject beings, close to nothing, empty husks. To be disabled in the cultural imaginary is to cease to function. Our highways are scattered with "disabled" vehicles—sad, static things of no use or importance. Lack of movement and autonomy equals lack of ability to act and to will. The lone girl in the power chair, failing to part the sea of human beings in a crowded hallway, comes to a halt, displaying infinite patience with the people in front of her, but she has little chance of being recognized as a person, of being addressed as a human being by those around her. "How many people," Nancy Mairs asks, "do you know who would willingly take home a television set that displayed only snow or a loaf of bread that had fallen from a shelf under the wheels of a shopping cart?" (1999, 47). Broken or discarded objects are rejected as belongings, the disabled do not belong, and rare is the human being who finds them appealing. People with disabilities are cast as objects of mourning. The feeling of grief directed at them exposes the idea that they have somehow disappeared—that they have become nothing, that they are dead—even though they may insist that they are not dead yet.

Mark O'Brien caught polio in 1955 at age six. He had the use of one muscle in his right foot, one muscle in his neck, and one in his jaw. He spent the rest of his life in an iron lung—a wind machine, replacing his lungs, drowning out the sound of human breathing with the rush of air propelled by the external contraption of shifting atmospheres. He knew that other people thought of him as nothing—a piece of "dried out bubble gum stuck on the underneath of existence," he called himself (1997, 5). What could he offer to them that would make them think otherwise? A poem, perhaps, one that speaks to the absence of shame in parts of his life, suggesting that this absence has to do with the fact that people with disabilities are not allowed human agency. The poem is called "Questions I Feared the Journalist Would Ask":

> When was your most recent orgasm?
> Were you by yourself?
> What did you fantasize?
> In this fantasy,
> while you were wearing the wig,
> the bra, the makeup,
> did you imagine what kind of person
> was pushing the vibrator up your ass?
> Why do you have this thing for Black men?
> But isn't that racist in itself?
> And why did you leave the curtain open?
>
> But she never asked me these,
> damn her to hell.[5]

The prying questions of journalists, no matter how shameless, reveal a dependence on a culture that targets those people—celebrities and politicians—thought to have the most power, allure, and agency. If O'Brien's speaker is not worth a prying question, it is because he is thought to have no worth. Having nothing to be ashamed of, then, is not a sign of either moral integrity or moral failure. It is a sign of social worthlessness. Any human being will display shame if only his or her social value is sufficient to merit asking a prying question.

The problem of social value is urgent in the case of people with disabilities and their sexual culture. Because they are thought to have no social value, they are not allowed to feel shame or do not feel it, and they are handled in an entirely different way from the nondisabled. A classic example pertains to the masturbation training sometimes used on people with disabilities who have been institutionalized. It has a variety of goals and entails specific exercises designed to teach a person how to attain the bodily sensations of arousal (Kaeser 298).[6] Its uses in the institutional setting are multiple, some for the benefit of better institutional control, some for the benefit of individual patients: (1) to help patients with mental disabilities understand that sexual acts should be private, allowing authorities to eliminate offensive behavior from public spaces; (2) to provide patients with a means of releasing tension and controlling frustration, creating a more passive and manageable population for caregivers; (3) to teach safer methods of masturbation to patients who are injuring themselves in the pursuit of sexual pleasure; and (4) to introduce the pleasures of sexuality as part of typical human existence to people for whom these pleasures are unknown. Because masturbation training is used most prominently on the mentally disabled, the issue of agency is paramount. It is usually not possible to obtain the consent of the patient. It is not always feasible to provide verbal instruction, and a hands-on approach may be the only possible method to teach an individual how to masturbate successfully (Kaeser 302). The potential for sexual abuse is high, and institutions make attempts to curb it by having a committee decide whether a patient requires masturbation training (Kaeser 304; Thompson 256).

Thomas Laqueur argues that masturbation defines the dirty little secret of liberal autonomy and its reliance on privatized subjectivity, and if he is right, masturbation training is not a neutral activity. It provides instruction in political agency in addition to helping the patient achieve sexual agency, declaring victory when the patient manages to achieve orgasm unassisted on a regular basis. For example, among the principal benefits claimed for successful masturbation training are a sense of greater agency in daily life and an understanding of cause-and-effect logic. "The person begins to learn," as Kaeser puts it, "how to regulate his own sexual responses and consequently, may come to understand that he is capable of effectuating changes in his life. It may be possible for him to learn that he can purposely alter the way he feels simply by touching and manipulating his genitals. This should assist him in learning the broader concept that if he creates some action an associated and reciprocal reaction will occur" (302). To fail in masturbation training is to fail to become an autonomous agent, but this failure has everything to do with prejudices against disability because achieving both political and sexual agency relies on the presupposition that the body and mind are nondisabled and will function properly if trained.

## The Private and Public Spheres

These people wear their bodies in downtown crowds
without embarrassment.
    —MARK O'BRIEN, "Sonnet #3"

A recurring motif in the literature on shame touches on the public confession of shameful emotion. Shame is terrifying because it relies on public exposure: the etymology of *shame* derives from a pre-Teutonic word that means to "cover oneself," being a natural expression of shame. But shame is also a sumptuous emotion for this reason. To stand out in public has its own delights. The feeling of shame, then, turns on the movement between the private and public realms, and this fact has a number of implications for people with disabilities. It implies access to the public sphere. It implies the possibility of privacy. The closet is the place of shame in gay culture, but it is not always obvious that "coming out" is about movement from one place to another. This movement is not always metaphorical. It also depends on access and mobility.

    What happens if one is always in the public eye? What if one has no privacy? What if the access between the private and public spheres is obstructed or blocked? What if one is not sufficiently mobile to move between them?

O'Brien's writings attack these questions in a variety of ways, providing examples of how the collapsing of the boundary between the private and public spheres affects the emotion of shame and practices of disabled sexuality. Two accounts by O'Brien are emblematic of the extremes imposed by the split between the private and public spheres and experienced by people with disabilities who want to express sexual feelings. In a remarkably generous and candid essay, "On Seeing a Sex Surrogate," he takes his readers step by step through his first experiences of sexual intercourse with a woman, including having to find an accessible and private venue, overcoming fears of being rejected, gaining the confidence to touch erotically and let himself be touched by another person, and managing the difficult physical positions necessary for sexual intercourse.[7] The paradigmatic moment arrives when O'Brien sees himself—literally in the mirror—for the first time as a sexual person:

> She got into the bed with me and began to stroke my thighs and cock. I climaxed instantly. I loathed myself for coming so soon, in the afterglow of my man-of-the-world fantasies. Undismayed, Cheryl began to stroke me, scratch me, and kiss me slowly. Reminding me of our previous session, she assured me that I could have a second orgasm. She said that she would rub the tip of my cock around her vagina. Then she would put it into her. I couldn't see what was going on down there and I was too excited to sort out the tactile sensations. Suddenly, I had another orgasm.
> "Was I inside of you?" I asked.
> "Just for a second," she said.
> "Did you come, too?"
> She raised herself and lay beside me,
> "No, Mark, I didn't. But we can try some other time if you want."
> "Yes, I want."
> After she got off the mattress, she took a large mirror out of her tote bag. It was about two feet long and framed in wood. Holding it so that I could see myself, Cheryl asked what I thought of the man in the mirror. I said that I was surprised I looked so normal, that I wasn't the horribly twisted and cadaverous figure I had always imagined myself to be. I hadn't seen my genitals since I was six years old. That was when polio struck me, shriveling me below my diaphragm

in such a way that my view of my lower body had been blocked by my chest. Since then, that part of me had seemed unreal. But seeing my genitals made it easier to accept the reality of my manhood.

O'Brien's first voluntary sexual experience with another person is only possible once he finds a way to live independently, and it is in fact delayed until he is thirty-seven because of his confinement at home and in institutions. O'Brien is fortunate to find someone as kind as Cheryl, someone who understands the importance of his being open with himself as much as with her. It would be easy to criticize his story, I suppose, for its acceptance of various stereotypes about masculinity, but O'Brien's sexuality is more complicated than this version suggests, as we will see in a moment, and it misses the point to think that the value of his story lies in critique rather than in the fullness of his description of the barriers, both physical and psychological, placed by institutionalization in the way of the sexual expression of disabled people. That O'Brien escaped confinement is the miracle that made it possible for him to express himself sexually.

O'Brien captures the other extreme—and the more stereotypical version of disabled sexuality—in "Marlene," a poem about sex with a nurse under the all-too-public conditions of the institution. It is difficult to tell whether the poem recounts an episode of sexual abuse or sexual generosity—a riddle made unfathomable, I suggest, by the fact of institutionalization itself:

My balls knew what was coming
when that washrag touched my hardening dick.
Seared by shame and lust,
I restrained myself until she turned me . . . .
The old black janitor stepped through the curtains,
wiped the come off the linoleum, not saying a thing.
Letting me down on my back,
she spanked my crotch,
her face stony with boredom.

My greatest fuck.
First of many, I assumed.
Wrong.
Last one ever.

(1997, 14)

The sponge bath as sexual adventure animates the cultural fantasies associated with the hospital stay. But the speaker in "Marlene" is not in the hospital, and his stay is neither short nor voluntary. O'Brien makes clear the difference between the fantasies associated with what one might call hospital pornography and the sexual imaginary created by institutionalization. If the first is utopian in its preservation of sexual privacy and excitement, the second pictures a dystopian world where privacy does not exist and no one cares—not because lack of privacy increases the excitement of sex but because sex in the institutional context is an effect of and cause for boredom. Sex only makes the floor dirtier, though it is nothing that a wet mop cannot fix.

---

### Dossier No. 18
*New York Times Online*
December 17, 2006

The Ethicist
Awkward Dance
By Randy Cohen

> *Last Christmas, I took my grandchildren to "The Nutcracker," a ballet I love. My enjoyment was severely marred by the appearance of a black snowflake and then, even worse, a black Snow King. The aesthetic incongruity was inconceivable. The entire ballet was spoiled. It is analogous to a one-legged midget playing Tarzan. Does this make me a racist?—Name withheld, Sewell, N.J.*
>
> This does make you a racist—not in the sense of exercising a virulent antipathy toward African-Americans but of being, like most of us, affected by feelings about race. . . .

---

The sexual experiences of people with disabilities, then, cast a different light on the boundary between the private and public spheres. A few more examples of the effect of institutionalization on sexual practices and values. The enlightened institutional position holds that masturbation is "normal" but should take place in private. However, the question arises whether there are opportunities for privacy available to people in institutions, especially people with cognitive disabilities. On homosexuality, the enlightened institutional position takes the form of making sure that homosexual acts are not the only sexual option.[8] A certain amount of experimentation is said to be "normal," but the institutional setting should not determine sexual orientation or behavior. Nevertheless, for people who have spent most of their life in a single-sex institution, discussion of options is irrelevant because the choice of sexual partners is predetermined. In an enlightened institution, an interest in pornographic materials is seen as a typical part of growing up. However, it is illegal to use pornographic materials in a public place like an institution where their appearance may sexually harass staff and other patients (Thompson 257).

The dependence of people with disabilities on personal attendants further complicates the relation between sexual behavior and the public sphere.[9] What are the sexual limits affecting the use of personal attendants? Does my attendant help me dress in sexy lingerie, arrange my partner and me in sexual positions, fetch the vibrator, take us to the bathroom afterward? We have trained professionals willing to spend their life helping people eat, go to the toilet, move from place to place, and bake cookies. Professionals are not trained to help someone masturbate or have sex. Irving Zola suggests how overwhelming is the sexual frustration of some people with disabilities and how little their opportunities for satisfaction. Here he transcribes remarks by a paralyzed man named Johan: "I can't do anything myself. I can't even masturbate. What can I do? How do you ask someone? If you ask it once, how do you ask again? What about them? What will they think of you? What will they say to others? And if they leave, what then? You will have to start all over again with someone else" (150).

Johan's frustration is not any less poignant for being a familiar feature of the sexual existence of some people with disabilities. It reveals that the distinction between the private and public spheres is a function of the able body and that people with disabled bodies are often forced to suppress feelings of shame caused by the erosion of privacy in their everyday life if they want to pursue sexual expression.

## Sex/Gender

Tracy called herself a fag hag
saying she liked pictures of gay men fucking
"Will you be my fag hag?" I asked, desperate.
          —MARK O'BRIEN, "Tracy would've been a pretty girl"

Jacques Lacan's famous parable of gender attribution imagines gender as a train destination. Owing to the necessity of satisfying natural needs away from home, restrooms are provided in public places. Lacan posits this convenience as a way of thinking about the assignment of gender. A train arrives at a station, and a little girl and little boy, sister and brother, look out the train window and see two different signs—"Ladies" and "Gentlemen." Each child believes that the sign names the train's destination, but the sign also reflects a gender destination. "For these children," Lacan concludes, "Ladies and Gentleman will be henceforth two countries towards which each of their souls will strive on divergent wings" (152). Lacan's parable provides a rich conception of the signifying practices of gender, although it does not require too much thought to realize that some behavior may go on behind these two doors that does not match the binary opposition of Ladies and Gentlemen (cf. Edelman).

Had Lacan visualized an accessible restroom at the train station, he would have had to tell a different story. More often than not accessible toilets are unisex. There are no Ladies and Gentlemen among the disabled because the ideology of ability conceives of people with disabilities as ungendered and asexual. Ladies and Gentlemen with disabilities see the sign on the door, but they cannot enter. The practice of using unisex accessible toilets exposes the fact that able-bodiedness overdetermines the assignment of gender. It also reflects the mainstream belief that people with disabilities must relinquish feelings of embarrassment or shame normally associated with being displayed to the so-called opposite sex.[10] In the game of signifying practices, the difference between ability and disability trumps the difference between Ladies and Gentlemen every time.[11]

The example of Lacan suggests that the presence of disability nullifies gender assignment, but it is equally critical to understand that the able body is itself a diacritical marker of sex/gender. The stereotypical idea of castration promoted by psychoanalysis gives the disabled body a unique role in gender differentiation. Psychoanalysis defines castration as the social wound that any one person must overcome to achieve psychological maturation and social integration, but since this social wound summons necessarily the imagination of physical wounding, castration also presents as the problem to which variation in gender identity is the answer. Whether any given variation is the right choice depends on value judgments driven by gender stereotypes, and part of the quandary of gender identity involves navigating with and against these stereotypes. Able-bodiedness usually connotes masculinity. It may be in Terry Galloway's words a "fictive able-bodiedness," but able-bodiedness it remains. Femininity supposedly represents lack, defect, and disability. These gender stereotypes obtain for both gay and straight orientations, but individual embodiments of them may vary from emotions of pride to shame to angry rebellion. That lesbian and straight women are often unashamed of their masculinity, while gay and straight men may be humiliated by their femininity, probably derives from the unequal social mobility and cultural access produced by the equation between femininity and disability.[12]

After living independently for twelve years, O'Brien began to experiment in the early 1990s with the sex/gender system through the practice of cross-dressing.[13] He began to wear lipstick, eyeliner, powder, rouge, eye shadow, a skirt, a blouse, and a wig of long, black hair as often as he dared and could arrange it with his attendants. He wrote about discovering a new sense of happiness and freedom in his dream of becoming a beautiful woman. In the same period, he finished a cycle of poems about womanliness in which he struggled against the stereotypical connections between sex/gender and disability. The poem, "becoming her," for example, appears at first glance to be a straightforward description of cross-dressing, until one looks more closely:

a slow process
dreary, difficult
suffocating me in suspense
black cups embrace my non-existing breasts
black lace presses my imaginary vulva
still, i am not yet her
breathing hard from exhaustion, excitement, fear
still i must wait
i brave the pencil point near my eyes
mascara, powder, rouge
the lipstick is nice
but i'm still not her until
the black ferocious wig
digs her claws thru the bobby pins and
a push here,
a twist there

i feel her becoming me,
i becoming her
the wig is firmly placed and
i smile her magic smile
my red, red lips proclaim
she's here.

(1997, 38)

"becoming her" is the only poem in O'Brien's corpus that suppresses capitalization. At the moment of becoming, the speaker of the poem is less than the typical "I." His body is passive as well, the object of many actions, some of them dangerous and violent. Without any action on his part, pieces of clothing, makeup, and a wig gather to his body and transform him—the result of his metamorphosis being happiness: "i smile her magic smile." If we ignore O'Brien's biography, we imagine an able-bodied man cross-dressing to make himself happy, and the diminished i's and passive constructions appear to compliment the stereotypical idea of woman as the weaker or more disabled gender. The poem gives witness to the transformation of man into woman, but it labels the price of his happiness as loss of able-bodiedness, virility, and power. Women are often objects of male violence and oppression, and once an able-bodied man becomes a woman, he becomes this object, too.

If we include details from O'Brien's life, however, the poem requires another interpretation, one that sets disability in play against sex/gender stereotypes. O'Brien's paralyzed body is the ultimate object because he rarely does anything to it. Other people handle him, move him from place to place, feed and dress him. The experience of dressing as receiving the embrace of clothing is an effect of total body paralysis, not a metaphor in which sleight of hand transforms one gender magically into another. The poem's speaker is out of breath and exhausted because he must be removed from the iron lung to be washed and dressed, and he cannot breathe for long outside of it. Thus, the poem's passive, formal features and descriptions of weakness are not necessarily comments on the cost to a man of becoming a woman; rather, they represent the everyday features of a disabled man's life in the context of gender play. More crucial, the poem does not picture the woman as disabled or weak. The "ferocious black wig," once donned, appears as a headdress of power—a Medusa ef-

fect that reverses the polarity of paralysis. Medusa turns to stone anyone
who looks at her; she is not the one who is paralyzed. The speaker's reward
for submitting to the pain and risk of transformation is not castration but
power and bodily integration.

"Femininity," perhaps the key poem in the cycle of works about womanliness written in the early 1990s, attempts a radical revision of stereotypical ideas about disability and sex/gender. The poem elicits several interpretations whose logic is made difficult, I want to assert, by the
ideology of ability and its effect on gender and sexed identity:

> Naked on the gurney
> in the hospital corridor,
> surrounded by nurses,
> tall, young, proud of their beauty,
> admiring my skinny cripple body.
> "You're so thin,
> you should've been a girl."
> "I wish my eyelashes
> were as long as yours."
> "Such pretty eyes."
> I thought
> or think I thought
> or wish I'd said,
> "But your bodies work,
> Get scissors,
> cut my cock and balls off.
> Make me a girl,
> without anaesthesia,
> make me a girl,
> make me a girl."
>
>                                         (1997, 39)

Part of the challenge of "Femininity" is to unpack the contradictions
that it is compelled to embrace because of the way that sex/gender stereotypes map onto disability. For the same reason, various interpretations of
the poem demonstrate not only contradictions with one another but internal contradictions as well. My strategy of interpretation, although
somewhat artificial, is to offer a series of readings as numerical steps in an

attempt to show where O'Brien's representation of disability collapses gender stereotypes based on the able body. My conclusion here is that research on the sexual culture of people with disabilities requires that more work be done on the sex/gender system.

According to a first reading, the poem represents disability identity as acceptance of lack. The male speaker, already symbolically castrated because disabled, invites real castration where most able-bodied, heterosexual men would balk. For the speaker, castration is the lesser of two evils because it is worse to be a disabled male than a nondisabled female: "But your bodies work, / Get scissors." The poem views femininity, then, as a device to restore the disabled, male body to able-bodiedness, but this device is only possible because of the disabled man's willingness to pay the physical price for the symbolic gain. His acceptance of lack helps him trade the physical disability of quadriplegia for the symbolic disability of womanliness—a net gain. A second reading of the poem understands disability as symbolic of femininity. The nurses hovering around the disabled speaker's body misunderstand disability as femininity, most obviously because they confuse the effects of paralysis with the characteristics of female beauty: "You're so thin, / you should've been a girl." Since the disabled man is already a symbolic woman, it is only a small step to embody the symbolism: "make me a girl, / make me a girl." Gender stereotypes admit of no such thing as disabled masculinity. Apparently, all disabled people are women in the society described by the poem.

There is only one problem with these two readings. A castrated man, no matter how insistent the stereotype, is not a woman, and a third reading of the poem would claim that there is, in point of fact, little room in "Femininity" for women. They are merely bystanders, part of the audience to which the disabled man makes his pitch, and although the pitch makes a mockery of gender stereotypes, its end result is not an embrace of femininity. I note immediately that the absence of femininity is not necessarily the effect of a chauvinistic choice made by O'Brien. The ideology of ability produces the effect. Indeed, it produces the same effect on masculinity because there is, in second point of fact, little room in "Femininity" for men. Men are merely bystanders—or better "Walkers"—part of the audience to which the disabled man is making his pitch. O'Brien describes the pitch to "Walkers," in the poem of this title, as "telling them the lies they need, / like disability's no big deal" and "Licking ass most skillfully" to win "all kinds of goodies . . . / chess sets, books, TVs, / maybe even our very own lives" (1997, 36). If the able body is one of the diacritical markers of gender, once the choice to embrace disability erases the marker, both femininity and masculinity as we know them disappear, and O'Brien stops representing gender as typically understood.

"Femininity," in this third reading, gives a place to neither femininity nor masculinity. Rather, the poem triangulates the able-bodied concepts of woman and man with disability to represent the speaker's identity as either castrated macho or virile female. The only sex/gender category close to these identities appears to be the classical concept of "effeminacy," a "category unto itself," according to David Halperin, who explains that it was for a long time "a symptom of an excess of what we would now call heterosexual as well as homosexual desire" (111). On the one hand, O'Brien exploits the ties of effeminacy to male sexual excess to represent virility, allowing the speaker of the poem to assert his male macho: "Get scissors, / cut my cock and balls off. / Make me a girl, / without anaesthesia." On the other hand, O'Brien uses effeminacy to represent womanliness, supporting the speaker's desire to become an attractive sexual object: "make me a girl, / make me a girl." My first two readings of the poem therefore require revision. First, the poem represents disability identity as acceptance of lack, but only insofar as lack appears as a marker of sexual power. The speaker's command that the nurses castrate him, "without anaesthesia," represents an excess that demands to be read as male sexual desire. Second, the poem understands femininity as symbolic of lack, but only insofar as lack appears specifically as the enactment of sexual attractiveness. The speaker's intention to mimic the nurses' sexual beauty reads as female desire. In both cases, O'Brien uses disability to confuse gender categories with sexual ones for the purpose of rejecting the stereotypical asexuality of disabled people and asserting that they desire to be both sexually active and attractive.

The sex/gender system as conceived by early feminists defined sex as the biological material on which the social construction of gender is based, and although the distinction has driven powerful and important critiques of women's oppression, it has been difficult to maintain in the face of new developments in gender and sexuality studies. Radical feminists claim that the oppression of women will never end until they control their own biologically distinctive capacity for reproduction, while LGBT theorists view

sex as an enormously complex, cultural array of sexual practices and orientations. For example, Judith Butler's *Gender Trouble* argues that a heterosexual matrix has always already gendered sex. The inclusion of disability, I want to suggest, further complicates the sex/gender system by putting
its terms into even greater motion. Disability studies makes clear that both
terms of the sex/gender system rely on the more fundamental opposition
between ability and disability. One of the critical stakes of sex/gender theory is, if we believe Sedgwick's argument in *The Epistemology of the Closet*,
to maintain as its crucial pivot point the simultaneous impossibility of separating sex and gender and the analytic necessity of making the attempt
(1990, 29).[14] I agree with this argument, but the inclusion of disability requires an adjustment. The simultaneous impossibility of separating sex
and gender and the analytic necessity of attempting it constitute not
merely a pivot point in the sex/gender system. Rather, the emergence of
contradiction in this system relies on a variety of pivot points, one of the
most significant being the fact that the reciprocal economy between sex
and gender depends on their reference to the able body.

Disability represents a significant pivot point where the difference between sex and gender becomes problematic. Gender in the presence of the
disabled body does not overlay sex in the typical way because the difference between ability and disability trumps the difference between Ladies
and Gentleman, suppresses the assignment of gender, and denies the presence of sexuality. In the case of the nondisabled body, the sex/gender system usually dictates, for better or worse, that the presence of sexual activity mandates the construction of gender identity; but in the case of the
disabled body, sexual behavior does not necessarily lead to a perception of
gender. For example, the repeated attempts by O'Brien to assert his sexuality fail to make other people imagine him as either man or woman. Instead, he remains only "a bad, filthy thing that belonged to the nurses"
(O'Brien and Kendall 2003, 23), and yet when he begins to experiment
with cross-dressing, he manages to assert his sexuality as well as that of his
disabled speakers.

Disability changes the analytic distinction between sex and gender
because it not only reverses the causal polarity of the system but also
shows that each pole is rooted in the ideology of ability. If an able-bodied
man succumbs to cross-dressing, it indicates that he has a "mental disease" that makes him oversexed. His effeminacy is an offense against gen-

der because it puts in question his masculinity.[15] If a disabled man tries cross-dressing, the result is different. It indicates the presence of sexual desire where none was perceived to exist previously. It is only by appearing oversexed that the disabled man appears to be sexed at all. His effeminacy is not an offense against gender because he has no gender identity to offend. Rather, his effeminacy is an offense against the ideology of ability and its imperative that disabled people have no sexual existence. O'Brien's gender play marks out the presence of sexual desire on the otherwise desexualized landscape of the disabled body by attacking the distinctions between sex, gender, and sexuality and by exposing their mutual dependence on stereotypes of the able body.

## Conclusion

Whooshing all day, all night
In its repetitive dumb mechanical rhythm,
Rudely, it inserts itself in the map of my body. . . .
    —MARK O'BRIEN, "The Man in the Iron Lung"

The ideology of ability shapes not only the existence of human beings and their susceptibility to shame but also whether a person becomes a person at all. It controls the capacity of disabled and nondisabled people to live independently and to act, and whether they have agency, sexual or other, in their own life. It defines the spheres of existence in which they dwell, determining how they have sex and when they pass between the private and public realms. It exerts enormous pressure on the assignment of gender and on whether a body is viewed as having sexual properties. Ablebodiedness represents an ideological horizon beyond which it is difficult to think or to move. Perhaps this is why disability cannot escape its association with shame, why we are tempted to use disability to illustrate the individualizing effects of shame, and why people with disabilities never know when and where they will be permitted to feel ashamed. We all share, it seems, Mark O'Brien's bed in the iron lung, our head poked outside, trying to think beyond the "pulsing cylinder" (1997, 2), our body held inside, stored in "metal hard reluctance" (2), obedient to a narrow map of assumptions about what a body is and can be.

## Chapter Nine

# Disability and the Right to Have Rights

The right to have rights, according to Hannah Arendt's valuable formulation, bases human rights on the right to belong to a political community in which individuals are judged by their actions and opinions.[1] Only this species of political belonging guarantees the recognition of individuals as members of humanity, with the consequence that the deprivation of human rights is manifested above all as the deprivation of the status of being human. Arendt first becomes aware of the need to have a right to have rights in her study of the dark implications of totalitarianism. The rise of totalitarian regimes in the first half of the twentieth century, she argues, made visible the "constitutional inability" of European nation-states to guarantee human rights, revealing the general weakening of the nation-state in the world order (269). Totalitarian governments found it useful to impose their values on neighboring states: for example, when Nazi Germany denationalized its victims, singling them out as pariahs, they were received as pariahs everywhere because their human rights had ceased to exist in the absence of state guarantee. Once driven from their homes, the victims of totalitarian regimes found it impossible to find new ones. The only practical substitute for their lost homeland became the internment camp. Totalitarianism reveals a crisis in human rights caused by "a new global political situation" (297), Arendt explains, but the solution to this crisis is not obvious:

> This new situation, in which "humanity" had in effect assumed the role formerly ascribed to nature or history, would mean in this context that the right to have rights, or the right of every individual to belong to humanity, should be guaranteed by humanity itself. It is by no means certain whether this is possible. (298)

According to Seyla Benhabib, Arendt's hesitation about whether it is possible for humanity to guarantee human rights has two sources. Benhabib suggests first of all that Arendt is insufficiently aware of the effects of globalization: transnational migration and the emergence of multicultural states make it difficult to base human rights on state-guaranteed citizenship. Arendt apparently doubts universal human rights and clings to citizenship rights because she does not understand that globalization has made state-guaranteed citizenship obsolete. Second, Benhabib ascribes Arendt's hesitation about universal human rights to a "certain melancholia." Notice that Benhabib does not define this melancholia as a psychological disability; rather, she calls it "an attitude of philosophical reflection and meditation about the fragility of human bonds and institutions, a new sense for the catastrophes and calamities of history, an appreciation for the profound contingency of those human institutions and practices which make freedom possible" (2000, 14).

The emphasis in Arendtian melancholia on the frailty of human bonds and institutions mirrors the theoretical perspective on human fragility associated with disability as a critical concept, but Benhabib does not make disability a part of human rights discourse. While recognizing the fragility of human bonds and practices in the global political context, she insists on incorporating citizenship claims into a universal rights discourse in which one's human status establishes one as a rights-bearing person. Benhabib sets as her goal the possibility of a transnational political community in which humanitarian interventions by NATO and the international human rights regime will enforce human rights. Nevertheless, Benhabib admits a moment of hesitation where the presence of disability does pose an obstacle to the system of universal rights based on human status. She notices that the institution of civil society in the European context defines citizenship not by a hierarchical decision from above but by whether "individuals show themselves to be worthy of membership in civil society through the exercise of certain *abilities*" (2000, 60; emphasis added). These "abilities" include, among others, minimal knowledge of the language of the host country, civil knowledge of laws and governmental forms, and economic sustainability through either independent wealth or employable talents and skills (2000, 60). Benhabib is careful on a number of occasions to explain that people without these abilities should not be excluded from political membership, but she offers no specific arguments for their inclusion, and the difficult question remains how disabled people might fit into a model of citizenship or human rights based on the ideology of ability.[2] In fact, closer attention to the philosophical melancholia of Arendt suggests that her hesitation about human rights derives from this same difficult question. Once freed from international law and based solely on the idea of humanity, human rights become vulnerable, Arendt complains, to arbitrary conclusions about what is best for humanity and who the best kinds of human beings are. "For it is quite conceivable," she writes, "that one fine day a highly organized and mechanized humanity will conclude quite democratically . . . that for humanity as a whole it would be better to liquidate certain parts thereof" (299). Arendt's melancholia has its source in the worry that human status will be summoned in the future as a principle of exclusion rather than inclusion.

I want to revisit Arendt's melancholia as a positive foundation for the right to have rights—a goal that requires disability to play a universal role as the guarantor of human rights. This guaranty is necessary because all known theories of human rights, whether based on humanity, social contract theory, utilitarianism, or citizenship, exclude individuals from the rights-bearing community if they do not possess the specific abilities required for membership. To acknowledge melancholia as a philosophical intuition about the fragility of human bonds and institutions is equally to acknowledge the fragility of human beings—a fragility long recognized by disability studies scholars—since the vulnerability of human bodies and minds underlies as a first cause that of human institutions. It is also to understand that human-rights discourse will never break free from the ideology of ability until it includes disability as a defining characteristic of human beings. The catastrophes and calamities of history do not destroy human institutions without first striking down human beings. It is the person who is truly fragile: bereft of the sheltering embrace of political community, human beings are reduced to "mere existence," Arendt contends, "all that which is mysteriously given us by birth and which includes the shape of our bodies and the talents of our minds" (301). Moreover, human identity is, as Alasdair MacIntyre explains, primarily "bodily identity," and it is by reference to this identity that "the continuities of our relationships to others" are mostly defined: "Among the various ills that affect us are those that disturb those continuities—loss of or damage to memory, for example, or disfigurement that prevents others from recognizing us—as well as those that disable us in other ways" (8). The fragility of body and mind defines us as human beings, determining the longevity of our institutions, enhancing the quality of our associations, and establishing our place in and responsibilities for the natural environment.

---

Dossier No. 19
*CNN.com*
July 18, 2006

Bodies lie wrapped at Memorial Medical Center in the aftermath of Hurricane Katrina.
"They pretended they were God"
Doctor, 2 nurses allegedly killed patients with lethal drug dose
By Drew Griffin and Kathleen Johnston

NEW ORLEANS, Louisiana (CNN)—In the desperate days after hurricane Katrina struck, a doctor and two nurses at a flooded New Orleans hospital allegedly killed four patients by giving them a lethal drug cocktail, Louisiana's top law enforcement official said Tuesday.

"We're talking about people that pretended that maybe they were God," Attorney General Charles C. Foti Jr. said, announcing second-degree murder charges against Dr. Anna Pou, Lori L. Budo and Cheri Landry.

"This is not euthanasia. It's homicide," Foti said. . . .

---

The problem today with using humanity as the basis for human rights is that it drags behind it outdated notions that define the human according to eighteenth-century ideals of rational cognition, physical health, and technological ability. When political membership relies on the ideology of ability, people with physical talents, the famous, and those considered geniuses have little difficulty maintaining and adjusting their citizenship status, even during times of great crisis.[3] But if a person does not display rational thinking, healthiness, or technical skills, that person risks being seen as less than human and losing the rights bestowed by membership in the human community. In the United States at this moment, disabled people are subject to forced confinement, deprived of the right to sue or to be sued in court, denied money damages against employment discrimination for state jobs, blocked from polling places by inaccessible architecture and obsolete voting rules, and severely limited in their ability to travel from place to place.[4] Moreover, Douglas Baynton demonstrates that one of the greatest obstacles in the modern era to the civil rights agenda of women, people of color, and immigrants has been the stigma of disability. The right to vote was withheld from women because of their supposed lack of higher reasoning. People of color had no chance to acquire civil rights as long as they were considered feeble-minded or diseased. The criminalization of refugees, asylum seekers, and immigrants continues today to rely on representing them as less than human, imagining them as diseased, disabled, or dishonest but primarily as the first two. The presence of disability further feminizes the female other, further racializes the racial other, and further alienates the alien other. In each case, the association of disability with a particular group justifies exclusion from the community of rights-bearing people. Disability, then, is a significant factor in the imagination of the right to have rights, but it serves usually as a negative operator. What difference to human rights would it make if we were to treat fragility, vulnerability, and disability as central to the human condition, if we were to see disability as a positive, critical concept useful to define the shared need among all people for the protection of human rights?

It has often been objected that "human" is not a category that applies across cultures because the distinction between human and nonhuman is historically and culturally variable. This objection must be answered if human rights are to be guaranteed globally on the basis of human status. Moreover, the practice of granting rights to only those people capable of demonstrating a prescribed level of physical and mental ability must be swept away if being human is to serve as a universal standard for political membership. Basing human rights on disability, however, presents a more minimum standard for universality. Bryan Turner has outlined a "minimal, thin theory of human rights" that uses a "minimum criterion" of commonality based on human frailty, seeking to avoid "rich theories of human culture, symbolic communication or reason" (505). He argues that human beings are frail because their "lives are finite," because they "typically exist under conditions of scarcity, disease and danger," and because they are "constrained by physical processes of ageing and decay" (501). Turner understands that some human rights thinkers may protest that the condition of frailty is also historically and culturally variable and that it cannot substitute for human status in the securing of rights. He nevertheless maintains that human life is "finite" and that the majority of the world's population lives under circumstances of scarcity—and despite the existence of institutions and technologies designed to reduce these circumstances, institutions and technologies that now appear as part of the problem, not the solution (501). World events appear to confirm his argument. The danger of an avian flu pandemic exposes the smallness of our planet as well as the fragility of global civil society. Hurricane Katrina has demonstrated the threat of internal statelessness to nations where there is no political will to care for those who have neither the economic nor physical ability to avoid catastrophe. Meanwhile, the emergence of technologies supposedly designed to improve human existence, such as industrial farming, mass manufactured housing, and oil refinement, have produced disabling conditions such as pollution and personal injury even as they seek to provide food and shelter for large numbers of people.[5] Nothing reveals the circuit of global flow and responsibility among nations with greater urgency and clarity than populations displaced and put at risk by natural disasters, famine, industrial pollution, and the spread of disease. Turner insists that rights as a system of mutual protection gain their motive force from the collective recognition of human frailty, offering a crucial adjustment to the call for a universal rights discourse based on human status (507).

---

### Dossier No. 20

*New York Times Online*

April 20, 2006

Learning to Savor a Full Life, Love Life

By Jane Gross

Mary Kate Graham's boyfriend, Gary Ruvolo, is fond of recounting every detail of their first date 13 years ago and each candlelight anniversary dinner since. "God help me," Ms. Graham said, rolling her eyes with affectionate indulgence.

Ms. Graham and Mr. Ruvolo, both 32, accept each other's foibles with tenderness. The one time their romance was in trouble—a girl "was spending too much time at Gary's house, and I didn't like it," Ms. Graham said—they went to couples' counseling and worked it out.

Their next hurdle will be moving from their family homes, both in Brooklyn, to a group residence. There, for the first time, Ms. Graham, who is mentally retarded, and Mr. Ruvolo, who has Down syndrome, will be permitted to spend time together in private.

The pair were coached in dating, romance and physical intimacy by a social service agency at the cutting edge of a new movement to promote healthy sexuality for the seven million Americans with mental retardation and related disabilities.

In what experts say is the latest frontier in disability rights, a small but growing number of psychologists, educators and researchers are promoting social opportunities and teaching the skills to enjoy them. . . .

---

The liberal tradition represents citizens as autonomous, rational beings who enter freely into social contracts by which they agree to be bound in return for rights and protections (Carey). The assumption remains, however, that these contracts are not necessary to human existence. Defined by an essential freedom and independence of existence, citizens are construed as autonomous beings who are fit to walk the earth in solitude if they so desire. The social contract works rather like an insurance policy to protect individuals against uncharacteristic descents into dependency. A focus on disability provides another perspective by representing human society not as a collection of autonomous beings, some of whom will lose their independence, but as a community of dependent frail bodies that rely on others for survival. Notice that dependence does not figure here as an individual character trait, as in the social contract model, but as a structural component of human society. In other words, my point is not that disabled persons are dependent because of their individual properties or traits. It is not a matter of understanding disability as weakness but of construing disability as a critical concept that reveals the structure of dependence inherent to all human societies. As finite beings who live under conditions of scarcity, we depend on other human beings not only at those times when our capacities are diminished but each and every day, and even at those moments when we may be at the height of our physical and mental powers. The human life cycle, even though it may differ from culture to culture due to economic resources, represents a universal experience familiar to all members of the human race and with which they may reach toward common political society.

Establishing the fragility of the mind and body as the foundation of a universal human rights has significant advantages. Of first importance, the principle previously used to exclude people from human status would become the principle used to include them. Accepting human fragility, vulnerability, and disability as the standard of inclusion for rights-bearing status generates a minimum, thin standard, one that would be difficult to use for exclusionary purposes. Second, a standard based on vulnerability is more adaptable, permitting a continuum of experiences elastic enough to include people with physical and mental disabilities, the poor, refugees, children, the elderly, and persecuted ethnicities. Third, by emphasizing embodied frailty, human rights discourse moves away from more abstract determinations of rights based on membership in a nation-state or on the philosophies of various institutions such as NATO, the United Nations, or the International Red Cross. Fourth, it exposes the widespread dependence of people and nations on one another, dispelling the dangerous myth that individuals or nations exist naturally in a state of autonomy and that those individuals or nations that fall into dependence are somehow inferior to others. Finally and most crucial, it locates the activation of human rights at the point of greatest need, requiring the recognition of humanity in those people at the greatest risk of losing their place in the world. Altruistic gestures on the international scene toward people in danger, such as Mexico's offer to receive homeless victims of Hurricane Katrina, would be the rule and not the exception. The HIV/AIDS epidemic would be a human rights problem for the world, not merely a dilemma for South Africa and other affected nations to solve. Communities victimized by racial or ethnic hatred would attract international attention and support. Populations displaced by natural disasters, violence, and disease and those seeking relief from poverty would have the right to immigrate to more secure locations and to be integrated into new communities. It would no longer make sense to maintain pockets of economically deprived populations in order to make use of cheap labor for economic gain in the world market. The exploitive circuit between cheap labor and robust consumerism would be broken—replaced by a flow of immigration based on greater economic opportunities and more secure and safer living conditions.

The major question is why should we help them, why should we include the fragile, vulnerable, and disabled in our communities—that is, aside from the not negligible consideration that we are they? The standard of reciprocity, of course, has stood at the origin of human rights discourse since the social contract model was invented, but the value of disability is worth pursuing in itself for another reason.[6] Ability as an ideology is about examining the potential of a person, making it known, and then granting admission or acceptance on what is known. The presence of this ideology explains why testing, whether for civic knowledge, medical health, or intelligence, is central to standards of political membership in the modern era. Starting from disability reverses the ideological expectation that human potential can be quantified for the simple reason that disability is variable and thus surprising, and surprise helps one to rethink human potential, producing an added bonus for human rights discourse. Michael Bérubé, for example, focuses on the surprising nature of disability in the story of his eleven-year-old son, Jamie, who has Down syndrome. Bérubé soon discovers in the course of life with his son that Jamie routinely exceeds expectations for him, despite the research about Down syndrome available from the medical establishment—about which Bérubé argues that the only expectation that Jamie meets is that he will surprise the people around him and from which an important inference must be drawn about human dignity:

> it might be a good idea for all of us to treat other humans as if we do not know their potential, as if they just might in fact surprise us, as if they might defeat or exceed our expectations. It might be a good idea for us to check the history of the past two centuries whenever we think we know what "normal" human standards of behavior and achievement might be. And it might be a very good idea for us to expand the possibilities of democracy precisely because democracy offers us unfinished and infinitely revisable forms of political organization that stand the best chance, in the long run, of responding

adequately to the human rights of the unpredictable creatures we humans are. That might be one way of recognizing and respecting something you might want to call our human dignity. (53)

Bérubé concludes that the rights of disabled people should not be understood as a "fringe addition to civil rights law but as its very fulfillment" (55). We must enlarge this claim, I believe, to understand disability rights as the fulfillment of human rights. My twofold conclusion is, first, that we can have no idea of human rights worth serious consideration in the absence of a theoretical and practical account of disability; and, second, that disability rights hold the key to universal human rights.

As a coda to my call for a new human rights discourse open to fragility, vulnerability, and disability, I offer the example of the city of Geel in Belgium, a society that provides if not a legal blueprint then a hopeful vision welcoming to citizens with disabilities (Airing; Goldstein and Godemont). Possibly since 600 AD and certainly since the thirteenth century, Geel has been a haven for people with mental disabilities. The earliest population records date from 1693. Legend has it that the King of Oriel, an island now part of County Tyrone in Ireland, decided upon the death of his wife to wed his own daughter, Dymphna. She fled from Ireland to the present site of Geel, where her father found and killed her. The king's actions were considered insane, and because Dymphna was able to resist his advances, it was believed that she had special powers over people with mental illness, and she became their patron saint. As the legend of St. Dymphna spread far and wide, Geel became increasingly known as a center for the treatment of mental disability. Its church installed an infirmary to house arrivals in 1430, but the facilities soon proved inadequate to the influx of people seeking a new home, and the arrivals began to board with the people of the city. In this way the population of Geel became accustomed to the mentally disabled and accepted their presence among them as a point of pride. The church continued guardianship of the facilities until 1852, when the state took control. By 1938, when the population of boarders reached its peak, approximately 3,800 people with mental disabilities were living in the homes of the 20,000 inhabitants of the town. The presence of mentally disabled people was so common that mental impairment lost its stigma, and the people of the town embraced the boarders as citizens of Geel. The boarders came and went as they pleased. They worked in the houses or fields if they wished or did nothing if they were so inclined. If they worked, their wages were entirely their own, including if they worked for the people with whom they lived. Most surprising perhaps, the disabled people were not only Belgian; among them were found Dutch, French, English, Spanish, and Russian boarders. Others came to Geel from Chile, China, and the United States. About forty-five languages or dialects were spoken by the boarders when their population was at its peak, and Geel was able to retain 80 percent of all persons sent there to live. Geel demonstrates no nationalistic attitudes toward boarders, requiring only that they be mentally disabled to gain entry as new citizens.

During and after World War II the population of boarders dropped by over half, and in subsequent years their numbers have continued to diminish. In 2003 there were 516 boarders living with 423 families. Researchers attribute the decrease to the growing medicalization of care for the mentally disabled and the belief that families should have formal training rather than the training of experience. Geel families shun the medical model when relating to their boarders, preferring to play the roles of supportive parent or teacher. For example, boarders were not even diagnosed according to the *Diagnostic and Statistical Manual of Mental Disorders* until 2002. In the psychological literature, however, Geel has become a model for community-based mental healthcare. Though the number of boarders is now small compared to previous years, Geel continues to display practices and attitudes that make it a community ideally suited to receive fragile, vulnerable, and disabled people. Inhabitants of the city acknowledge and accept the human needs of the boarders, respond to those needs rather than act on unfounded fears, and recognize new arrivals as members of their community. The townspeople know the boarders by name and know where they live. The entire population protects, apparently without regard for its own interests, the members of their community least likely to be accepted elsewhere.

# Chapter Ten
# Conclusion

Because children symbolize, for better or worse, the future of humanity, their appearance in the world is tied to a collective vision of what is to come. The birth of any child is an ideological moment fraught with anxiety not only about its ability to move through life but also about the shapes and abilities of future human beings. Questions therefore arise, and these questions provide revealing indications about ability as an ideology. When a baby is born, its mother asks, "Is it a boy or a girl?" Her second question is, "Does it have all of its fingers and toes?" The questions seem to address different curiosities. The first question asks about gender; the second asks about disability. In fact, the questions voice the same inquiry in different rhetorical guises, as exposed by another age-old turn of phrase. Ask a pregnant woman whether she wants a boy or a girl, and she will reply, like clockwork, "I don't care if it is a boy or a girl as long as it is healthy." The question—"Is it a boy or a girl?"—is not only about gender, then, but also about health, reproductive ability, and genital integrity because standard gender identity is unrecognizable in the absence of ability as a marker. If the child has "ambiguous genitalia," the child supposedly has no gender—and we, potentially, no future—and such a child will soon confront what doctors call "gender assignment surgery," unless the child's parents have the good sense to leave well enough alone (see Colligan;

Valentine and Wilchins). Gender assignment surgery is not based on the child's gender identity, since the child is assumed not to have one. It depends on surgical parameters: if the child's genitals are easier to assign as a penis, the surgeon will make that choice; if as a vagina, it will be the choice. The goal is always to give the appearance of the able body, salted with the hope that the organs will still function in their altered state.

In the absence of ability, gender identity has no future and risks to disappear entirely. Disability effects similar transformations on racial, sexed, and class identities not only because they, too, rely on ability as a marker but also because disability appears at first glance to be so individualizing that it overwhelms any sense of group identity, and without identity, it is nearly impossible to project a future. The radical individuality of disability apparently threatens the very possibility of a shared political future among people, cutting an easy path to solipsism and political isolation. A major obstacle to the identity politics of disabled people, we have seen, is the individuality of impairment itself. While disabled people confront the same concerns as other minority groups about the authenticity of their experiences, an added problem arises because of the individualization of disability: it may be argued that women alone understand feminine experience, or African Americans, black experience, and that only they should be allowed to represent the political concerns of their respective groups, but disability activists struggle both to represent the experience of disability in general and the experience of different disabilities in particular. The question confronting the disability community is not only how to design a unified political coalition among people with different impairments but how to determine when a blind person, for example, may represent a deaf person in a political debate.

Such questions would arise less often if disability did not serve as a differential in the creation of identity, if it were not thought to generate an onslaught of suffering that awakens a mysterious psychological mechanism rendering individuals defective as social and political actors. This consequence arises, I hasten to add, not because disability and pain are equivalent. Rather, disability is nearly always interpreted in our society as a personal tragedy, as inherently individual, and in a manner similar to pain. Neither disability nor pain, however, differentiates the individual. They do not for the most part belong to one person alone. They are social inventions, external to people, that mark them as individual. The dominant social representation of disability in the West is the individual alone in pain, and it is difficult to find alternative representations, especially those that reveal pain's social origins. What would it mean to conceive of pain not as an individual or private sensation—as a feeling owned by one person—but as a socially mediated identity, as a product of social forces operating external to individuals?

Feelings of pain, however dependent on biological causes, become meaningful due to their social mediation, and the identities that people embody based on these mediations therefore exist in objective social locations. Such identities are reducible exclusively neither to origins in the natural world nor to their function in the social world. Identities theorize both. They consist of representations and actions that spring from neither organic nor psychological causes; their existence has no specific origin in individual anatomy or consciousness. Rather, their existence references a combination of factors. Identities evolve relative to collective organization, gaining their specific properties as part of a whole at the macro level. Identities are real because they represent direct responses to distinct and often verifiable conditions of society, both positive and negative, but since they are not specifically individualist, organic, or functionalist, they may survive beyond the time of their usefulness or acquire other uses difficult to name. Their value seems determined by their ability both to provide higher organization for particular groups and to help individuals navigate such organizations, although there also exist identities that organize through actions of violence and exclusion particular to communities, and the value of these identities is dubious, despite their ability to spark and to preserve social cohesion. Most significant, identities possess two characteristics usually considered mutually exclusive on the current theoretical scene: they are both socially constructed and reference social reality.

Some leading theorists of disability studies already conceive of disability identity as a constructed and yet objective social location. Carrie Sandahl's recent work reconciles this seeming contradiction in the idea of "a solo performer's ability to forge community," arguing that Lynn Manning's disability pieces display identities that are "both real and constructed"—"epistemically significant, on the one hand, and variable, nonessential, and radically historical, on the other" (2006, 582). Snyder and Mitchell define "cultural locations of disability" as sites "in which disabled people find themselves deposited, often against their will" and which represent "a saturation point of content about disability that has been produced by those who share certain beliefs about disability as an aspect of human difference" (2006, 3). Most important, they explain that "impairment is both human variation encountering environmental obstacles *and* socially mediated difference that lends group identity and phenomenological perspective" (2006, 10). Discriminatory practices deposit people with disabilities in social locations that are less accessible to the goods, resources, services, and benefits enjoyed by nondisabled people, and these practices affect the reality of disabled people's identities. The disabled in the United States often cannot vote because polling places are inaccessible; they cannot always take their grievances to court because courtrooms are not designed for their bodies; disabled people are among the highest unemployed and the lowest in income due to discrimination in the workplace; they face the possibility of involuntary confinement in institutions because there are economic restrictions on home care (see, for example, Johnson 62–63). A society with a universally accessible built environment and laws designed to offer equal protection to all people would produce far fewer disabled citizens in the future.

Disability identity exposes two features crucial to all minority identity. First, the pain of identity derives from inequitable social location; second, this pain may produce a new political awareness critical of societies based on inequality and oppression. Far from being a feeling that corrupts or disables people as political actors, suffering may serve as a political index for social injustice, prejudice, and cruelty, creating incentives for future coalition-building and political action. Nevertheless, traditional attitudes and opinions about pain are extremely narrow, rooted as they are in the belief that pain belongs uniquely to the individual, and they make it difficult to see how pain might metamorphose from a personal sensation to an experience supportive of strong and positive political values. If the personal is not automatically political in the case of pain—and all indications seem to suggest that pain is the exception that confirms the usual rule—how does suffering shift from a motive force affecting the individual body to one that sustains a new body politic?

Consider the example of Gretchen Anne Schaper, a paraplegic and performance artist, who decided one day to leave her wheelchair behind and to crawl to all her college classes as an experiment "about the unexpected, about speed, height, disability, endurance, strangers, pain and the

3. Gretchen Schaper Ryan, *Crawling Performance Piece*. 2000.
(Photograph by Kate Drendel.)

human condition" (Corbet). Her experiment produces an immediate impact on her social surroundings because she crawls out of her usual social
location, the wheelchair, in which she moves at about the same pace as
walking persons and remains above the taboo level of the ground—the
zone set apart in Western societies for animal life, dirt, infants, and the human down and out (see fig. 3). We may think of a person in a wheelchair
as on display, but crawling on the ground, according to Schaper, exhibits
her disabled status in full. She becomes a social pariah after only a few moments of dragging herself across campus by her arms, her paralyzed legs
splayed behind her. Skateboarders rattle past without acknowledging her.
Groundskeepers give her a wide berth as if she were contagious. Specta-
tors stare at her but pretend not to. Traveling without the aid of her mechanical chair establishes her as a social deviant, marking her as a target
for the hostility of the people surrounding her. "I did feel hostility," she remarks in the postperformance interview. "I really did. A lot of scoffing.

Like four people addressed me directly all day. It was amazing how many people pretended they didn't see me. And a lot of, 'Oh, she just wants attention.'"

---

### Dossier No. 21
*New Republic*
April 3, 2006

The Art of Losing
*Edgar Allan Poe & The Juke-Box:*
*Uncollected Poems, Drafts, and Fragments*
*By Elizabeth Bishop*
Edited by Alice Quinn
By Helen Vendler

This book should not have been issued with its present subtitle of "Uncollected Poems, Drafts, and Fragments." It should have been called "Repudiated Poems." For Elizabeth Bishop had years to publish the poems included here, had she wanted to publish them. They remained unpublished (not "uncollected") because, for the most part, they did not meet her fastidious standards (although a few, such as the completed love poem "It is marvelous to wake up together," may have been withheld out of prudence). Students eagerly wanting to buy "the new book by Elizabeth Bishop" should be told to go back and buy the old one, where the poet represents herself as she wished to be known. . . .

In the long run, these newly published materials will be relegated to what Robert Lowell called "the back stacks," and this imperfect volume will be forgotten, except by scholars. The real poems will outlast these, their maimed and stunted siblings.

---

The reactions of people in the street are hurtful to Schaper, but the suffering also provides an opportunity to transform the pain of her impairment. At first the sensation of crawling is physical: she drags herself painfully and with difficulty across the concrete pavement, stopping occasionally to arrange her legs into a sitting position and to catch her breath. Soon, however, her thoughts turn from physical pain to feelings of social isolation and suffering. "What was so scary was the physical exposure," she explains, "and what those people would think of my crippled body once it was separated from its camouflaging chair. I began asking, for the first time, why I was filled with so much shame. Why I cared what they thought; why they were upset by my presence." Schaper begins to understand the political dimension of her identity. It is a source of a different kind of pain, one unrelated to individual psychological development and determined by society, and consequently, no intervention at the individual psychological level, no psychoanalytic session, can soothe it. This pain requires social action, political change, and the recognition that she is not alone in her suffering.

Critics of identity politics who associate pain with politicized identity tend to address pain at the individual, psychological level, when an explanation at the social level is required. The sense of pain crucial to identity politics is not individual physical or psychological suffering, driven by personal anatomy or complexes, but the product of a growing social awareness that is best described as a new identity. While the pain of impairment is real, it nevertheless undergoes a redescription that changes its meaning when it is politicized by identity claims. Only a metapsychology requiring that suffering be represented as uniquely owned by an individual makes this change in the epistemology of suffering difficult to trace. Most people tend to assume that physical pain leads automatically to mental pain and vice versa—pain always and only remaining within the threshold of the individual. Consequently, to develop from one's physical or mental suffering a different kind of pain—a political pain, transformative of one's primary physical condition—seems incoherent, but this is exactly what the emergence of politicized identity accomplishes. The feelings of injury apparent in identity politics do not derive from bodily wounds, and it is a bad metaphor to call identity politics "wounded attachments" (Brown 52–76). Rather, the feelings of injury central to identity politics reflect the emergence of a new and oppositional social identity. Pain under the pressure of identity politics changes from a feeling of private suffering into a theoretical position, a political identity, from which the person in pain may join with others to reexamine the world, the better to fight the oppression of minority people and to create a future for them.

The shift to political identity represents a crucial resource for social change, even though the shift may have little effect at first glance on individual gestures, ideas, and feelings. It is the multiplication of associations through the many that joins individuals in political community. Schaper's experiment with the nether zone of physical immobility, for example, makes an implicit political statement about social inequity by claiming solidarity with the "many people in the world" who do not have wheelchairs; their only choice is to hide themselves or to crawl in public, opening themselves to humiliations particular to their cultures. But how much more forceful was the energy released by one of the most effective political protests in disability history where the experiences of a few were amplified by the many. In spring 1990 three dozen wheelchair users, representing ADAPT (American Disabled for Accessible Public Transit), threw aside their chairs and crawled up the eighty-three marble steps of the Capitol building to demonstrate for the passage of the ADA (see fig. 4). Their struggle to gain entrance to the inaccessible Capitol building was as grueling as Schaper's painful experiment, but the result was not a discovery of personal pain but a new political consciousness. Although the national press tried to put the focus on the individual suffering of the protestors, in the end the vision of so many disabled people dragging themselves up the Capitol steps gave expression to the collective political suffering felt by disabled people denied access to their own country, laws, and government. The result was a political vision of accessibility that the Congress had to embrace. For those who claim that identity politics offers only self-victimization and political paralysis, the example of ADAPT provides irrefutable evidence to the contrary.

Unfortunately, people with disabilities still have a great deal of political work to do if they are going to build a different future for their children. Recently in the *New York Times,* an essay appeared that marshals in one location almost every stigma and stereotype used historically to target people with disabilities and their desire to live a life in common free from violence, discrimination, and oppression. The essay reports on the use of preimplantation genetic diagnosis (PGD) by deaf and little people. Some of them are choosing not to screen out their genetic traits but to select for them, inviting their children, whom the author of the essay calls "genetic freaks," to carry forward their rich disability culture (Sanghavi). PGD creates test-tube babies and then analyzes their DNA before they are transferred to a woman's uterus. A survey of clinics found that 3 percent, or four clinics, permitted PGD tests to select an embryo for the presence of a disability, despite the fact that the procedure was designed originally with

4. Capitol Crawl Up protest, 1990. (Photograph by Tom Olin.)

the intention of eliminating people with disabilities. Some providers are now banning requests to use the test "for selecting deafness or dwarfism" (Sanghavi), a procedure that *Slate* magazine calls "the deliberate crippling of children" (Saletan). "If we make a diagnostic tool," one medical professional comments, "the purpose is to avoid disease," the implication being that people with disabilities are diseases best prevented (Senghavi).

As of this writing, the essay has solicited 183 readers' comments from which erupts an explosion of disgust, name-calling, and hatred directed at the parents with disabilities. The comments deserve a place in our dossier, but I will refrain, paraphrasing them instead, as I hope that they would be too agonizing by this time for my readers to absorb. The writers of the comments cannot conceive of disability as other than a lifetime of pain and suffering, and they attack the parents with every epithet used traditionally to pour scorn on disabled people. The parents are "narcissistic," "evil," "twisted," "emotionally disturbed," "in need of psychiatric help," "stupid," "abusive," "sick," "angry," "brutally unfair," "appalling," "crazy," "immoral," "cruel," "a disgrace to humanity," "freaks." Their "sick plea for attention" and "selfishness," according to the comments, cause "permanent harm" to their children, and the children themselves, called repeatedly an "unjust burden," will supposedly grow up to "make excessive demands on society" and increase "the cost on our already overburdened system." The commentators believe, despite the fact that they will some day join their ranks, that increasing the number of disabled people will lead only to a "culture of suffering." But these loving disabled parents consider their culture neither painful nor harmful to their children but a way of life—complete with positive identities, common interests and experiences, shared knowledge, and feelings of community and happiness—for which their children represent the future. Until everyone agrees that these children have a future, people with disabilities will remain the largest minority population subject to unjust and unrecognized oppression.

# Acknowledgments

My first and earliest debt is to David Mitchell and Sharon Snyder, without whose interest and example I would never have entered the field of disability studies. They remain in many ways the readers for whom I write. Rosemarie Garland-Thomson also embraced my early, awkward efforts, gave me encouragement, and became a valued colleague and friend. I thank Michael Bérubé for reading what I write and for the gift of his work; I have been in conversation with him, in imaginary and real ways, for many years and hope to continue the conversation for many more. Brenda Brueggemann, Michael Davidson, and Lennard Davis welcomed me into disability studies as a valued colleague and gave me advice, attention, and opportunities. Robert McRuer is a critic of my work in the best sense, taking my arguments seriously and sharing his own expertise. I thank Catherine Kudlick and Carrie Sandahl for their good company, thoughtfulness, and honesty, and Riva Lehrer for making images that delight the eye.

At the University of Michigan, I am indebted to the students who have taken Topics in Disability Studies over the years and to those who shared their ideas with me about disability as an intellectual pursuit, especially Renée Echols, Claire Decoteau, Roxana Galusca, D. Ohlandt-Ross, Scott St. Pierre, and Cynthia Wu. I thank Kristine Mulhorn and Margaret Somers for sharing the classroom with me and for teaching me new subjects. Most of the materials in this book were first presented to the First Draft Club, to whose members, especially David Halperin, Valerie Traub, and John Whittier-Ferguson, I express gratitude for their comments and criticisms. The academic initiatives that I administer at Michigan have given my work a context in which to develop. I thank Earl Lewis, Terrence McDonald, and Janet Weiss for their support of the Global Ethnic Literatures Seminar; Philip Hanlon, Lester Monts, and Teresa Sullivan for their support of the Future of Minority Studies at Michigan; and Paul Courant, June Howard, Earl Lewis, Terrence McDonald, Marvin Parnes, and Teresa Sullivan for their support of the University of Michigan Initiative on Disability Studies. I am grateful to all my colleagues at Michigan, past and present, who have supported the growth of disability studies: Susanna Blumenthal, Susan Brown, Paul Courant, Jeffrey Evans, Laurence Goldstein, Linda Gregerson, Daniel Herwitz, June Howard, Martha Jones, Anna Kirkland, James Knox, Petra Kuppers, Joanne Leonard, Earl Lewis, Terrence McDonald, Jonathan Metzl, Lester Monts, Kristine Mulhorn, Michael Myatt, Richard Price, Els Nieuwenhuijsen, Marvin Parnes, Martin Pernick, Michael

Schoenfeldt, Sidonie Smith, Margaret Somers, Teresa Sullivan, and Janet Weiss. I thank as well Jim Magyar, Peg Ball, and the other people at the Ann Arbor Center for Independent Living for teaching me about the day-to-day reality of the disability community and for getting me out of the ivory tower and into the streets.

Many of the ideas in this book evolved in conversation with members of the Future of Minority Studies National Research Project—a collaborative community that thinks about the historical oppression of minority peoples, the politics of minority representation, and the ways that minority studies might contribute to the future of progressive democratic reform. I thank Linda Martín Alcoff for her intellectual example, ideas, and serenity; Johnnella Butler for her leadership and enthusiasm; Michael Hames-García for thoughts both fugitive and insightful; Ernesto Martínez for his sincerity and seriousness; Amie MacDonald and Susan Sánchez-Casal for putting pedagogy first; Chandra Talpade Mohanty for her graciousness and political wisdom; Satya Mohanty for his leadership and sense of humor; Uma Mohanty for her appreciation of Beethoven; Paula Moya for letting me in the door, despite first impressions, and giving me friendship and advice; John Su for teaching the teacher; and Sean Teuton for his ability to think outside the box. I want to acknowledge the entire FMS community, in particular the graduate student and assistant professor caucus.

Finally, I am grateful for the love and support of my family. Jill, each new day with you is sweeter than the last. Thank you for your intelligence, energy, patience, wit, and gentle heart. Claire and Pierce, thank you for bringing art, beauty, and music into our home and for making me more than I am. May all good things come to you.

Permission to reprint materials has been generously granted by the Modern Language Association for "Tender Organ, Narcissism, and Identity Politics," *Disability Studies: Enabling the Humanities,* ed. Brenda Jo Brueggemann, Sharon L. Snyder, and Rosemarie Garland-Thomson (New York: MLA, 2002); by *American Literary History* for chapter 3; by Palgrave Macmillian for "Disability Studies and the Future of Identity Politics," *Identity Politics Reconsidered,* ed. Linda Martín Alcoff, Michael Hames-Gárcia, Satya P. Mohanty, and Paula M. L. Moya (New York: Palgrave-Macmillan, 2006); by *Literature and Medicine* for chapter 5; by Indiana University Press for chapter 6; by University of Chicago Press for "Sex, Shame, and Disability Identity: With Reference to Mark O'Brien," *Gay Shame,* ed. David Halperin and Valerie Traub (Chicago: University of Chicago Press, 2008); and by *Disability Studies Quarterly* for chapter 9. All materials have been substantially revised. I thank the following individuals and organizations for illustrations and the permission to reproduce them: Foundation Le Corbusier and Artists Rights Society for Le Corbusier's *Modulor;* Henry Dreyfuss Associates for *Josephine and Joe Jr.;* Gretchen Schaper Ryan and Kate Drendel for the photograph of the *Crawling Performance Piece;* and Tom Olin for the photograph of the Capitol Crawl Up.

# Notes

1. The nature of pain and the methodology of its study are diverse because they involve the definition of emotion and consciousness. Aydede collects a strong sampling of contemporary views about pain, one of which, the perceptual theory, appeals to the idea that pain has the capacity to signal changes in states of reality (59–98).

2. Snyder and Mitchell express this view powerfully throughout *Cultural Locations of Disability*. For example: "As Darwin insisted in *On the Origin of Species*, variation serves the good of the species. The more variable a species is, the more flexible it is with respect to shifting environmental forces. Within this formulation, one that is central to disability studies, variations are features of biological elasticity rather than a discordant expression of a 'natural' process gone awry" (2006, 70).

3. The literature on intersectionality is now vast. Some key texts relating to disability include Barbee and Little; Beale; Butler and Parr; Fawcett; Hayman and Levit; Ikemoto; Jackson-Braboy and Williams; Martin; O'Toole (2004); and Tyjewski.

4. While not aware of disability studies per se, Johnny Williams provides an excellent intersectional analysis of stereotypical conflations of race and class, arguing that American society explains the social and economic failures of minority groups in terms of personal "inabilities," while maintaining the belief that "social arrangements are fundamentally just" (221).

5. Catherine Kudlick proposed, on the DS-HUM listserve, an exercise similar to this one to replace traditional and biased disability simulations often used by classroom instructors. I am indebted to her discussion.

6. Philosophical realism has a number of varieties. The particular lineage of interest to me focuses on Hilary Putnam in philosophy and Richard Boyd in the philosophy of science. Satya P. Mohanty imports Boyd's ideas into the humanities in general and critical theory in particular, putting the concept of realism in the service of minority studies in novel and convincing ways. Other important figures in philosophical realism working in the humanities include Linda Martín Alcoff, Michael Hames-García, Paula M. L. Moya, and Sean Teuton.

CHAPTER TWO

1. In _The Mirror of Medusa,_ I trace the peculiar logic of narcissistic accusation from its appearances in classical mythology to its use in psychoanalysis and anthropology; the introduction to the revised edition (2000) takes up the question of narcissism relative to disability.

2. The most famous attacks against black studies and women's studies are the most exaggerated, but their exaggeration is only rhetorical, not an exaggeration of content, since the same arguments are made by feverish and subtle commentators alike. Frequently, the accusation of narcissism is just below the surface of the attack. William Bennet blasted the educational community for giving in to "special interests" such as ethnic studies and women's studies, while Lynne Cheney called for a return to a past in the United States untainted by intrusive discussions of race and gender. "Just at the moment," Allan Bloom has said of black studies, "when everyone else has become a 'person,' blacks have become blacks. . . . They stick together" (92). Nathan Glazer, another critic of affirmative action, understands that multiculturalism is about race relations in the United States, but he makes his case against it by arguing that multiculturalism inflates certain parts of the self at the expense of others. "There are multiple selves," he concludes. But only one self is dominant in multiculturalism: "Consequently, it is not necessary to represent the musical, athletic, regional, class, or religious self, because the racial or ethnic self is central and decisive" (49). For Camille Paglia, black studies, women's studies, and gay studies are only about self-interest: "each has simply made up its own rules and fostered its own selfish clientele, who have created a closed system" (1994, 99–100). Paglia singles out women's studies in particular as narcissistic: "women's studies is a comfy, chummy morass of unchallenged groupthink . . . sunk in a cocoon of smug complacency" (1992, 242); it is a "prisoner of its own futile, grinding, self-created discourse" (243).

3. Certainly, disability studies owes a large debt to recent trends in identity politics, for good and for bad. It has learned lessons from black studies and women's studies in particular, embracing the desire for empowerment, the strategy of representing marginality through first-person accounts, and the need to criticize practices of cruelty and injustice. But, of course, critics of disability studies have also profited from the negative rhetoric developed by critics of black studies and women's studies, with the result that disability studies, while new to the scene, finds the rhetoric of its enemies fully formed, even while its own self-description is not.

4. Christopher Lasch, among others, makes this point in _The Culture of Narcissism_ (253).

5. In _The Subject and Other Subjects,_ I discuss political subjectivity at greater length. One point is worth restating here. Politics always operates according to exclusionary principles insofar as it requires "borders": "Politics justly lays down the limits of inclusion for communities, whether it involves groups internal to its borders or whether it is policing external borders. There can be no political community without a serious conception of borders" (1998c, 132).

6. Contrary to Freud's views, Turner and McLean show more recently that people with disabilities do experience heightened anxiety.

7. Freud argues that narcissists "become inaccessible to the influence of psychoanalysis and cannot be cured by our efforts" (14:74). He compares narcissists to "primitive peoples," in addition to people with disabilities, especially in their capacity to consider their thoughts omnipotent (14:75).

8. A selection of reading in which the connection between disability and narcissism is suggested includes Coleman and Croake; Cubbage and Thomas; Fichten and Amsel; Greenacre; Jacobson; Lussier; Niederland; Ogden; Thomas; and Yorke.

9. I derive my language here from another case study, where Edith Jacobson analyzes the narcissistic behavior of both people with disabilities and beautiful able-bodied women with respect to the character type of "the exception" derived from Freud's 1916 essay, "Some Character-Types Met with in Psychoanalytic Work." Freud's paradigmatic figure of the narcissist is Richard III, whose disability justifies thinking of himself as a exceptional person permitted to wreak violence against other people to attain his own ends.

10. Harris and Wideman make this point (117). They also note that the impact of the psychoanalytic approach for people with disabilities has been largely punitive (121).

11. In Yorke's words, for some patients, "physical disability is hypercathected and becomes a physical coat-hanger on which to put a whole psychopathological wardrobe" (188).

12. For example, see Kleck et al.; Stiller; and Fichten and Amsel. Grier comes at the difference of the therapist from a different but related angle.

13. Asch and Rousso conclude that patients are more accepting of therapists with disabilities than the therapists' able-bodied colleagues (10–11). A development parallel to that between therapist and patients with disabilities exists in the relation between the mother and the child with a disability and between able-bodied children and parents with disabilities. The psychological literature tends to conclude that greater narcissistic injury results from having a child or parent with a disability than from having a disability oneself. For example, Lussier finds that "the psychologically weak father is not a condition creating a traumatic impact, no matter how frustrating and anxiety provoking, while the crippled father does in some way, at one stage or another" (184). See also Greenacre.

14. "The most common methodological approach to the question of disability in the humanities," note Mitchell and Synder, "is the analysis of cognitive and physical differences that symbolize other social conditions" (1997, 21). See also Mitchell and Snyder 2000.

15. I explore this symbolism in, among other places, "Kant and the Politics of Beauty."

16. The Right and the Left misunderstand the relation between disability and identity politics as a result. The underlying assumption on the Left is that groups in themselves create false ideals of the unified self. In short, the Left's attacks against identity politics favor individuality. The Right, of course, counters that identity politics is too individualistic. Disability studies requires a form of identity that resists both models because the Left's insistence on lone-wolf ideals of the self reproduces the medicalized view of disability and the Right's refusal to acknowledge difference leaves people with disabilities without any political position from

which to speak about their civil rights. See Bickford for a discussion of this problem in the context of feminism.

CHAPTER THREE

1. Disability studies may be in the position to offer significant adjustments to current theories of the body, especially the gendered and sexed body. Some of this work has already begun. See, for example, Shakespeare et al. and chapters 6, 7, and 8 below.

2. This little list runs the gamut of mythologies and realities connected with the representation of the disabled body, from freak show to mundane to metaphorical, and might serve as a warm-up for thinking about how different bodies transform language. A specific and provocative example of how the attributes of bodies affect the process of representation can be found in the recent work of transgender and intersex activists ("intersex" being the accepted term among these theorists for "hermaphrodites"). Intersex bodies, Valentine and Wilchins argue, defy the basis of existing categories, requiring new languages that seem confusing but more accurately represent their biology. For example, *his* or *her* is replaced with *hir*. Other examples of new linguistic usage appear in the email signatures of two transgender activists: "just your average, straight white guy with a cunt who really digs lezzie chicks like me" and "just your average butch lesbian intersexed white guy with a clitoral recession and a vaginoplasty who wants her dick back" (218).

3. Disability scholars are currently debating whether people with disabilities were better off before the inception of modernity, and this debate usually relies on the social construction argument. One example among many is found in Lennard J. Davis's pathbreaking study of deafness, *Enforcing Normalcy:* "This study aims to show that disability, as we know the concept, is really a socially driven relation to the body that became relatively organized in the eighteenth and nineteenth centuries. This relation is propelled by economic and social factors and can be seen as part of a more general project to control and regulate the body that we have come to call crime, sexuality, gender, disease, subalternity, and so on. Preindustrial societies tended to treat people with impairments as part of the social fabric, although admittedly not kindly, while postindustrial societies, instituting 'kindness,' ended up segregating and ostracizing such individuals through the discursivity of disability" (1995, 3). See also Linton et al., 6; Edwards; Oliver (1990); and Trent.

4. Pain is a notoriously complex issue in disability studies. On the one hand, a focus on pain risks to describe disability as if it were related exclusively to the physical body and not to social barriers, suggesting that disability is only and always about physical limitation. On the second hand, people with disabilities often complain that the social construction argument denies the pain of impairment and suggests that it can be overcome simply by changing cultural attitudes. On the third hand, some people with disabilities are not in physical pain and dispute the association between pain and disability. A politically effective theory of pain needs to mediate between these three alternatives. For more on the role of pain in disability studies, see Oliver (1996, chap. 3).

5. A major exception is Scarry, who makes it clear that pain is physical, but her own commitments make her work less useful than it could be for disability studies because she is more interested in describing how physical pain disturbs the social realm than the individual body. Her major examples of pain are torture and warfare, and these have a powerful impact on her theory. According to Scarry, pain is a "pure physical experience of negation, an immediate sensory rendering of 'against,' of something being against one, and of something one must be against. Even though it occurs within oneself, it is at once identified as 'not one-self,' 'not me,' as something so alien that it must right now be gotten rid of" (52). The subjective effects of pain, then, are objectified in the other, and consequently the gap between self and other widens to the point where it causes an enormous tear in the social fabric. Pain unmakes the world precisely because it usually lodges the source of suffering in the social realm. This idea of pain works extremely well for torture and warfare, where the presence of the torturer or enemy easily em-bodies otherness, but less so for disability, where suffering has to do not specifically with the destruction of the social realm but with the impairment of the body. Rather than objectifying their body as the other, people with disabilities often work to identify with it, for only a knowledge of their body will decrease pain and permit them to function in society. Unfortunately, this notion of the body as self has been held against people with disabilities. It is represented in the psychological literature as a form of pathological narcissism, with the result that they are represented as mentally unfit in addition to being physically unfit. On this last point, see chapter 2.

6. A notable exception, important for disability studies, is the feminist dis-course on rape; it rejects the idea that pain translates into pleasure, insisting that physical pain and feelings of being dominated are intolerable.

7. For other critiques of Haraway, see Wendell (44–45) and Mitchell and Snyder (1997, 28–29 n. 33).

8. Freud also had an exaggerated idea of prostheses, although he had an inkling that they do not always eliminate physical suffering. "Man has, as it were, become a kind of prosthetic God," he wrote. "When he puts on all his auxiliary or-gans he is truly magnificent; but those organs have not grown on to him and they still give him much trouble at times" (21: 91–92). Many persons with a disability who wear a prosthesis know that it soothes one kind of suffering only to return payment of another. When prostheses fit well, they still fit badly. They require the surface of the body to adjust—that is rarely easy—and impart their own special wounds. My mother wore a false eye; it fit at first, but as the surrounding tissue be-gan to shrink, it soon twisted and turned in its orbit, inflaming her eyesocket and becoming easily infected. I wear a plastic brace. It quiets the pain in my lower back, but I have developed a painful bunion, and the brace rubs my calf raw, es-pecially in the heat of summer.

9. Donna Haraway, although eschewing the language of realism, makes a case for the active biological agency of bodies, calling them "material-semiotic generative nodes" (200). By this last phrase, she means to describe the body as both constructed and generative of constructions and to dispute the idea that it is merely a ghostly fantasy produced by the power of language.

10. In 1990, when the ADA was passed, the number of Americans with dis-

abilities was estimated at 43 million. That number falls well short if one includes the one in three Americans who wear glasses or the 50 million who take medicine for hypertension. See Greenhouse (1999a), and also Kaufman (1999), who concludes her report on the legal issues posed to the Supreme Court as follows: "If the court decides that poor eyesight or hypertension are equally limiting, millions more Americans might wake up this spring to find themselves on the rolls of the disabled." Predictably, the Supreme Court found that 43 million disabled Americans were enough and ruled to restrict the definition of disability established by the ADA (Greenhouse 1999b).

## CHAPTER FOUR

1. A related phenomenon is the demand that people with disabilities live in their mind and not their body. Anne Finger's *Past Due* describes it superbly: "The world tells me to divorce myself from my flesh, to live in my head. Once someone showed me, excitedly, a postage stamp from Nicaragua: a man in a wheelchair, working alone, peering into a microscope. There's a US postage stamp that's almost exactly the same. It's always someone working alone, preferably male, brilliant, fleshless, a Mind" (1990, 18). And elsewhere: "I feel my disability as a physical reality, not just a social condition" (1990, 86).

2. Brown in fact disagrees with Nietzsche at the conclusion of chapter 3 by calling for a new politics that departs from the resentment of identity politics. This new politics would "release" pain in the hope of future healing. It would be oriented not toward individual "want" but toward what Brown calls "being." She is right to call for a shift, but her remarks, even when disagreeing with Nietzsche, continue to rely on individual psychology, notably on the theory of individual catharsis familiar to students of psychoanalysis. More disturbing in the case of the identity politics of people with disabilities is Brown's insistence that "wounded attachments" are an inherently undesirable state of affiliation.

3. The rhetoric of narcissism, as I argue in chapter 2, has been used against people with disabilities to degrade their participation in identity politics. Lennard Davis extends my reading of narcissism in *Bending over Backwards* to an interpretation of recent Supreme Court rulings, showing that the belief in the selfishness of disabled people limits the Court's ability to rule impartially on the ADA (see chap. 7).

4. See, for example, Potok, *A Matter of Dignity:* "When I talk to nondisabled people, they mostly identify me according to their learned and largely unthought-about attitudes and definitions. My physical disability, blindness, dominates and skews the ablebodied person's process of sorting out perceptions and forming a reaction. The relationship is often strained because of fear, pity, fascination, revulsion or merely surprise, none of which is easily expressed within the constraints of social protocol. Should the nondisabled person offer assistance? . . . For my part, am I only or mostly my disability?" (90). See also the classic theorist in the field, Robert A. Scott, *The Making of Blind Men,* who argues that "Blindness . . . is a social role that people who have serious difficulty seeing or who cannot see at all must learn to play" (3).

5. Other discussions important to realism and identity politics include Alcoff (1996, 2006); Alcoff et al.; and Moya and Hames-García.

6. On the social and moral value of identity, see my *Morals and Stories*, esp. chaps. 2 and 4.

7. Fredric Jameson defines the political unconscious as a collective impulse that situates the experience of the human group as "the absolute horizon of all reading and all interpretation" (17). See also my use of Jameson in "What Can Disability Studies Learn from the Culture Wars?" (2003).

8. I note that human factors engineering evolves considerably over time, from a time where different growth patterns between historical periods are stressed to one where differently abled bodies gain importance. See the ADA compliant update by Dreyfuss Associates' designer, Alvin R. Tilley, *The Measure of Man and Woman*.

9. Eva Feder Kittay takes up the idea that "mental retardation" may be liberalism's limit case because some people with disabilities may not be capable of participating in rational deliberation. Her essay provides a good background to the political issues raised by people with mental disabilities, although her conclusion about new ideas of caring justice is not entirely satisfying—not, I note, because she has not considered the question of cognitive disability thoroughly but because it is a difficult question. Other sources on the role played by cognitive disability in U.S. history include Snyder and Mitchell (2002) and Trent.

10. The classic political description of a world without an outside is the essay "Perpetual Peace," where Kant argues against political secrecy and standing armies and calls for a "league of nations" to ensure world peace. For an in-depth analysis, see my *The Subject and Other Subjects* (1998c, 115–30). Please note, however, that the world spectator position is often placed outside the purview of its own vision, despite the idea that there is no outside to the world.

11. See the conclusion to *Beyond the Pleasure Principle*, where Freud quotes Rückert: "Was man nicht erfliegen kann, muss man erhinken. . . . Die Schrift sagt, es ist keine Sünde zu hinken" (23:64).


CHAPTER FIVE

1. On the rhetoric of coming out as a person with a disability, see Brueggemann (50–81, 81–99); Brueggemann and Kleege; Kleege; Michalko; and Tepper (1999). On the limits of coming-out discourse, see Samuels.

2. Newton, *Mother Camp*, provides a counterexample, explaining that drag queens represent the shame of the gay world because they most visibly embody the stigma (3).

3. For a discussion of passing as a method of creating and establishing alternative narratives, see the essays in Sánchez and Schlossberg.

4. My focus is on connections between disability studies and queer theory, but I owe an enormous debt to the literature on racial passing as well. A good introduction to the complexities of racial passing is "Passing for White, Passing for Black," where Piper argues several crucial and paradoxical points about race worth accenting in the context of disability. First, racial identity, like disability

identity, does not depend on shared physical characteristics (30). Rather, identity of any kind is a function of "passing" because the person presents identifying characteristics to the world. Therefore, the decision to pass for white is "more than a rejection of black identity"; it is a rejection of the pain, disability, and alienation of "black identification" (13). Second, the affirmation or exaggeration of black identity may be a countermeasure designed to deal with the alienation of this identity (14). Here Piper's own "Self-Portrait Exaggerating My Negroid Features" might provide the starting point for a discussion of the relation between racial and disability masquerade.

Other important treatments of racial passing include McDowell, who opened the question of passing for literary study; Harper, who considers passing in the context of gender; Wiegman, who reports on the attention to anatomy in racial identification; Sollers, who tracks the etymology and usage of "passing" in nineteenth- and twentieth-century American literature; Dyer, who explains how whiteness passes for "universal"; and Wald, who provides a rich reading of theories of passing in the context of film, journalism, and literature.

Finally, it is worth mentioning that the tension in racial passing between "crossing the color line" and achieving "color-blind" or "race-blind" societies needs some day to be interrogated from a disability perspective alert to the metaphor of blindness.

5. Although feminists and queer theorists have not cited Goffman's theories when applying Riviere's ideas, it is clear that the masquerade serves in many of these applications as a strategy for managing stigma because its purpose is said to create effects subversive to male power by exaggerating stereotypes of womanliness. Doane (1982, 1988–89) uses Riviere to make the case that the masquerade exposes a distance or gap between the feminine self and its stereotypes, thereby questioning structures of male power. De Lauretis claims that the masquerade, even when required, gives subversive pleasure to the performer (17), while Castle uses Bakhtin's concept of the carnivalesque to propose that the masquerade throws accepted identities into disarray. Most recently, Garber argues that the masquerade challenges "easy notions of binarity, putting into question the categories of 'female' and 'male'" (10).

6. Robert McRuer adjusts Rich's theories to argue that our culture makes it compulsory to assume that "able-bodied perspectives are preferable and what we all, collectively, are aiming for" (2002, 93).

7. Of course, Riviere may be masquerading herself. Heath makes the case that her liminal relation to Ernest Jones and Freud, as an object of their sexual fantasies, underlies the theory of the masquerade.

8. These phrases belong to very different and opposing views, ones that nevertheless come to agreement about the so-called psychological deficiency of minority groups. The academic Right and Left often share the tendency to view psychological flaws as underlying the desire to form political identity groups, with the result that critics of identity politics often reproduce the descriptions of political minorities used by their oppressors, labeling them as wounded, resentful, power hungry, or narcissistic. See Bloom and Brown. On the accusation of narcissism against people with disabilities, see chapter 2.

9. Garland-Thomson discusses "coming out" as a coming into political con-

sciousness, referring to the process of writing *Extraordinary Bodies* "This book is the consequence of a coming-out process. . . . Being out about disability has enabled me both to discover and to establish a field of disability studies within the humanities and to help me consolidate a community of scholars who are defining it" (1997, ix).

10. Another example of improvisation comes from a personal communication with David Mitchell, who recounts his experience at the University of Michigan in the late 1980s when handicapped parking permits were distributed by university parking services. He had to go the office of parking services where a woman made him walk across the room in order to establish that he needed the permit. He confesses exaggerating his difficulty in order to fail the test and to make up for the lack of understanding shown by the woman who seemed to have no conception that walking distance is a factor in mobility as much as the ability to walk across a room. Note that Sandahl refers in a superb analysis of disability performance art to certain actions that seem to resemble Mitchell's tactic as "charity case" behaviors (2003, 41). No doubt, charity is being courted in some cases, but it is a strategic and ironic invocation of charity designed to meet and overcome lack of understanding in the nondisabled community. Its goal is neither unfair personal advantage nor pity but social justice.

11. Disability drag also invites connections to drag kinging. Halberstam argues that kinging, unlike queening, is not commensurate with camp, although it sometimes has similar effects. Disability masquerade relies even less on camp. Camp draws attention to itself and provokes imitation. It asks for crossover effects by which its power is transmitted from countercultural sites to mainstream publics. Disability drag, however, does not provoke feelings of imitation in the mainstream public. It maintains the stigma of people with disabilities, focusing attention through structures of objectification rather than imitation. On kinging and queening, see Halberstam (1998, 231–66; 2001, 427).

12. Contrast *The Idiots* (1998) by Lars von Trier, a film that is controversial but thought-provoking on the issue of able-bodied actors playing people with mental disabilities. The plot follows the adventures of a group of Danes who pretend to be cognitively disabled for reasons of social experimentation. They want to release their "inner idiot" as a resistance to technology and bourgeois culture but also enjoy poking fun at people's reactions to mental disability. They "spaz out" among themselves as well, often as a means of expressing both heightened and subtle emotions. Since the pretense of disability is a function of the plot, *The Idiots* has a different effect from *Rain Man* or *I Am Sam,* although the film is similar in its embrace of mental disability as a device to reform one's personality. It shows less investment in the character development of its protagonists as disabled and greater interest in how society reacts to disability and how the characters use the masquerade to manage their own emotional and interpersonal problems. Consequently, the act of playing disabled often appears integrated with the other actions performed by the characters, merging nondisabled and disabled features in a single personality. In the final scene, for example, Karen "spazzes" in front of her family, but only after we learn for the first time that she had just lost her daughter and left home the day before the funeral to join the group of pretenders. Her masquerade looks to be as much an expression of her terrible grief as a per-

formance of disability. Please note, however, that von Trier does not suggest that the pretenders acquire any great moral lessons from the masquerade. In the one scene where they interact with cognitively disabled actors, the pretenders are as condescending as other people are toward them when they are masquerading.

13. Marks suggests that the real reason for using nondisabled actors for disabled parts is to reassure the audience that disability is not real (160).

## CHAPTER SIX

1. The Court ruled in *Board of Trustees of Univ. of Ala. v. Garrett* that the Eleventh Amendment bars private money damages for state violations of ADA Title I, which prohibits employment discrimination against the disabled.

2. Scott prefers the use of discourse theory for writing alternative histories to gathering the evidence of experience. However, if the problem with experience is its constructed state, resorting to discourse does not present an advantage because discourse is no less socially constructed.

3. Emblematic of a second-wave theory of minority experience is Moya, *Learning from Experience* (2002).

4. Bruno Latour, for example, tracks how radical constructivist critique has been turned to reactionary ends and stresses the importance of embracing realist alternatives for progressive, political results.

5. On the realism of lived and complex embodiment as a point of departure for social change, see chapters 3 and 4.

6. For realist arguments about experience, see Moya (2002); Moya and Hames-García; and especially in this context the response by William S. Wilkerson to Scott's critique of Delany. On the realist implications of feminism, see Alcoff (2000, 2006).

7. Mario Perniola offers an argument complementary to mine, claiming that sexuality and suffering "constitute great challenges for postmodernism" because they "relate to the body understood as something given" (32).

8. The concept of "visitability," the application of which has not been widespread, extends accessibility to private housing beyond the needs of renters or property owners, while the Fair Housing Amendment of 1988 mandates basic architectural access in new, multifamily housing, although its enforcement has been weak. No law currently requires accessibility to single-family dwellings. For an overview, see "Laws on Disability Access to Housing."

9. My point is not to criticize Delany, who maintains a laudable openness to people with disabilities throughout his memoir. Two episodes are worth mentioning in particular. In one episode he is mistaken for a mute, mentally disabled man, pushed into a backroom, and awkwardly raped, after which he wonders "if this was what happened to the mute or simple-minded wandering New York" (140). In the second episode, he meets a man in a subway lavatory whose penis has its tip cut off and does not withdraw from the sexual encounter: "He came very fast. I wanted to talk with him afterward, but he zipped up once we were finished and hurried away. I never saw him again, although I looked for him" (188).

10. I am indebted to the discussion of Chang and Eng's sexuality by Cynthia Wu.

11. See Johnson for an unfanciful description of disability on the margins.

## CHAPTER SEVEN

1. A number of other discussions touching minimally on sexual citizenship are worth noting. Sonia K. Katya proposes the idea of "sexual sovereignty" to address various battles on the fault line between culture, identity, and sexuality, claiming that the Supreme Court decision in *Lawrence v. Texas* "serves as a starting point with which to build a theoretical model for global sexual autonomy that encompasses many of the anti-essentialist critiques offered by human rights discourse, critical race theory, and queer theory" (1435). Nevertheless, her theory of sexual sovereignty builds on ideas of "independence, personhood, autonomy, and impermeability" (1461), without considering their relation to disabled people as a sexual minority. Lisa Duggan offers an incisive analysis of the use of gay marriage and reproductive rights to advance the reconfiguration of American citizenship rights, arguing that the Right seizes on such cultural issues to conceal its determination to stimulate upward redistribution rather than downward redistribution of economic resources and power. Finally, Eithne Luibhéid focuses on immigrant sexual minorities, noting that sexuality is an especially dense intersection for power relations bearing on citizenship and noncitizenship.

2. In most cases, however, the women's worries turn out not to be true: "Wherever and whenever the first intercourse took place, all women recollected it as a positive experience: 'I was relieved that my rape-fantasies were wrong'" (Westgren and Levi 312).

## CHAPTER EIGHT

1. Michael Warner's ethics of gay shame also bears on disability. He draws a direct connection between disease transmission and gay shame, arguing that shame salts sex with the thrill of death (198). Gay people have a hard time reflecting on the risk of HIV/AIDS, he concludes, because their desires are clouded by shame (215). For Warner, the only solution is to embrace an actively funded and fully committed campaign of HIV prevention that combats shame rather than sex (218).

2. See also the interpretation of Sedgwick's theory of shame by Douglas Crimp (65, 67), who defines shame specifically as a positive emotion by which we feel sympathy for the oppressed.

3. Sedgwick adds the reference to the disabled man in the revision of the essay used in *Touching Feeling* where it follows an autobiographical account of her struggles as a "person living with a grave disease" (2003, 34). It is difficult to understand Sedgwick's rhetorical usage of the "half-insane man" in the context of her own disability identity as a cancer survivor and its transformative effect on her teaching and scholarship.

4. While we are on the subject of private acts in public, consider this account by O'Brien, *How I Became a Human Being,* of his first stay in the hospital at age six: "when I needed what the nurses called a 'BM,' I had to call for a nurse and ask her to lay me on top of a big steel bedpan, always an awkward procedure. To reach the state of calm needed to empty my bowels, I had to ignore the tumult on the ward as well as the cold, hard steel of the bedpan digging into my lower back. Afterward, being taken off the bedpan was painful and embarrassing. . . . The penalties for failing to shit every day included the insertion of suppositories, enema tubes, and nurses' gloved fingers. Whatever sense of privacy and dignity I had developed by age six were destroyed" (O'Brien and Kendall 2003, 23).

5. "Questions I Feared the Journalist Would Ask," Mark O'Brien Papers, BANC MSS 99/247 c, Bancroft Library, University of California, Berkeley. Copyright 1999, Lemonade Factory, Berkeley, CA. Used by permission. My thanks to Susan Schweik for obtaining materials from this archive for me and to Susan Fernback for giving me permission to use them.

6. It is worth remarking that masturbation training is usually a same-sex activity, except for the rare situation when the patient has declared a same-sex orientation, in which case a trainer of the opposite sex is assigned (Kaeser 302, 305).

7. O'Brien, "On Seeing a Sex Surrogate" (1990), a revised version of which also appears in O'Brien, *How I Became a Human Being,* chap. 13.

8. For example: "it is necessary to be satisfied that a situation has not been created in which homosexuality is the only option" (Thompson 257).

9. For a good introduction to the issues, see Stoner.

10. It is also the case, however, that some people experience the genderless zone of the unisex toilet as a safe space apart from the scrutiny and requirements of able-bodied society.

11. The ideology of ability also exercises its power on gender identity beyond the heterosexual world of Ladies and Gentlemen. The lesbian community accepted lesbians with disabilities early in its history, while disabled gay males have a hard time joining the gay community to this day, although the AIDS crisis has had enormous influence on the ethical relation of the gay community to disability. See Brownworth and Raffo for a sense of the rich history of lesbians with disabilities. Kenny Fries provides examples of the difficulties facing gay men with disabilities (101, 110–15, 123).

12. On drag kinging, see Halberstam (1998); on drag queening, see Newton.

13. The Mark O'Brien web page traces this development, including both accounts by him and photographs of his cross-dressing: www.pacificnews.org/marko/shriek.html (accessed April 29, 2005).

14. I rely in this section on Sedgwick's account of the history of the sex/gender system (1990, 27–30).

15. I take inspiration and language for this discussion from David Halperin's analysis of the effeminate male in *How to Do the History of Homosexuality* (34, 36–37).

CHAPTER NINE

1. My ideas about citizenship and human rights have benefited enormously from conversations with Margaret Somers.

2. Benhabib (2004, 13–14) mentions a system of moral advocacy for human rights that includes, among others, the "differently abled" and "mentally ill."

3. As Arendt notes, a difficult but certain way of avoiding the loss of citizenship rights is to be recognized as a genius: "a much less reliable and much more difficult way to rise from an unrecognized anomaly to the status of recognized exception would be to become a genius" (287).

4. On the forced confinement of disabled people, see Johnson. On legal restrictions for disabled people, see S. Blumenthal (2002). The Supreme Court ruled in *Board of Trustees of Univ. of Ala. v. Garrett* that the Eleventh Amendment bars private money damages for state employment discrimination against the disabled, regardless of the evidence.

5. For an exposé on the impact of the chemical and oil industries on health, see Allen.

6. See Nussbaum for a tough-minded and ambitious critique of social contract theory that reaches toward a vision of human rights for disabled people, poor nations, and animals on the basis of the capabilities approach. Her theory is a work in progress, however, and in that spirit, I add a few criticisms here. Nussbaum rightly bases human rights theory on freestanding ethical principles rather than on natural law, reciprocity, utility, or the ability to make contracts. Nevertheless, her principles fall noticeably short in two areas, both of which demonstrate too much reliance on previous theories. First, she establishes, similar to social contract theory, a threshold level of capability beneath which individuals are given human rights only as charity cases (71). For example, people who fall below the threshold through disease or accident become "former" human beings, and some people, such as those born with severe cognitive disabilities, never rise above the threshold (181). Second, Nussbaum represents the avoidance of pain, as does utilitarianism, as the standard by which to judge the success of a given policy or society. Here she cites Peter Singer favorably, a philosopher whom disability activists rightly disdain for his argument that certain disabled people should be put to death to ease their suffering. It is one thing to want to avoid pain; it is another to use it to decide whether another person should continue to exist as a human being. Finally, it must be noted that these two difficulties arise because of a fundamental ambiguity in the meaning of the capabilities themselves. Nussbaum refers to them variously as primary goods, entitlements, and freestanding principles, but they seem to resemble "abilities" more than anything else. Retaining ability as the standard used to determine whether an individual should be a rights-bearing person relies unnecessarily on the ideology of ability.

# Works Cited

Adam, Barry D. 1978. *The Survival of Domination: Inferiorization and Everyday Life*. New York: Elsevier.

Airing, C. D. 1974. "The Gheel Experience: Eternal Spirit of the Chainless Mind!" *JAMA* 230:998–1001.

Albrecht, Gary. 1992. *The Disability Business: Rehabilitation in America*. Newbury Park, Calif.: Sage.

Alcoff, Linda Martín. 1996. *Real Knowing: New Versions of Coherence Theory*. Ithaca, N.Y.: Cornell University Press.

Alcoff, Linda Martín. 2000. "Who's Afraid of Identity Politics?" *Reclaiming Identity: Realist Theory and the Predicament of Postmodernism*. Ed. Paula M. L. Moya and Michael R. Hames-García. Berkeley and Los Angeles: University of California Press. Pp. 312–44.

Alcoff, Linda Martín. 2006. *Visible Identities: Race, Gender and the Self*. New York: Oxford University Press.

Alcoff, Linda Martín, Michael Hames-García, Satya P. Mohanty, and Paula M. L. Moya, eds. 2006. *Identity Politics Reconsidered*. New York: Palgrave Macmillan.

Allen, Barbara L. 2003. *Uneasy Alchemy: Citizens and Experts in Louisiana's Chemical Corridor Disputes*. Cambridge: MIT Press.

Arendt, Hannah. 1976. *The Origins of Totalitarianism*. New York: Harcourt.

Asch, Adrienne. 2001. "Critical Race Theory, Feminism, and Disability: Reflections on Social Justice and Personal Identity." *Ohio State Law Journal* 62.1:391–423.

Asch, Adrienne, and Michelle Fine. 1988. *Women with Disabilities: Essays in Psychology, Culture, and Politics*. Philadelphia: Temple University Press.

Asch, Adrienne, and Harilyn Rousso. 1985. "Therapists with Disabilities: Theoretical and Clinical Issues." *Psychiatry* 48:1–12.

Aydede, Murat, ed. 2005. *Pain: New Essays on Its Nature and the Methodology of Its Study*. Cambridge: MIT Press.

Barbee, L. Evelyn, and Marilyn Little. 1993. "Health, Social Class and African-American Women." *Theorizing Black Feminisms: The Visionary Pragmatism of Black Women*. Ed. Stanlie M. James and Abena P. A. Busia. London: Routlege. Pp. 182–99.

Baynton, Douglas C. 2001. "Disability and the Justification of Inequality in American History." *The New Disability History: American Perspectives*. Ed. P. Longmore and L. Umansky. New York: NYU Press. Pp. 33–57

Beale, Frances. 1995. "Double Jeopardy: To Be Black and Female." *Words of Fire: An Anthology of African-American Feminist Thought.* Ed. Beverley Guy-Sheftall. New York: New Press. Pp. 146–55.

Benhabib, Seyla. 2000. *Transformation of Citizenship.* Amsterdam: Kohinklijke Van Gorcum.

Benhabib, Seyla. 2004. *The Rights of Others: Aliens, Residents, and Citizens.* Cambridge: Cambridge University Press.

Bennet, William J. 1984. *To Reclaim a Legacy: A Report on the Humanities in Higher Education.* Washington, D.C.: National Endowment for the Humanities.

Bersani, Leo. 1988. "Is the Rectum a Grave?" *AIDS: Cultural Analysis, Cultural Activism.* Ed. Douglas Crimp. Cambridge: MIT Press.

Bérubé, Michael. 2003. "Citizenship and Disability." *Dissent* (Spring): 52–57.

Bickford, Susan. 1997. "Anti-anti-identity Politics: Feminism, Democracy, and the Complexities of Citizenship." *Hypatia* 12.4:111–31.

Bloom, Allan. 1987. *The Closing of the American Mind: How Higher Education Has Failed Democracy and Impoverished the Souls of Today's Students.* New York: Simon and Schuster.

Bloom, Harold. 1994. *The Western Canon: The Books and School of the Ages.* New York: Riverhead Books.

Blumenthal, Ralph. 2002. "An Artist's Success at 14, Despite Autism." *New York Times Online,* January 16 (accessed September 13, 2006).

Blumenthal, S. L. 2002. "Law and the Modern Mind: The Problem of Consciousness in American Legal Culture, 1800–1930." Ph.D. diss., Yale University.

2001. *Board of Trustees of Univ. of Ala. v. Garrett.* 531 U.S. 356. Pp. 1–17.

Bordo, Susan. 1993. *Unbearable Weight: Feminism, Western Culture, and the Body.* Berkeley and Los Angeles: University of California Press.

Bornstein, Melvin. 1977. "Analysis of a Congenitally Blind Musician." *Psychoanalytic Quarterly* 46:23–77.

Boyd, Richard. 1988. "How to Be a Moral Realist." *Essays on Moral Realism.* Ed. Geoffrey Sayre-McCord. Ithaca, N.Y.: Cornell University Press. Pp. 181–228.

Brewer, Geoffrey. 2000. "Oh, the Psyches and Personalities He Has Seen." *New York Times Online,* April 19 (accessed September 13, 2006).

———. 2003. *Brief for the American Bar Association as Amicus Curaie Supporting Respondents.* No. 02–1667. Pp. 1–25.

Brown, Wendy. 1995. *States of Injury: Power and Freedom in Late Modernity.* Princeton, N.J.: Princeton University Press.

Brownworth, Victoria A., and Susan Raffo. 1999. *Restricted Access: Lesbians on Disability.* Seattle: Seal Press.

Brueggemann, Brenda Jo. 1999. *Lend Me Your Ear: Rhetorical Constructions of Deafness.* Washington, D.C.: Gallaudet University Press.

Brueggemann, Brenda Jo, and Georgina Kleege. 2003. "Gently Down the Stream: Reflections on Mainstreaming." *Rhetoric Review* 22.2: 174–84.

Burlingham, Dorothy. 1961. "Some Notes on the Development of the Blind." *Psychoanalytic Study of the Child* 16:121–45.

Butler, Judith. 1993. *Bodies That Matter: On the Discursive Limits of "Sex."* New York: Routledge.

Butler, Judith. 1997. *The Psychic Life of Power: Theories in Subjection.* Stanford: Stanford University Press.

Butler, Judith. 1999. *Gender Trouble: Feminism and the Subversion of Identity.* New York: Routledge.

Butler, Ruth, and Hester Parr, eds. 1999. *Mind and Body Spaces: Geographies of Illness, Impairment and Disability.* London: Routledge.

Carey, Allison. 2003. "Beyond the Medical Model: A Reconsideration of 'Feeblemindedness,' Citizenship, and Eugenic Restrictions." *Disability and Society* 18.4: 411–30.

Castells, Manuel. 2004. *The Power of Identity.* 2nd ed. Oxford: Blackwell, 1997.

Castle, Terry. 1986. *Masquerade and Civilization: The Carnivalesque in Eighteenth-Century English Culture and Fiction.* Stanford, Calif.: Stanford University Press.

Cheney, Lynne V. 1988. "Scholars and Society." *ACLS Newsletter* 1.3: 5–7.

Christian, Barbara. 1987. "The Race for Theory." *Cultural Critique* 6:51–63.

Cohen, Adam. 2004. "Editorial: Can Disabled People Be Forced to Crawl Up the Courthouse Steps?" *New York Times,* January 11, sec. 4, p. 14.

Coleman, Richard L., and James W. Croake. 1987. "Organ Inferiority and Measured Overcompensation." *Individual Psychology* 43.3: 364–69.

Colligan, Sumi. 2004. "Why the Intersexed Shouldn't Be Fixed: Insights from Queer Theory and Disability Studies." *Gendering Disability.* Ed. Bonnie G. Smith and Beth Hutchison. New Brunswick, N.J.: Rutgers University Press. Pp. 45–60.

Collins, Patricia Hill. 1998. "Learning from the Outsider within Revisited." *Fighting Words: Black Women and the Search for Justice.* Minneapolis: University of Minnesota Press. Pp. 3–10.

Collins, Patricia Hill. 2003. "Some Group Matters: Intersectionality, Situated Standpoints, and Black Feminist Thought." *A Companion to African-American Philosophy.* Ed. Tommy L. Lott and John P. Pittman. Malden: Blackwell. Pp. 205–29.

Corbet, Barry. 1999. "A Disability in Full." *New Mobility,* October, http://newmobility.com/review_article3.cfm?id=196&action=browse&type=REG&order_id=new (accessed July 15, 2005).

Corbett Sara. 2004. "The Permanent Scars of Iraq." *New York Times Magazine,* February 15, 34–41, 58, 60, 66.

Crimp, Douglas. 2002. "Marlo Montez, for Shame." *Regarding Sedgwick: Essays on Queer Culture and Critical Theory.* Ed. Stephen M. Barber and David L. Clark. New York: Routledge. Pp. 57–70.

Cubbage, Maxwell E., and Kenneth R. Thomas. 1989. "Freud and Disability." *Rehabilitation Psychology* 34.3: 161–73.

Davies, Dominic. 2000. "Sharing Our Stories, Empowering Our Lives: Don't Dis Me!" *Sexuality and Disability* 18.3: 179–86.

Davis, Lennard J. 1995. *Enforcing Normalcy: Disability, Deafness, and the Body.* London: Verso.

Davis, Lennard J. 2001. "Identity Politics, Disability, and Culture." *Handbook of Disability Studies.* Ed. Gary L. Albrecht, Katherine D. Seelman, and Michael Bury. Thousand Oaks, Calif.: Sage. Pp. 535–45.

Davis, Lennard J. 2002. *Bending over Backwards: Disability, Dismodernism, and Other Difficult Positions.* New York: New York University Press.

Delany, Samuel R. 2004. *The Motion of Light in Water: Sex and Science Fiction in the East Village.* Minneapolis: University of Minnesota Press.

De Lauretis, Teresa. 1986. "Issues, Terms, and Contexts." *Feminist Studies, Critical Studies.* Ed. Teresa de Lauretis. Bloomington: Indiana University Press. Pp. 1–19,

Doane, Mary Ann. 1982. "Film and the Masquerade: Theorising the Female Spectator." *Screen* 23.3–4: 74–87.

Doane, Mary Ann. 1988–89. "Masquerade Reconsidered: Further Thoughts on the Female Spectator." *Discourse* 11:42–54.

Duggan, Lisa. 2003. *The Twilight of Equality: Neoliberalism, Cultural Politics, and the Attack on Democracy.* Boston: Beacon Press.

Dworkin, Anthony Gary, and Rosalind J. Dworkin, eds. 1976. *The Minority Report: An Introduction to Racial, Ethnic, and Gender Relations.* New York: Praeger.

Dyer, Richard. 1998. "White." *Screen* 29.4: 44–64.

Edelman, Lee. 1994. "Tearooms and Sympathy; or, The Epistemology of the Water Closet." *Homographesis: Essays in Gay Literary and Cultural Theory.* New York: Routledge. Pp. 148–70.

Edwards, Martha. 1996. "The Cultural Context of Deformity in the Ancient Greek World." *Ancient History Bulletin* 10.3–4: 79–92.

Fawcett, Barbara. 2000. *Feminist Perspectives on Disability.* Harlow: Prentice Hall.

Ferris, Jim. 1998. "Uncovery to Recovery: Reclaiming One Man's Body on a Nude Photo Shoot." *Michigan Quarterly Review* 37.3:503–18.

Fichten, Catherine S., and Rhonda Amsel. 1988. "Thoughts Concerning Interaction between College Students Who Have a Physical Disability and Their Nondisabled Peers." *Rehabilitation Counseling Bulletin* 32 (September): 22–40.

Fiduccia, Barbara Waxman. 2000. "Current Issues in Sexuality and the Disability Movement." *Sexuality and Disability* 18.3: 167–74.

Fine, Michelle, and Asch, Adrienne, eds. 1988. *Women with Disabilities: Essays in Psychology, Culture, and Politics.* Philadelphia: Temple University Press.

Finger, Anne. 1990. *Past Due: A Story of Disability, Pregnancy, and Birth.* Seattle: Seal Press.

Finger, Anne. 1992. "Forbidden Fruit." *New Internationalist* 233:8–10.

Flores, Juan. 2005. "Reclaiming Left Baggage: Some Early Sources for Minority Studies." *Cultural Critique* 59:187–206.

Foucault, Michel. 1980. *The History of Sexuality.* Vol. 1: *An Introduction.* Trans. Robert Hurley. New York: Vintage.

Foucault, Michel. 1984. "Des Espaces autres." *Architecture, Mouvement, Continuité* 5 (October): 46–49.

Foucault, Michel. 1995. *Discipline and Punish: The Birth of the Prison.* Trans. Alan Sheridan. New York: Vintage.

Fraser, Nancy. 2000. "Rethinking Recognition." *New Left Review* 3 (May–June): 107–20.

Freud, Sigmund. 1953–74. *The Standard Edition.* Ed. James Strachey. 24 vols. London: Hogarth Press.

Fries, Kenny. 1998. *Body, Remember: A Memoir.* New York: Blume.

Fox, H., M. Daniels, and H. Wermer. 1964. "Applicants Rejected for Psychoanalytic Training." *Journal of the American Psychoanalytic Association* 12:692–716.

Funk, Robert. 1987. "Disability Rights: From Caste to Class in the Context of Civil Rights." *Images of the Disabled, Disabling Images.* Ed. Alan Gartner and Tom Joe. New York: Praeger. Pp. 7–30.

Garber, Marjorie. 1992. *Vested Interests: Cross-Dressing and Cultural Anxiety.* New York: Routledge.

Garland-Thomson, Rosemarie. 2002. "The Politics of Staring: Visual Representations of Disabled People in Popular Culture." *Disability Studies: Enabling the Humanities.* Ed. Brenda Jo Brueggemann, Sharon L. Snyder, and Rosemarie Garland-Thomson. New York: PMLA. Pp. 56–75.

Gill, Carol J. 2000. "Health Professionals, Disability, and Assisted Suicide: An Examination of Relevant Empirical Evidence and Reply to Batavia." *Psychology, Public Policy, and Law* 6.2: 526–45.

Glazer, Nathan. 1997. *We Are All Multiculturalists Now.* Cambridge: Harvard University Press.

Goffman, Erving. 1963. *Stigma: Notes on the Management of Spoiled Identity.* Englewood Cliffs, N.J.: Prentice-Hall.

Goldberg, Carey. 2000. "For These Trailblazers, Wheelchairs Matter." *New York Times Online,* August 17, http://query.nytimes.com/gst/fullpage.html?res=9E0CE3DA173EF934A2575BC0A9669C8B63&sec=health&spon=&pagewanted=all (accessed December 22, 2006).

Goldstein, J. L., and M. M. L. Godemont. 2003. "The Legend and Lessons of Geel, Belgium: A 1500-Year-Old Legend, a 21st-Century Model." *Community Mental Health Journal* 39.5:441–58.

Goodheart, Eugene. 1996. *The Reign of Ideology.* New York: Columbia University Press.

Grealy, Lucy. 2001. "In the Realm of the Senses." *Nerve,* October 25, nerve.com/dispatches/Grealy/RealmOfTheSenses/ (accessed April 7, 2004).

Greenacre, Phyllis. 1958. "Early Physical Determinants in the Development of the Sense of Identity." *Journal of American Psychoanalytic Association* 6:612–27.

Greenhouse, Linda. 1999a. "Justices Wrestle with the Definition of Disability: Is It Glasses? False Teeth?" *New York Times Online,* April 28 (accessed September 12, 2006).

Greenhouse, Linda. 1999b. "High Court Limits Who Is Protected by Disability Law." *New York Times,* June 23, A1, A16.

Grier, William. H. 1967. "When the Therapist is Negro: Some Effects on the Treatment Process." *American Journal of Psychiatry* 123:1587–92.

Grigely, Joseph. 2000. "Postcards to Sophie Calle." *The Body Aesthetic: From Fine Art to Body Modification.* Ed. Tobin Siebers. Ann Arbor: University of Michigan Press. Pp. 17–40.

Hahn, Harlan. 1987. "Civil Rights for Disabled Americans: The Foundation of a Political Agenda." *Images of the Disabled, Disabling Images.* Ed. Alan Gartner and Tom Joe. New York: Praeger. Pp. 181–203.

Halberstam, Judith. 1998. *Female Masculinity.* Durham, N.C.: Duke University Press.

Halberstam, Judith. 2001. "Oh Behave! Austin Powers and the Drag Kings." *GLQ* 7.3:425–52

Halley, Janet E. 1999. *Don't: A Reader's Guide to the Military's Anti-Gay Policy.* Durham, N.C.: Duke University Press.

Halperin, David. 2002. *How to Do the History of Homosexuality.* Chicago: University of Chicago Press.

Hamilton, Toby. 1979. "Sexuality in Deaf Blind Persons." *Sexuality and Disability* 2.3: 238–46.

Haraway, Donna J. 1991. *Simians, Cyborgs, and Women: The Reinvention of Nature.* New York: Routledge.

Harding, Sandra. 1986. *The Science Question in Feminism.* Ithaca, N.Y.: Cornell University Press.

Harper, Phillip Brian. 1996. *Are We Not Men? Masculine Anxiety and the Problem of African American Identity.* New York: Oxford University Press.

Harris, Adrienne, and Dana Wideman. 1988. "The Construction of Gender and Disability in Early Attachment." *Women with Disabilities: Essays in Psychology, Culture, and Politics.* Ed. Michelle Fine and Adrienne Asch. Philadelphia: Temple University Press. Pp. 115–38.

Hayles, N. Katherine. 1999. *How We Became Posthuman: Virtual Bodies in Cybernetics, Literature, and Informatics.* Chicago: University of Chicago Press.

Hayman, Robert L. Jr., and Nancy Levit. 2002. "Un-Natural Things: Constructions of Race, Gender, and Disability." *Crossroads, Directions, and a New Critical Race Theory.* Ed. Francisco Valdes, Jerome McCristal Culp, and Angela P. Harris. Philadelphia: Temple University Press. Pp. 157–86.

Heath, Stephen. 1986. "Joan Riviere and the Masquerade." *Formations of Fantasy.* Ed. Victor Burgin, James Donald, and Cora Kaplan. London: Methuen. Pp. 45–61

Hevey, David. 1992. *The Creatures Time Forgot: Photography and Disability Imagery.* London: Routledge.

Ikemoto, Lisa C. 1997. "Furthering the Inquiry: Race, Class, and Culture in the Forced Medical Treatment of Pregnant Women." *Critical Race Feminism: A Reader.* Ed. Katherine Adrien Wing. New York: New York University Press. Pp. 136–43.

Imrie, Rob. 1996. *Disability and the City: International Perspectives.* London: Paul Chapman.

Irigaray, Luce. 1985. *This Sex Which Is Not One.* Trans. Catherine Porter. Ithaca, N.Y.: Cornell University Press.

Jackson-Braboy, Pamela, and David R. Williams. 2006. "The Intersection of Race, Gender, and SES: Health Paradoxes." *Gender, Race, Class, and Health: Intersectional Approaches.* Ed. Amy J. Schulz and Leith Mullings. San Francisco: Jossey-Bass. Pp. 131–62.

Jacobson, Edith. 1965. "The 'Exceptions': An Elaboration of Freud's Character Study." *Psychoanalytic Study of the Child* 20:135–54.

Jameson, Fredric. 1981. *The Political Unconscious: Narrative as a Socially Symbolic Act.* Ithaca, N.Y.: Cornell University Press.

JanMohamed, Abdul, and David Lloyd. 1987a. "Introduction: Toward a Theory of Minority Discourse." *Cultural Critique* 6:5–12.

JanMohamed, Abdul, and David Lloyd. 1987b. "Introduction: Minority Discourse—What Is to Be Done?" *Cultural Critique* 7:5–17.

Jeffreys, Mark. 2002. "The Visible Cripple: Scars and Other Disfiguring Displays Included." *Disability Studies: Enabling the Humanities.* Ed. Brenda Jo Brueggemann, Sharon L. Snyder, and Rosemarie Garland-Thomson. New York: PMLA. Pp. 31–39.

Job, Jennifer. 2004. "Factors Involved in the Ineffective Dissemination of Sexuality Information to Individuals Who Are Deaf or Hard of Hearing." *American Annals of the Deaf* 149.3: 264–73.

Johnson, Harriet McBryde. 2003. "The Disability Gulag." *New York Times Magazine,* November 23, 58–64.

Jones, Megan. 1997. "'Gee, You Don't Look Handicapped . . .' Why I Use a White Cane to Tell People I'm Deaf." *Electric Edge,* July–August, www.ragged-edge-mag.com/archive/look.htm (accessed September 13, 2006).

Kaeser, Frederick. 1996. "Developing a Philosophy of Masturbation Training for Persons with Severe or Profound Mental Retardation." *Sexuality and Disability* 14.1: 295–308.

Kant, Immanuel. 1983. *Perpetual Peace and Other Essays.* Trans. Ted Humphrey. Indianapolis: Hackett.

Katya, Sonia K. 2006. "Sexuality and Sovereignty: The Global Limits and Possibilities of *Lawrence.*" *William and Mary Bill of Rights Journal* 14:1429–92.

Kaufman, Leslie. 1999. "From Eyeglasses to Wheelchairs: Adjusting the Legal Bar for Disability." *New York Times Online,* April 18 (accessed September 12, 2006).

Kaufman, Miriam, M. D., Cory Silverberg, and Fran Odette, eds. 2003. *The Ultimate Guide to Sex and Disability.* San Francisco: Cleis.

Kirkland, Anna. 2006. "What's at Stake in Fatness as a Disability?" *Disability Studies Quarterly* 26.1, www.dsq-sds.org/_articles_html/2006/winter/kirkland .asp (accessed November 17, 2006).

Kittay, Eva Feder. 2001. "When Caring Is Just and Justice Is Caring: Justice and Mental Retardation." *Public Culture* 13.3:557–79

Kleck, Robert, Hiroshi Ono, and Albert H. Hastorf. 1966. "The Effects of Physical Deviance upon Face-to-Face Interaction." *Human Relations* 19:425–36.

Kleege, Georgina. 2002. "Disabled Students Come Out: Questions without Answers." *Disability Studies: Enabling the Humanities.* Ed. Sharon L. Snyder, Brenda Jo Brueggemann, and Rosemarie Garland-Thomson. New York: PMLA. Pp, 308–16.

Lacan, Jacques. 1977. *Écrits: A Selection.* Trans. and ed. Alan Sheridan. New York: W. W. Norton.

Laqueur, Thomas W. 2003. *Solitary Sex: A Cultural History of Masturbation.* New York: Zone Books.

Lasch, Christopher. 1979. *The Culture of Narcissism: American Life in an Age of Diminishing Expectations.* New York: Warner Books.

Latour, Bruno. 2004. "Why Has Critique Run out of Steam? From Matters of Fact to Matters of Concern." *Critical Inquiry* 30.2:225–48.

2004. "Laws on Disability Access to Housing: A Summary." www.con cretechange.org/ laws_overview.htm (accessed November 11, 2006).

Lester, J. C. 2002. "The Disability Studies Industry." *Libertarian Alliance,* September 26, www.la-articles.org.uk/dsi.htm (accessed November 11, 2006).

Linton, Simi. 1998. *Claiming Disability: Knowledge and Identity.* New York: New York University Press.

Linton, Simi, Susan Mello, and John O'Neill. 1995. "Disability Studies: Expanding the Parameters of Diversity." *Radical Teacher* 47:4–10.

Longmore, Paul. 2003. *What I Burned My Book and Other Essays on Disability.* Philadelphia: Temple University Press.

Luibhéid, Eithne. 2002. *Entry Denied: Controlling Sexuality at the Border.* Minneapolis: University of Minnesota Press.

Lussier, André. 1980. "The Physical Handicap and the Body Ego." *International Journal of Psycho-Analysis* 61:179–85.

Lyotard, Jean-François. 1988. *The Differend: Phrases in Dispute.* Trans. Georges Van Den Abbeele. Minneapolis: University of Minnesota Press.

MacIntyre, Alaisdair 1999. *Dependent Rational Animals: Why Human Beings Need the Virtues.* Chicago: Open Court.

Mairs, Nancy. 1996. *Waist-High in the World: A Life among the Nondisabled.* Boston: Beacon.

Mairs, Nancy. 1999. "Sex and the Gimpy Girl." *River Teeth* 1.1: 44–51.

Marks, Deborah. 1999. *Disability: Controversial Debates and Psychosocial Perspectives.* London: Routledge.

Martin, Emily. 2006. "Moods and Representations of Social Inequality." *Gender, Race, Class, and Health: Intersectional Approaches.* Ed. Amy J. Schulz and Leith Mullings. San Francisco: Jossey-Bass. Pp. 60–88.

McDowell, Deborah. 1986. "Introduction." In Nella Larson. *Quicksand* and *Passing.* New Brunswick, N.J.: Rutgers University Press. Pp. ix–xxxv.

McRuer, Robert. 2002. "Compulsory Able-Bodiedness and Queer/Disabled Existence." *Disability Studies: Enabling the Humanities.* Ed. Sharon L. Snyder, Brenda Jo Brueggemann, and Rosemarie Garland-Thomson. New York: PMLA. Pp. 88–99.

McRuer, Robert. 2003. "As Good as It Gets: Queer Theory and Critical Disability." *GLQ* 9.1–2:79–105

Michalko, Rod. 1998. *The Mystery of the Eye and the Shadow of Blindness.* Toronto: University of Toronto Press.

Mitchell, David T. 1997. "Invisible Bodies and the Corporeality of Difference." *Minnesota Review* 48–49:199–206.

Mitchell, David T., and Sharon L. Snyder. 1997. "Introduction: Disability Studies and the Double Bind of Representation." *The Body and Physical Difference: Discourses of Disability.* Ed. David T. Mitchell and Sharon L. Snyder. Ann Arbor: University of Michigan Press. Pp. 1–31.

Mitchell, David T., and Sharon L. Snyder. 2000. *Narrative Prosthesis: Disability and the Dependencies of Discourse.* Ann Arbor: University of Michigan Press.

Mohanty, Satya P. 1997. *Literary Theory and the Claims of History: Postmodernism, Objectivity, Multicultural Politics.* Ithaca, N.Y.: Cornell University Press.

Montgomery, Cal. 2001. "A Hard Look at Invisible Disability." *Ragged Edge Magazine Online* 2, www.ragged-edge-mag.com/0301/0301ft1.htm (accessed September 13, 2006).

Moya, Paula M. L. 2002. *Learning from Experience: Minority Identities, Multicultural Struggles*. Berkeley and Los Angeles: University of California Press.

Moya, Paula M. L. N.d. "Response to Juan Flores's 'Reclaiming Left Baggage.'" Unpublished paper. Pp. 1–12.

Moya, Paula M. L., and Michael R. Hames-García, eds. 2000. *Reclaiming Identity: Realist Theory and the Predicament of Postmodernism*. Berkeley and Los Angeles: University of California Press.

Nancy, Jean-Luc. 1993. *The Birth to Presence*. Trans. Brian Holmes et al. Stanford: Stanford University Press.

Newton, Esther. 1972. *Mother Camp: Female Impersonators in America*. Englewood Cliffs, N.J.: Prentice-Hall.

Niederland, William G. 1965. "Narcissistic Ego Impairment in Patients with Early Physical Malformations." *Psychoanalytic Study of the Child* 20:518–34.

Nussbaum, Martha C. 2006. *Frontiers of Justice: Disability, Nationality, Species Membership*. Cambridge: Harvard University Press.

O'Brien, Mark. 1990. "On Seeing a Sex Surrogate." *The Sun* 174 (May), www.pacificnews.org/marko/sex-surrogate.html (accessed April 29, 2005).

O'Brien, Mark. 1997. *The Man in the Iron Lung*. Berkeley, Calif.: Lemonade Factory.

O'Brien, Mark. N.d. "Questions I Feared the Journalist Would Ask." Mark O'Brien Papers, BANC MSS 99/247 c. Bancroft Library, University of California, Berkeley.

O'Brien, Mark, with Gillian Kendall. 2003. *How I Became a Human Being: A Disabled Man's Quest for Independence*. Madison: University of Wisconsin Press.

Ogden, Thomas Henry. 1974. "A Psychoanalytic Psychotherapy of a Patient with Cerebral Palsy: The Relation of Aggression to Self and Body Representation." *International Journal of Psychoanalytic Psychotherapy* 3:419–23.

Oliver, Michael. 1990. *The Politics of Disablement: A Sociological Approach*. New York: St. Martin's Press.

Oliver, Michael. 1996. *Understanding Disability: From Theory to Practice*. New York: St. Martin's Press.

Olson, Walter. 1997. *The Excuse Factory: How Employment Law Is Paralyzing the American Workplace*. New York: Martin Kessler.

O'Toole, Corbett Joan. 2000. "The View from Below: Developing a Knowledge Base about an Unknown Population." *Sexuality and Disability* 18.3: 207–24.

O'Toole, Corbett Joan. 2004. "The Sexist Inheritance of the Disability Movement." *Gendering Disability*. Ed. Bonnie G. Smith and Beth Hutchison. New Brunswick, N.J.: Rutgers University Press. Pp. 294–300.

O'Toole, Corbett Joan, and Tanis Doe. 2002. "Sexuality and Disabled Parents with Disabled Children." *Sexuality and Disability* 20.1: 89–101.

Paglia, Camille. 1992. *Sex, Art, and American Culture*. New York: Vintage.

Paglia, Camille. 1994. *Vamps and Tramps*. New York: Vintage.

Perniola, Mario. 2004. *Art and Its Shadow*. Trans. Massimo Verdicchio. New York: Continuum.

Phillips, Marilynn J. 1990. "Damaged Goods: Oral Narratives of the Experience of Disability in American Culture." *Social Science and Medicine* 30:849–857.

Piper, Adrian. 1992. "Passing for White, Passing for Black." *Transition* 58:4–32.

Plummer, Kenneth. 2003. *Intimate Citizenship: Private Decisions and Public Dialogues*. Seattle: University of Washington Press.

Potok, Andrew W. 2002. *A Matter of Dignity: Changing the World of the Disabled*. New York: Bantam.

Putnam, Hilary. 1990. *Realism with a Human Face*. Cambridge: Harvard University Press.

2006. "Readers' Comments: Wanting Babies Like Themselves, Some Parents Choose Genetic Defects." *New York Times Online*, December 5, http://news.blogs.nytimes.com/?p=100 (accessed December 8, 2006).

Rich, Adrienne. 1980. "Compulsory Heterosexuality and Lesbian Existence." *Women: Sex and Sexuality*. Ed. Catharine R. Stimpson and Ethel Spector Person. Chicago: University of Chicago Press. Pp. 62–91.

Riviere, Joan. 1991. "Womanliness as a Masquerade." *The Inner World and Joan Riviere: Collected Papers 1920–1958*. Ed. Athol Hughes. London: Karnac Books. Pp. 90–101.

Saletan, William. 2006. "Deformer Babies: The Deliberate Crippling of Children." *Slate*, September 21, http://www.slate.com/id/2149772/ (accessed December 8, 2006).

Samuels, Ellen Jean. 2003. "My Body, My Closet: Invisible Disability and the Limits of Coming-Out Discourse." *GLQ* 9.1–2:233–55.

Sánchez, María Carla, and Linda Schlossberg, eds. 2001. *Passing: Identity and Interpretation in Sexuality, Race, and Religion*. New York: New York University Press.

Sandahl, Carrie. 2003. "Queering the Crip or Cripping the Queer? Intersections of Queer and Crip Identity in Solo Autobiographical Performance." *GLQ* 9.1–2:25–56.

Sandahl, Carrie. 2006. "Black Man, Blind Man: Disability Identity Politics and Performance." *Theatre Journal* 56:579–602.

Sanghavi, Darshak. 2006. "Wanting Babies Like Themselves, Some Parents Choose Genetic Defects." *New York Times Online*, December 5, http://www.nytimes.com/2006/12/05/health/05essa.html (accessed December 8, 2006).

Scarry, Elaine. 1985. *The Body in Pain: The Making and Unmaking of the World*. New York: Oxford University Press.

Scott, Joan W. 1991. "The Evidence of Experience." *Critical Inquiry* 17:773–97.

Scott, Robert A. 1969. *The Making of Blind Men: A Study of Adult Socialization*. New York: Russell Sage Foundation.

Sedgwick, Eve Kosofsky. 1990. *Epistemology of the Closet*. Berkeley and Los Angeles: University of California Press.

Sedgwick, Eve Kosofsky. 1993. "Queer Performativity: Henry James's The Art of the Novel." *GLQ* 1.1:1–16.

Sedgwick, Eve Kosofsky. 2003. *Touching Feeling: Affect, Pedagogy, Performativity*. Durham, N.C.: Duke University Press.

Seidman, Steven, ed. 1996. *Queer Theory/Sociology*. Oxford: Blackwell.

Shakespeare, Tom. 1996. "Disability, Identity and Difference." *Exploring the Divide: Illness and Disability*. Ed. Colin Barnes and Geof Mercer. Leeds: Disability Press. Pp. 94–113.

Shakespeare, Tom. 1999. "The Sexual Politics of Disabled Masculinity." *Sexuality and Disability* 17.1: 53–64.

Shakespeare, Tom. 2000. "Disabled Sexuality: Toward Rights and Recognition." *Sexuality and Disability* 18.3: 159–66.

Shakespeare, Tom, Kath Gillespie-Sells, and Dominic Davies. 1996. *The Sexual Politics of Disability: Untold Desires.* London: Cassell.

Shapiro, Joseph. 1993. *No Pity: People with Disabilities Forging a New Civil Rights Movement.* New York: Three Rivers Press.

Shapiro, Joseph. 1994. "Disability Policy and the Media: A Stealth Civil Rights Movement Bypasses the Press and Defies Conventional Wisdom." *Policy Studies Journal* 22.1: 123–32.

Shuttleworth, Russell P. 2000. "The Search for Sexual Intimacy for Men with Cerebral Palsy." *Sexuality and Disability* 18.4: 263–82.

Siebers, Tobin. 1992. *Morals and Stories.* New York: Columbia University Press.

Siebers, Tobin. 1998a. "Kant and the Politics of Beauty." *Philosophy and Literature* 22.1: 31–50.

Siebers, Tobin. 1998b. "My Withered Limb." *Michigan Quarterly Review* 37.2:196–205.

Siebers, Tobin. 1998c. *The Subject and Other Subjects: On Ethical, Aesthetic, and Political Identity.* Ann Arbor: University of Michigan Press.

Siebers, Tobin. 1999. "*The Reign of Ideology* by Eugene Goodheart." *Modern Philology* 96.4:560–63.

Siebers, Tobin. 2000. *The Mirror of Medusa.* Rev. ed. Christchurch, New Zealand: Cybereditions.

Siebers, Tobin. 2003. "What Can Disability Studies Learn from the Culture Wars?" *Cultural Critique* 55:182–216.

Singer, Peter. 1979. *Practical Ethics.* Cambridge University Press.

Sollers, Werner. 1997. *Neither Black Nor White Yet Both: Thematic Explorations of Interracial Literature.* New York: Oxford University Press.

Somers, Margaret R. 2006. "Citizenship, Statelessness, and Market Fundamentalism: Arendtian Lessons on Losing the Right to Have Rights." *Migration, Citizenship, Ethnos: Incorporation Regimes in Germany, Western Europe, and North America.* Ed. Y. M. Bodemann and G. Yurdakul. New York: Palgrave Macmillan. Pp. 35–62.

Sontag, Susan. 2001. *Illness as Metaphor* and *AIDS and Its Metaphors.* New York: Picador.

Snyder, Sharon L., and David T. Mitchell. 1996. *Vital Signs: Crip Culture Talks Back.* Marquette, Mich.: Brace Yourselves Productions.

Snyder, Sharon L., and David T. Mitchell. 2002. "Out of the Ashes of Eugenics: Diagnostic Regimes in the United States and the Making of a Disability Minority." *Patterns of Prejudice* 26.1: 79–103.

Snyder, Sharon L., and David T. Mitchell. 2006. *Cultural Locations of Disability.* Chicago: University of Chicago Press.

2004. *State of Tennessee v. George V. Lane et al.* 541 U.S.

Stiller, Jerome. 1984. "The Role of Personality in Attitudes toward Those with Physical Disabilities." *Current Topics in Rehabilitation Psychology.* Orlando, Fla.: Grune and Stratton. Pp. 201–26.

Stoner, Kyle. 1999. "Sex and Disability: Whose Job Should It be to Help Disabled People Make Love?" *Eye,* August 12, www.eye.net/eye/issue/issue_08.112.99/news/sex.html (assessed June 8, 2004).

Taylor, Charles. 1987. *Sources of the Self: The Making of Modern Identity.* Cambridge: Harvard University Press.

Teuton, Sean. 2008. *Red Land, Red Power: Grounding Knowledge in the American Indian Novel.* Durham, N.C.: Duke University Press.

Tepper, Mitchell S. 1997. "Discussion Guide for the Sexually Explicit Educational Video *Sexuality Reborn: Sexuality Following Spinal Cord Injury.*" *Sexuality and Disability* 15.3: 183–99.

Tepper, Mitchell S. 1999. "Coming Out as a Person with a Disability." *Disability Studies Quarterly* 19.2: 105–6.

Thomas, Kenneth R. 1997. "Countertransference and Disability: Some Observations." *Journal of Melanie Klein and Object Relations* 15.1: 145–61.

Thompson, Simon B. N. 1994. "Sexuality Training in Occupational Therapy for People with a Learning Disability, Four Years On: Policy Guidelines." *British Journal of Occupational Therapy* 57.7: 255–58

Thomson, Rosemarie Garland. 1997. *Extraordinary Bodies: Figuring Physical Disability in American Culture and Literature.* New York: Columbia University Press.

Tilley, Alvin R. *The Measure of Man and Woman.* New York: Wiley, 2002.

Trent, James W., Jr. 1984. *Inventing the Feeble Mind: A History of Mental Retardation in the United States.* Berkeley and Los Angeles: University of California Press.

Turner, Bryan S. 1993. "Outline of the Theory of Human Rights." *Sociology* 27.3:489–512.

Turner, R. Jay, and P. D. McLean. 1989. "Physical Disability and Psychological Distress." *Rehabilitation Psychology* 34.4: 225–42.

Tyjewski, Carolyn. 2003. "Hybrid Matters: The Mixing of Identity, the Law and Politics." *Politics and Culture* 3, aspen.conncoll.edu/politicsandculture/page.cfm?key=240 (accessed August 3, 2004).

Vahldieck, Andrew. 1999. "Uninhibited." *Nerve,* November 19, www.nerve.com/PersonalEssays/Vahldieck/uninhibitied/ (accessed April 7, 2004).

Valentine, David, and Riki Anne Wilchins. 1997. "One Percent on the Burn Chart: Gender, Genitals, and Hermaphrodites with Attitude." *Social Text* 52–53.3–4: 215–22.

Vincent, Norah. 1998. "Disability Chic: Yet Another Academic Fad." *New York Press,* February 11–17, 40–41.

Wade, Cheryl Marie. 1994. "It Ain't Exactly Sexy." *The Ragged Edge: The Disability Experience from the Pages of the First Fifteen Years of the Disability Rag.* Ed. Barrett Shaw. Louisville, Ky.: Advocado Press. Pp. 88–90.

Wald, Gayle. 2000. *Crossing the Line: Racial Passing in Twentieth-Century U. S. Literature and Culture.* Durham, N.C.: Duke University Press.

Ward, Amy Paul. 2006. "Rape." *Encyclopedia of Disability.* Ed. Gary L. Albrecht. 5 vols. Thousand Oaks, CA: Sage. Pp. 1348–51.

Warner, Michael. 1999. *The Trouble with Normal: Sex, Politics, and the Ethics of Queer Life.* New York: Free Press.

Weeks, Jeffrey. 1998. "The Sexual Citizen." *Theory, Culture, and Society* 15.3–4: 35–52.

Wendell, Susan. 1996. *The Rejected Body: Feminist Philosophical Reflections on Disability.* New York: Routledge.

Westgren, Ninni, and Richard Levi. 1999. "Sexuality after Injury: Interviews with Women after Traumatic Spinal Cord Injury." *Sexuality and Disability* 17.4: 309–19.

Wiegman, Robyn. 1995. *American Anatomies: Theorizing Race and Gender.* Durham, N.C.: Duke University Press.

Wilensky, Amy. 2001. "The Skin I'm In." *Nerve,* October 24, www.nerve.com/personal/Essays/Wilensky/skin/ (accessed April 7, 2004).

Wilkerson, Abby. 2002. "Disability, Sex Radicalism, and Political Agency." *NWSA Journal* 14.3: 33–57.

Wilkerson, William S. 2000. "Is There Something You Need to Tell Me? Coming Out and the Ambiguity of Experience." *Reclaiming Identity: Realist Theory and the Predicament of Postmodernism.* Ed. Paula M. L. Moya and Michael R. Hames-García. Berkeley and Los Angeles: University of California Press. Pp. 251–78.

Williams, Johnny E. 2000. "Race and Class: Why All the Confusion?" *Race and Racism in Theory and Practice.* Ed. Berel Lang. Lanham, Md.: Littlefield. Pp. 215–24.

Williams, Patricia J. 1991. *The Alchemy of Race and Rights: Diary of a Law Professor.* Cambridge: Harvard University Press.

Wu, Cynthia. 2004. "'The Mystery of Their Union': Cross-Cultural Legacies of the Original Siamese Twins." Ph.D. diss., University of Michigan.

Yorke, Clifford. 1980. "Some Comments on the Psychoanalytic Treatment of Patients with Physical Disabilities." *International Journal of Psycho-Analysis* 61:187–93.

Young, Iris. 2005. *On Female Body Experience: "Throwing Like a Girl" and Other Essays.* Cambridge: Oxford University Press.

Zola, Irving. 1982. *Missing Pieces: A Chronicle of Living with a Disability.* Philadelphia: Temple University Press.

# Index

Able-bodiedness, 4, 6, 8, 102, 116, 118, 168, 169, 170, 172, 175. *See also* Ideology of ability
Abortion, 4, 66
Accessibility/inaccessibility, 32, 46, 85, 92, 94, 109, 124, 127–28, 194, 208
Adam, Barry, 117–18
ADAPT, 106, 194
Airports, 96, 108
Alcoff, Linda Martín, 2, 12–13, 15, 105, 125, 199, 205, 208
Americans with Disabilities Act, 31, 35, 43, 45, 69, 98, 106, 120–22, 194, 203–5, 208
Animal rights, 92
Apartheid, 18, 21–22
Architecture, 23, 84–89, 124, 127, 132, 180
  and sex, 127–31
  *See also* Built environment
Arendt, Hannah, 176–79, 211
Asch, Adrienne, 30, 40, 43, 142, 201
Assisted suicide, 4, 66
Autism, 100, 112, 115

Baynton, Douglas, 6, 180
Benhabib, Seyla, 177–78, 211
Bérubé, Michael, 184–85
Biological inferiority, 12, 123
Black studies, 35–37, 47, 200
Blindness, 29, 40, 45–46, 48, 50, 52–53, 56, 57, 60, 69, 71–73, 77, 81, 83, 102, 106–7, 111–12, 117, 124, 142, 188, 204, 206
Body theory, 1, 30, 54, 58, 61–65, 67, 74

Brown, Wendy, 79–80, 193, 204, 206. *See also* Wounded attachments
Built environment, 3, 5, 25, 27, 31, 44, 73, 80, 84, 85, 94, 100, 123, 128, 134, 148, 152, 190
Butler, Judith, 13, 55–56, 61–62, 75–77, 79–80, 174, 199

Capitol crawl-up protest, 106, 194–95
Castration complex, 103, 107
Citizenship, 43, 46, 59, 73, 78, 95, 135, 152, 154, 177–78, 180, 209, 211
  in liberal tradition, 182
Citizenship rights, 95, 154, 177, 209, 211
Civil rights, 18, 45, 55, 60, 67, 73, 106, 120, 180, 185, 202
Closet, 97, 98, 99, 100, 101, 163. *See also* Passing
Collins, Patricia Hill, 28–29
Coming out, 97, 163, 206
Complex embodiment, 9, 22–33, 48, 65, 77, 100, 148, 208
  defined, 25
  as intersectional identity, 27–30
  and social construction, 30–33
Critical race studies, 1, 3, 27, 101
Cross-dressing, 169, 170, 174–75, 210
Cultural studies, 1, 121
Cultural theory, 1–3, 11, 13, 133, 159

Davis, Lennard J., 58, 73, 202, 204
Deafness, 4, 24, 29, 45–46, 53, 74, 77, 81, 83, 100, 102, 114, 117, 124, 142, 188, 194, 196, 202
Delany, Samuel, 127, 130, 208
Democracy, 4, 15, 56, 70, 92, 93, 156, 184